Frontiers in Horticulture

(Volume 2)

Eurasian Geophytes: A Review

Edited by

Sibel Day
Department of Field Crops
Faculty of Agriculture
Ankara University
Ankara, Türkiye

Frontiers in Horticulture

(Volume 2)

Eurasian Geophytes: A Review

Editor: Sibel Day

ISSN (Online): 2588-7882

ISSN (Print): 2588-7874

ISBN (Online): 979-8-89881-057-3

ISBN (Print): 979-8-89881-058-0

ISBN (Paperback): 979-8-89881-059-7

Published by Bentham Science Publishers Pte. Ltd. Singapore, in collaboration with Eureka Conferences, USA. All Rights Reserved.

First published in 2025.

need for a court order if at any point you breach any terms of this License Agreement. In no event will any delay or failure by Bentham Science Publishers in enforcing your compliance with this License Agreement constitute a waiver of any of its rights.

3. You acknowledge that you have read this License Agreement, and agree to be bound by its terms and conditions. To the extent that any other terms and conditions presented on any website of Bentham Science Publishers conflict with, or are inconsistent with, the terms and conditions set out in this License Agreement, you acknowledge that the terms and conditions set out in this License Agreement shall prevail.

Bentham Science Publishers Pte. Ltd.
No. 9 Raffles Place
Office No. 26-01
Singapore 048619
Singapore
Email: subscriptions@benthamscience.net

BENTHAM SCIENCE

CONTENTS

FOREWORD

The book describes several geophytes, their characteristics, and their cultivation. Geophytes have been part of our daily lives since ancient times. They are used as ornamental plants, food, and medicine. The book covers the origin, distribution, morphology, and cultivation of geophytes. Pests and diseases are also described. The chapters are well structured, and several geophytes are described. This information will be useful in these changing climatic conditions.

I congratulate the editor, Dr. Sibel Day, and all the contributors of different chapters for bringing out this publication. I hope that the book will be of great use to students, researchers, scientists, and others interested in geophytes.

Nilgün Bayraktar
Department of Field Crops
Ankara University
Ankara, Türkiye

PREFACE

Geophytes are plants with underground organs that can survive, while their above-ground parts wither after the growing season. These botanical organisms, known for their specialized underground storage organs, display a wide variety of morphological adaptations essential for retaining nutrients, storing water, and surviving in diverse environmental conditions.

While our understanding of geophytes is slowly improving, especially in terms of the evolution of underground traits and the environmental factors affecting their distribution, heightened attention is needed for the scientific exploration of these taxa due to their economic and evolutionary significance.

In this book, we present a collection of 8 chapters written by experts in the field of geophytes. The information presented in this book demonstrates the features of geophytes, cultivation, some important families, and their importance.

I am extremely grateful to all our contributors for accepting the invitation to share their knowledge and research. Their expertise from diverse fields has been invaluable in composing the chapters, and their enduring editorial suggestions have helped to produce this project. I would also like to express my thanks to the Bentham team for their generous cooperation at every stage of the book production.

Sibel Day
Department of Field Crops
Faculty of Agriculture
Ankara University
Ankara, Türkiye

List of Contributors

Burak Tüzün	Department of Crop and Animal Production, Sivas Technical Sciences Vocational School, Sivas Cumhuriyet University, Sivas, Türkiye
Esra Uçar	Department of Crop and Animal Production, Sivas Technical Sciences Vocational School, Sivas Cumhuriyet University, Sivas, Türkiye
Ezgi Oguz	Department of Field Crops, Faculty of Agriculture, Ankara University, Ankara, Türkiye
Gülşen Güçlü	Department of Health Programmes, Health Services Vocational School, Sivas Cumhuriyet University, Sivas, Türkiye
Muhammet Cagri Oguz	Department of Field Crops, Faculty of Agriculture, Ankara University, Ankara, Türkiye
Mustafa Yildiz	Department of Field Crops, Faculty of Agriculture, Ankara University, Ankara, Türkiye
Nilüfer Koçak Şahin	Department of Field Crops, Faculty of Agriculture, Ankara University, Ankara, Türkiye
Sibel Day	Department of Field Crops, Faculty of Agriculture, Ankara University, Ankara, Türkiye

CHAPTER 1

An Overview of Geophytes: Features and Cultivation

Sibel Day[1,*]

[1] *Department of Field Crops, Faculty of Agriculture, Ankara University, Ankara, Türkiye*

Abstract: Geophytes, the specialised stems, are classified as true bulbs, onion bulbs, tubers, corms, and rhizomes. Their scientific exploration heightened attention due to their economic and evolutionary significance. Their morphology and cultivation methods show a wide diversity all over the world. Depending on species and genera, their environmental requirements show differences. Improving cultivation practices and conservation efforts for geophytes is important due to anthropogenic pressure. By recognizing the value of geophytes and implementing effective conservation measures, we can safeguard these botanical treasures for future generations.

Keywords: Bulbs, Corms, Morphology, Production methods, Tubers.

INTRODUCTION

Geophytes are biennial or perennial plants that have organs that can continue to live underground, even though their above-ground organs dry up and die after completing their development during the growing season. These specialised stems have the ability to store nutrients under the soil. The primary function of underground organs is to store nutrients and moisture for growth and to ensure the survival of the species. Geophytes are often referred to as bulbs. Researchers categorise them as true bulbs, onion bulbs, tubers, corms (bulb-like tubers), and rhizomes. However, the term 'bulb' is an appropriate label for all geophytes, regardless of whether they are bulbous, tuberous, or rhizomatous. Therefore, geophytes are commonly known as bulbous plants [1]. Bulbs can be a skin (*Tulipa* spp. and *Narcissus* spp., *etc.*) or without a skin (*Fritillaria* spp. and *Lilium* spp., *etc.*).

---

* **Corresponding author Sibel Day:** Department of Field Crops, Faculty of Agriculture, Ankara University, Ankara, Türkiye; E-mail: day@ankara.edu.tr

Geophytes, botanical organisms renowned for their possession of specialised underground storage organs, exhibit a rich diversity of morphological adaptations that are crucial for nutrient retention, water storage, and survival in varied environmental conditions.

While our understanding of geophytes is gradually advancing, particularly with regard to the evolution of underground traits [1 - 4] and the ecological determinants of their distribution [5 - 7], the scientific exploration of these taxa warrants heightened attention due to their economic and evolutionary significance.

So far, the focus of research on the evolution of geophytes has been mainly on specific taxonomic groups [1 - 3, 5, 8, 9] or geographical regions [6, 7, 10 - 14]. However, comprehensive studies examining the evolution of these traits on a global scale are lacking, hindering a holistic understanding of the evolutionary drivers of geophytism and the diversity of growth forms observed today.

GEOPHYTE MORPHOLOGY: ADAPTATIONS OF UNDERGROUND STORAGE ORGANS

Geophytes, plants with underground storage organs, exhibit diverse morphological adaptations that are essential for survival, growth, and ecological niche. These adaptations are evident in various aspects of their morphology, including storage organs, shoot systems, root systems, reproductive structures, and adaptations to environmental conditions. A comprehensive understanding of geophyte morphology is elucidated through botanical studies, contributing to broader insights into plant evolution, ecology, and horticulture.

Storage Organs

Storage organs such as bulbs, corms, tubers, rhizomes, and tuberous roots (Fig. **1**) are prominent features of geophyte morphology [15]. These organs serve as reservoirs of nutrients and water, facilitating survival during adverse conditions and supporting new growth [16]. The diversity of storage organs reflects the adaptive strategies of geophytes to different environmental niches and climatic conditions [17].

Bulbs

Bulbs, characterised by modified, underground stems covered by succulent scale leaves, have been extensively studied in the botanical literature [16]. The basal plate of bulbs serves as the point of root attachment, while the central axis facilitates shoot emergence, often shielded by protective scale leaves [15].

Notable geophytes associated with bulbs include species such as *Tulipa*, *Narcissus*, and *Lilium* [17].

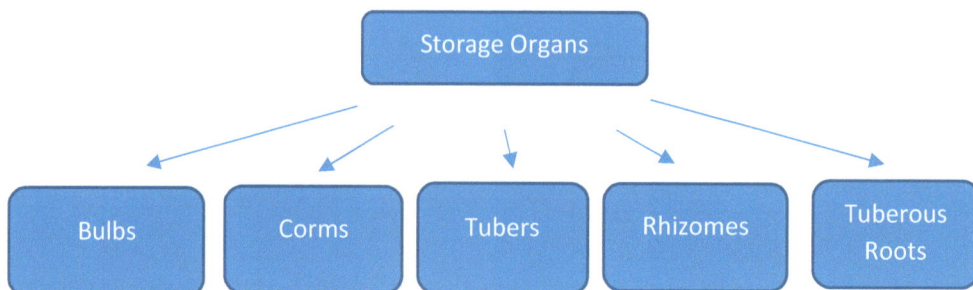

Fig. (1). Storage organs.

Corms

The bulbous tuber (corm) is an enlarged body (basal plate) with scattered nodes and internodes. It is not shaped like onion scales. The basal plate is integrated with many shells and contains spreading root buds. In bulbous tubers, the storage organ is the basal plate. At the top of the bulbous stem is the apical shoot bud, which will later form the leaves and flower shoots. Corms, stout underground stems devoid of fleshy scale leaves, represent another prevalent form of storage organ in geophytes [18]. Surrounded by dry tunics, corms exhibit a solid interior with a centrally located growing point [19]. Botanical investigations have highlighted the significance of corms in species such as *Crocus, Gladiolus,* and *Crocosmia* [15].

Tubers

Tubers, characterised by enlarged underground stems that serve as reservoirs for energy reserves, have been extensively studied in the botanical literature [20]. Tubers, whether of stem or root in origin, have multiple eyes or buds for shoot emergence [21]. Well-known geophytes with tuberous storage organs include *dahlia, Solanum tuberosum,* and *cyclamen* [22].

Rhizomes

Rhizomes, horizontal underground stems that facilitate storage and vegetative propagation, have garnered significant attention in botanical research [23]. Rhizomes produce shoots and roots at nodes along their length, showcasing varied morphological adaptations [24]. Botanical studies have elucidated the role of rhizomes in geophytes such as *Iris, Zingiber officinale,* and *Asparagus officinalis* [25].

Tuberous Roots

Tuberous roots, characterised by thickened, fleshy structures for nutrient storage, are subject to extensive botanical investigation [26]. These roots, often featuring multiple growth points, contribute to the propagation of geophytes [27]. Botanical literature documents the prevalence of tuberous roots in species such as *Anemone*, *Begonia*, and *Dahlia imperialis* [28].

These storage organs, meticulously documented in the botanical literature, underscore the adaptive significance of geophytes in diverse ecological contexts and highlight their central role in plant biology and ecosystem dynamics.

Shoot System

Geophytes often possess modified shoot systems adapted for emergence from underground storage organs [23]. Shoots may consist of stems, leaves, flowers, or combinations thereof and vary in size, shape, and texture among species [24]. Seasonal growth patterns, including dormancy and active growth phases, characterise the shoot systems of geophytes [15].

Root System

Geophytes typically develop fibrous root systems for anchorage, water absorption, and nutrient uptake [20]. Adventitious roots may arise from storage organs or along stems, contributing to resource acquisition and stability [26]. Root systems exhibit adaptations to soil structure, moisture levels, and nutrient availability, optimising plant performance in diverse habitats [22].

Reproductive Structures

Flowers play a vital role in the reproduction of geophytes, often featuring specialized structures for pollination [29]. Flower morphology varies widely among species, reflecting adaptations to pollinators, breeding systems, and environmental conditions [25]. Geophytes employ sexual and asexual reproductive strategies, including seed production and vegetative propagation *via* offsets, rhizomes, or tubers [28]. Flowers of geophytes play a significant role in supporting pollinators, especially in early spring. Their colours and nectars make them an attractive food source for bees, butterflies, and other insects.

ADAPTATIONS TO ENVIRONMENT

Geophytes exhibit morphological adaptations to diverse environmental conditions, including temperature, moisture, light availability, and soil composition [19]. Variations in leaf size, shape, and texture reflect adaptations to water conservation, light capture, and herbivory deterrence [21].

Morphological traits such as succulence, pubescence, and root morphology contribute to the ecological success and resilience of geophytes in different habitats [27].

Botanical studies of geophyte morphology provide valuable insights into plant form-function relationships, ecological interactions, and conservation strategies. By elucidating the intricate adaptations of underground storage organs and associated structures, researchers contribute to the conservation and sustainable management of geophyte species worldwide.

PRODUCTION METHODS OF GEOPHYTES

Geophytes are produced by generative and vegetative methods. Vegetative propagation techniques are used for large-scale production.

Generative Production

The technique described is for seed propagation. After flowering, fully mature seeds are harvested and promptly sown or stored under appropriate conditions until the optimal sowing period. Seed propagation requires a thorough understanding of maturation times, germination periods, germination rates, and germination temperatures required. Genera such as *Allium, Begonia, Chionodoxa, Cyclamen, Eranthis, Freesia, Fritillaria, Liatris, Muscari, Sparaxis, Tigrida*, and *Ranunculus* are commonly propagated *via* seed. The optimal germination temperatures vary according to the genus. For instance, *Cyclamen* seeds require temperatures of 16-18°C, while *Muscari* and *Chionodoxa* seeds necessitate temperatures of 5-7°C. Certain *Lilium* species, such as *Lilium ledebourii*, commence germination at 26-29°C, gradually shifting to 14-17°C, whereas *Colchicum macrophyllum* benefits from an initial treatment at 20°C, followed by temperatures of 10-15°C in a dark environment for effective germination [30 - 36].

In seed propagation, it is possible to obtain a large number of plants; however, certain drawbacks may arise, such as the obtained plants not resembling the parent plant, some species failing to produce sufficient seeds, and the prolonged duration required to obtain a plant of sufficient size to flower from seed sowing.

Furthermore, the soil pH for seed sowing ranges between 5 and 6.5 and varies according to the species. The duration necessary to obtain a bulb of flowering size from seed sowing varies by genus. According to studies conducted under optimal conditions, it has been determined that *Alliums* require 2 years, *Eranthis* requires 4 years, *Fritillarias* require 4-5 years, *Galanthus* requires 4-5 years, *Liliums* require 2-4 years, *Ornithogalums* require 3 years, and *Leucojums* require 2-4 years to achieve this stage [33, 34].

Vegetative methods

Geophytes are predominantly propagated vegetatively. In generative propagation, vegetative methods are often preferred due to reasons such as certain species having low seed-forming capacities and the prolonged duration required to obtain a plant of flowering size from seed sowing. Vegetative propagation methods can be categorized into seven groups. These include:

Production with Bulblets

It is the most commonly used method among vegetative propagation techniques. In this method, the daughter bulbs formed alongside the mother bulbs during the growing season are used for propagation. The daughter bulbs adjacent to the mother bulb are removed from the soil when physiological activity is minimised, and the leaves are yellow and dry. They are then separated from the mother bulb, graded according to size, and planted in prepared planting sites to obtain bulbs of flowering size [37].

This method is typically applied in genera such as *Fritillaria, Galanthus, Leucojum, Narcissus, Iris, Lilium,* and *Tulipa.* Generally, it takes 1-3 years to obtain bulbs of sufficient size to produce flowers using this method. The quantity of daughter bulbs obtained from the mother bulb depends on factors such as the species of the plant, the region where production is conducted, and the size of the mother bulb. On average, *Narcissus* species produce about 1.6 daughter bulbs per year, *Tulipa* and *Iris* produce 5 daughter bulbs per year, and *Lilium* species produce 2 daughter bulbs per year.

Production by Dividing Tubers, Rhizomes, and Bulbous tubers

In this method, the divided parts from the tuber and rhizome should contain the shoot eye, and the part divided from the bulb should contain the root base. These divided parts should be applied with fungicide to prevent rot.

Several studies on plants like *Anemones, Eranthis, Erythronium,* and *Triteleia bridgesii* indicate that plant division can have notable effects on flowering [33 - 40].

Production with Axillary Bulbils (Aerial Stem Bulbils)

Production is carried out using bulbils formed in leaf axils, stems, and roots. This method is commonly applied in species such as *Lilium sargentiae, Lilium sulphureum*, and *Lilium tigrinum*. In these species, bulbils formed in leaf axils are collected when they are fully mature, while those formed in the roots are collected in autumn [41].

Production with Bulb Scales (Scaling)

This technique, known as scaling, involves planting each scale removed from a bulb to obtain a new plant. Scaling is commonly used in the production of *Lilium* species. The bulb scale is separated in a manner that includes the root area at the base of the bulb, and after treatment with fungicide against diseases, they are planted. The outermost wrinkled and dehydrated scales are not used. It is recommended to use the first two or three rows of bulb scales from the outside inward. Adventitious bulblets develop at the base of each scale. Generally, 3-5 bulblets are obtained from each scale. Apart from *Lilium* species, this method is also applied in *Hyacinthus*, certain *Fritillaria* species, *Muscari*, and *Scilla* [32 - 34].

Chipping and Twin-scaling

Chipping, or slicing the bulb into sections, is a method used to obtain a large quantity of bulbs. It involves cutting the bulb vertically into equal-sized pieces to create segments. This method takes advantage of the meristematic region in the basal plate of the bulb, where cell division occurs, allowing for the production of new bulbs. It is commonly applied in genera such as *Galanthus, Fritillaria, Leucojum, Narcissus, Chionodoxa, Nerine, Scilla*, and *Sternbergia* [42]. Bulbs with well-developed basal plates, preferably round in shape, are typically chosen as the material for this method, aiming to produce bulbs of flowering size.

Depending on the size of the bulb, it is divided into segments, with the number of segments being 4, 12, 16, or 32. The divided bulbs are subjected to surface sterilization and then placed in polyethylene bags containing perlite or vermiculite moistened with water. These bags are kept in a dark environment (incubator) for 12 weeks. The incubation temperatures may vary between 18-23 °C depending on the species. For example, temperatures of 15-20°C are found to be effective for *Galanthus elwesii*, while for *Sternbergia lutea, Leucojum aestivum*, and *Leucojum vernum*, 20°C is recommended [33, 34, 43 - 45]. Additionally, Dhiman [46] stated that in *Lilium*, an increase in the ratio of bulblets/scales, bulblet diameter, and weight occurred in a mixture of sand and vermiculite medium.

In the slicing method, the fewer the number of slices, the larger the bulb segment, and it reaches flowering size earlier. As the number of slices increases, the size of the bulb segment decreases, resulting in a delay in flowering. In *Leucojum vernum, Leucojum aestivum, Fritillaria imperialis*, and *Sternbergia lutea*, it has been noted that larger bulb sizes and the application of division (into 4 parts) are effective [33, 34, 43, 45, 47]. On the other hand, in *Fritillaria persica*, it has been found that bulbs divided in the middle produce more daughter bulbs compared to slicing into 4 or 8 parts [48].

The Twin-Scaling method, also known as dividing the bulb into pairs, is an ancient technique that has been practiced since around 1935. It is considered a progression from the slicing method.

It is commonly applied in species such as *Galanthus, Fritillaria, Leucojum, Hyemanthus, Pancratium, Sternbergia, Allium, Chionodoxa, Lachenalia, Muscari, Ornithogalum, Scilla, Veltheimia, Iris, Hyacinthus, Narcissus*, and others. Depending on the size of the bulbs, after the slicing process, each slice is divided into segments consisting of pairs of bulb scales, with a portion connecting two scales at the bottom. Depending on the size of the bulb, each slice is divided into 3 or 4 twin scales. The incubation period is conducted similarly to the slicing method. The duration of incubation varies according to temperature, genus, and species. Generally, temperature ranges of 15-22 °C and a period of 12-16 weeks are applied. The time required for bulbs to reach flowering size varies according to species, typically ranging from 3 to 4 years. In some species, such as *Urginea maritima*, this period may be longer (up to 6 years) [34, 37, 43, 49].

Production by Cutting the Bulb Base

For this production technique, healthy bulbs with larger basal plates are used. There are two different methods used for cross-section: center excision and base hollowing of the bulb.

Cross-cutting

In this method, first, the roots on the bulb base are removed, and then the bulbs are left to dry. After drying, the bulb base is cut with a sharp knife, making 3 or 4 cross-sections depending on the size of the bulb. The cuts should be made so that the bulb base can be separated. The prepared bulbs are then kept at 25°C with the cut sections facing upwards. Sand is sprinkled over the cut area and then covered with a layer of sand about 5 cm thick. Approximately one week later, a thin layer of fungus forms on the cut area, and the bulbs are removed to check whether they are healthy. The bulbs are then planted in production rooms at 20-32 °C for 2.5-3 months, with the cut sections facing downwards to allow for the formation of bulbils. The bulbils, along with the parent bulbs, are then planted in open areas. In the first year, the parent bulbs disintegrate, and in subsequent years, the bulbils are grown. Every year, the bulbils are sorted, with those reaching flowering size being separated. This method can be used for *Hyacinthus* [34, 33].

Removing the Center and Hollowing out the Bulb Base (Scooping)

In this method, large and mature bulbs are harvested after the leaves turn yellow and are initially stored at 25°C. Once removed from storage, the bulbs are cleaned, treated with pesticides, and dried. Subsequently, the roots of the bulbs are trimmed, and the base portion of the bulb is scooped out using a spoon or knife. This cutting is made at the boundary where the bulb scales meet the base of the bulb. The prepared bulbs are then kept in the storage for several weeks with the cut sides facing upwards initially and, later, kept flat. Bulblets develop from the wounds on the base of the bulb. This method is applied in *Hyacinthus, Muscari, and Scilla*.

In center excision, the growth cone located at the center of the bulb is removed. This directs the growth potential of the bulb towards the formation of daughter bulbs at the basal plate of the bulb. After the center excision process, the bulbs are stored in the same manner as in the slicing method, initially with the cut side facing upwards and then downwards. This method can be applied to *Hyacinthus* and *Fritillaria*.

It has been reported that with the scooping method in *Hyacinthus*, an average of 60 bulblets can be obtained, but it takes 4-5 years for flowering to occur. On the other hand, with the cross-section method, 20-25 bulblets can be obtained, and flowering occurs in 3-4 years [34, 33].

Production Through Tissue Culture

Plant tissue culture is the process of producing new tissues, plants, or plant products from whole plants, cells (such as meristematic cells, suspension or callus cells), tissues (various plant parts = explants), or organs (apical meristem, roots, *etc.*) under controlled light and temperature conditions in culture vessels, using artificial nutrient media. Modified environments such as Gamborg (B5) and Murashige and Skoog (MS) are more commonly used in the tissue culture of geophytes [50 - 52].

Tissue culture production can be achieved for genera such as *Lilium, Tulipa, Hyacinthus, Muscari, Fritillaria, Colchicum, Iris, Crocus, Galanthus, Sternbergia, Leucojum, Eranthis, Anemone, Cyclamen, Scilla*, and *Oxalis* [53].

GEOPHYTES' GROWING CONDITIONS, PLANTING, AND MAINTENANCE TECHNIQUES

Environmental Requirements

Species and genera of geophytes have different light requirements. For optimal flowering, they typically require 8-10 hours of light, with a minimum of 6 hours. In terms of light preferences:

- **Shady environments:** *Triteleia* and *Arum*.
- **Intense light environments:** *Eremurus, Acidanthera, Achimenes, Dahlia, Gladiolus, Sparaxis, Canna, Galtonia, Hyacinthus, Ipheion, Polianthes, Sternbergia,* and *Tulipa*.
- **Light to partial shade environments:** *Agapanthus, Triteleia, Scilla, Allium, Anemone, Chionodoxa, Crocus, Eranthis, Erythronium, Iris, Galanthus, Muscari, Oxalis, Ornithogalum, Caladium, Camassia, Colchicum, Fritillaria, Lilium, Leucojum, Narcissus, Ornithogalum, Oxalis,* and *Zantedeschia*.
- **Semi-shaded environments:** *Cyclamen, Begonia,* and *Hyacinthoides* [54 - 60].

The temperature requirements of geophytes vary according to genus and species. Tulips require temperatures between 5-13°C, while *Hyacinthus, Sternbergia, and Lilium* species prefer temperatures between 20-25°C. For *Iris* and *Allium* species, temperatures ranging from 9-13°C are necessary for flowering. Extremely high temperatures can delay flowering [61].

In addition to high temperatures, low temperatures also have an impact. Matsubara *et al.* [62] noted that temperatures around -5°C adversely affected species such as *Canna* and *Freesia*, as well as *Oxalis purpurea, Muscari armeniacum,* and *Narcissus tazetta* var. *chinensis*, to the extent of causing plant death. However, low temperatures can have positive effects on certain genera and species. For example, it has been reported that bud formation occurs at low temperatures in the *Eranthis* genus, and there is an increase in the number of buds at temperatures ranging from 8-14°C in the *Anemone blanda* species [63].

Geophytes prefer light and warm soils in terms of soil preferences. They can grow in almost any type of soil with sufficient permeability and pore volume. Well-drained, sandy-loamy, or loamy-sandy soils with high moisture retention capacity during the growing season are the most suitable soil types. Additionally, for the excavation of bulbs, the soil should be free of stones. Soil with high clay content can be made suitable by mixing it with organic materials. The soil pH should be between 6-7, and the soil temperature during planting should be 5-10 °C [54, 58].

Cultivation practices

Planting time for geophytes generally covers a period from September to October in cold climates and from October to January in temperate climates. Especially for genera such as *Gladiolus, Dahlia,* and *Ranunculus,* which bloom in summer, they are usually planted in spring. However, more cold-resistant genera like *Lilium* can be planted earlier.

As a general rule, planting depth should be 1-2 times the size of the bulb or tuber. Specifically, for genera such as *Amaryllis* and *Calla,* the bulb should be planted with one-third exposed; for *Anemone, Muscari, Scilla,* and *Cyclamen,* it should be planted at a depth of 5 cm; for *Crocus, Galanthus,* and *Caladium,* it should be planted at a depth of 6-8 cm; for *Allium, Gladiolus, Dahlia,* and *Eremurus,* it should be planted at a depth of 8-10 cm; and for *Lilium, Narcissus, Freesia,* and *Tulipa* species, planting depth can range from 10-20 cm.

Shallow planting can hinder root development, resulting in weak growth and an increased risk of frost damage. Conversely, deeper planting may delay emergence. Additionally, it is noted that planting depth can vary depending on soil type, and deeper planting is possible in sandy soils compared to clayey soils [32, 55, 58, 64, 65].

Geophytes are low-maintenance plants. While they generally rely on natural rainfall for growth and development, it is important to ensure moist soil conditions, especially for autumn-planted bulbs, following planting for root formation and growth. During dry periods, when the soil becomes dry, irrigation is recommended to facilitate this process. If irrigation is necessary, it is advised to water frequently but with small amounts, both after planting and throughout the growing season [58, 65].

Organic mulching can be applied from the planting of bulbs to prevent weed growth and protect against winter frosts. Mulching helps retain soil moisture and temperature. Mulch is typically removed in early spring, but a thin layer of mulch can be applied after the plants emerge above the soil surface [55, 58, 64].

To encourage bulb or tuber growth rather than seed production, it is recommended to remove faded flowers from the plant. Deadheading is also suggested for certain genera like *Narcissus* and *Tulipa* to extend the flowering season [55, 58, 64].

Storage

Geophytes that bloom in spring enter a dormant period after flowering, during which their bulbs are either left in the soil or stored under controlled conditions.

Removed bulbs should be stored in conditions with controlled temperature and humidity, and regular ventilation should be provided. Suitable storage temperatures vary depending on the species, but generally, they are around 20 °C. For example, *Alliums* can be stored at 20-23°C, *Anemones* at 17-20°C, *Chionodoxa* and *Crocus* at 20°C, *Galanthus* at 17°C, *Muscari* at 23-25°C, *Fritillaria* at 9°C, *Lilium* at 3-5°C, and *Cyclamen* at 8-10°C.

Geophytes that bloom in summer are sensitive to winter cold and frost, so after their leaves dry out in autumn, they should be dug up from the soil and stored under controlled conditions. Storage temperatures vary depending on the species but generally range from 20-25°C.

If the air humidity in the storage environment is insufficient, it is advisable to keep the bulbs slightly moist in vermiculite or peat. *Colchicums* should be stored at 17-20°C, *Dahlias* at 5-9°C, *Galtonia* at 17-20°C, and *Sprekelias* at 20°C [32, 49, 64].

Anthropogenic Pressure on Geophytes

Anthropogenic pressure, including inappropriate herbivory and habitat destruction (overgrazing, road construction, mining activities, overexploitation, war and terrorism, diseases, insects, rodents, birds, small animals, and climate change), is taking a toll on these underground marvels, jeopardizing their survival and the ecosystems they support.

Overgrazing

Overgrazing poses direct and indirect threats to geophytes. Trampling by livestock can damage the underground organs of geophytes, such as bulbs and tubers, disrupting their ability to store nutrients and water. As a result, weakened geophyte plants may struggle to survive, reproduce, or compete with other plant species. Additionally, excessive grazing pressure can remove vegetation cover, exposing geophyte populations to erosion, soil compaction, and increased vulnerability to invasive species [66, 67].

Overgrazing poses a significant threat to geophyte populations, with far-reaching implications for ecosystem integrity and biodiversity. By recognizing the ecological importance of geophytes and implementing sustainable land management practices, we can mitigate the impacts of overgrazing and safeguard these underground treasures for future generations. Through collaborative efforts and concerted action, we can ensure the resilience and vitality of ecosystems where geophytes thrive, preserving their beauty and ecological value for years to come [68].

Habitat Destruction

One of the most significant threats to geophytes is habitat destruction, driven primarily by urbanization, agriculture, mining, and infrastructure development. Many geophyte-rich habitats, such as grasslands, woodlands, and meadows, are being converted into urban areas or agricultural fields, leading to the loss of critical habitats.

As bulldozers clear land for construction or plow fields for farming, the delicate balance that sustains geophyte populations is disrupted, often irreversibly [69].

Overexploitation

The allure of geophytes, with their vibrant flowers and unique forms, has made them targets for overexploitation. Harvesting for ornamental purposes, pharmaceuticals, and culinary uses has put immense pressure on wild populations. In some regions, rare and endangered geophyte species are illegally collected for the horticultural trade, further endangering their survival. Unregulated harvesting practices not only deplete populations but also disrupt pollination dynamics and seed dispersal mechanisms, hindering the natural regeneration of these plants [70].

Climate Change

Climate change poses additional challenges to geophyte survival. These plants are finely attuned to seasonal cues, relying on temperature and precipitation patterns to emerge, bloom, and reproduce. However, shifting climate patterns, including unpredictable rainfall, extreme temperatures, and altered growing seasons, can disrupt these delicate rhythms. Geophyte species that are adapted to specific climatic conditions may struggle to survive in rapidly changing environments, leading to population declines and local extinctions.

Conservation Efforts

To mitigate the impact of anthropogenic pressure on geophytes, concerted conservation efforts are crucial. Conservation organizations and governmental agencies must prioritize the protection of geophyte-rich habitats through the establishment of reserves, protected areas, and habitat restoration initiatives. Public awareness campaigns can educate communities about the ecological importance of geophytes and the need for sustainable harvesting practices [71].

Furthermore, the implementation of legal frameworks and regulations to control the trade and collection of geophytes is essential for preventing overexploitation. Engaging local communities in conservation efforts can foster stewardship of natural resources and promote alternative livelihoods that are compatible with geophyte conservation [68].

Moreover, addressing climate change through mitigation and adaptation strategies is paramount for the long-term survival of geophytes and the ecosystems they inhabit. Efforts to reduce greenhouse gas emissions and enhance ecosystem resilience can help mitigate the adverse effects of climate change on geophyte populations [69].

CONCLUSION

Geophytes, with their remarkable adaptations and ecological significance, enrich our natural landscapes in ways both seen and unseen. However, anthropogenic pressure, driven by habitat destruction, overexploitation, and climate change, threatens the survival of these underground wonders. Urgent action is needed to conserve geophyte diversity and ensure the resilience of the ecosystems they support. By recognizing the value of geophytes and implementing effective conservation measures, we can safeguard these botanical treasures for future generations.

REFERENCES

[1]   Patterson TB, Givnish TJ. Phylogeny, concerted convergence, and phylogenetic niche conservatism in the core Liliales: insights from rbcL and ndhF sequence data. Evolution 2002; 56(2): 233-52.
[PMID: 11926492]

[2]   Wilson CA. Patterns in evolution in characters that define *Iris* subgenera and sections. Aliso J Syst Florist Bot 2006; 22(1): 425-33.
[http://dx.doi.org/10.5642/aliso.20062201.34]

[3]   Sosa V, Cameron KM, Angulo DF, Hernández-Hernández T. Life form evolution in epidendroid orchids: Ecological consequences of the shift from epiphytism to terrestrial habit in *Hexalectris*. Taxon 2016; 65(2): 235-48.
[http://dx.doi.org/10.12705/652.2]

[4]   Stoughton TR, Kriebel R, Jolles DD, O'Quinn RL. Next-generation lineage discovery: A case study of tuberous *Claytonia* L. Am J Bot 2018; 105(3): 536-48.
[http://dx.doi.org/10.1002/ajb2.1061] [PMID: 29672830]

[5]   Evans M, Aubriot X, Hearn D, *et al.* Insights on the evolution of plant succulence from a remarkable radiation in Madagascar (Euphorbia). Syst Biol 2014; 63(5): 697-711.
[http://dx.doi.org/10.1093/sysbio/syu035] [PMID: 24852061]

[6]   Cuéllar-Martínez M, Sosa V. Diversity patterns of monocotiledonous geophytes in Mexico. Bot Sci 2016; 94(4): 699.
[http://dx.doi.org/10.17129/botsci.763]

[7]   Sosa V, Loera I. Influence of current climate, historical climate stability and topography on species richness and endemism in Mesoamerican geophyte plants. PeerJ 2017; 5: e3932.
[http://dx.doi.org/10.7717/peerj.3932] [PMID: 29062605]

[8]   Perret M, Chautems A, Spichiger R, Kite G, Savolainen V. Systematics and evolution of tribe Sinningieae (Gesneriaceae): evidence from phylogenetic analyses of six plastid DNA regions and nuclear *ncpGS*. Am J Bot 2003; 90(3): 445-60.

[http://dx.doi.org/10.3732/ajb.90.3.445] [PMID: 21659138]

[9]   Oberlander KC, Emshwiller E, Bellstedt DU, Dreyer LL. A model of bulb evolution in the eudicot genus *Oxalis* (Oxalidaceae). Mol Phylogenet Evol 2009; 51(1): 54-63.
[http://dx.doi.org/10.1016/j.ympev.2008.11.022] [PMID: 19070669]

[10]   Pate JS, Dixon KW. Tuberous, cormous and bulbous plants: Biology of an adaptive strategy in Western Australia. Beaverton, Oregon, USA: International Scholarly Book Services Inc. 1982.

[11]   Rundel PW. Monocotyledonous geophytes in the California flora. Madrono California Botanical Society 1996; 355-68.

[12]   Hoffmann AJ, Liberona F, Hoffmann AE. Distribution and ecology of geophytes in Chile. Conservation threats to geophytes in Mediterranean-type regions. Landsc Disturb Biodivers Mediterran Type Ecosyst 1998; 231-53.
[http://dx.doi.org/10.1007/978-3-662-03543-6_13]

[13]   Parsons RF. Monocotyledonous geophytes: comparison of California with Victoria, Australia. Aust J Bot 2000; 48(1): 39-43.
[http://dx.doi.org/10.1071/BT98056]

[14]   Parsons RF, Hopper SD. Monocotyledonous geophytes: comparison of south-western Australia with other areas of mediterranean climate. Aust J Bot 2003; 51(2): 129-33.
[http://dx.doi.org/10.1071/BT02067]

[15]   Kamenetsky R, Okubo H, Ornstein K, Gamrasni D. Dormancy release in geophytes. Geophytes: From basic science to horticultural applications. CRC Press. 2019; pp. 207-25.

[16]   Rees AR. Ornamental bulbous plants. Handbook of Flowering 2018; 259-308.

[17]   Dafni A, Cohen D, Noy-Mier I. Life-cycle variation in geophytes. Ann Mo Bot Gard 1981; 68(4): 652-60.
[http://dx.doi.org/10.2307/2398893]

[18]   Singh G. Plant systematics: an integrated approach. CRC Press 2019.

[19]   Khan MA, Naseer S, Nagoo S, Nehvi FA. Behaviour of saffron (*Crocus sativus* L.) corms for daughter corm production. J Phytol 2011; 3(7)

[20]   Peterson RL, Barker WG, Howarth MJ. Development and structure of tubers. Potato Physiol 1985; 123-52.
[http://dx.doi.org/10.1016/B978-0-12-447660-8.50009-0]

[21]   Grun P, Hebelstrup KH. Metabolic adjustments in stem tubers of potato under different light intensities. Plant Physiol Biochem 2016; 101: 14-24.

[22]   Ferguson TU. Tuber development in yams; physiological and agronomic implications. Third Symp Int Soc Trop Root Crops. 72-7.

[23]   Mauseth JD. Botany: An Introduction to Plant Biology. Jones & Bartlett Learning 2016.

[24]   Fahn A. Plant Anatomy. Pergamon Press, Oxford, UK 1982; p. 544.

[25]   Rudall P. Anatomy and systematics of Iridaceae. Bot J Linn Soc. Bloomsbury Publishing. 1994; 114: pp. (1)1-21.

[26]   Zierer W, Rüscher D, Sonnewald U, Sonnewald S. Tuber and tuberous root development. Annu Rev Plant Biol 2021; 72(1): 551-80.
[http://dx.doi.org/10.1146/annurev-arplant-080720-084456] [PMID: 33788583]

[27]   Fukuda T, Tashiro RM, Tani N, Hara T. Changes in microstructure and carbohydrate metabolism in tuberous roots of *Ipomoea batatas* during development. Sci Hortic (Amsterdam) 2020; 272: 109571.

[28]   Hosoki T, Yamamoto H, Suzuki S, Taira S. Tuber formation in lotus (*Nelumbo nucifera* Gaertn.) and functional classification of tuberous organs. J Plant Res 2018; 131(2): 287-97.

[29]   Baskaran V, Misra RL, Abirami K. Effect of plant growth regulators on corm production in *gladiolus*. J Hortic Sci 2009; 4(1): 78-80.
[http://dx.doi.org/10.24154/jhs.v4i1.563]

[30]   Dotterweich B, Röber R. The influence of temperature upon germination of some Primulaceae. Int Symp Propag Ornamental Plants. 226: 247-54.

[31]   Corbineau F, Neveur N, Côme D. Seed germination and seedling development in *Cyclamen persicum*. Ann Bot (Lond) 1989; 63(1): 87-96.
[http://dx.doi.org/10.1093/oxfordjournals.aob.a087732]

[32]   Rees AR. The physiology of ornamental bulbous plants. Bot Rev 1966; 32(1): 1-23.
[http://dx.doi.org/10.1007/BF02858583]

[33]   Zencirkıran M, Mengüç A. The effects of twin scale and chipping techniques on bulblet production in *Galanthus elwesii* Hook. II. National Ornamental Plants Congress. 24-8.Antalya. 2002; pp.

[34]   Aksu E, Görür G, Çelikel F. A study on cultural propagation of *Leucojum aestivum* bulbs using vegetative methods. II. National Ornamental Plants Congress. 29-34.Antalya. 2002; pp.

[35]   Dehkaei MP, Khalighi A, Moosavi RN. Effect of alternating and constant temperature on seed germination of chelcheragh liliy (*Lilium ledebourii*) in Iran. Acta Hortic 2005; 28(6731)

[36]   Antonidaki-Giatromanolaki A, Dragassaki M, Papadimitriou M, Vlahos I. Effects of stratification, temperature and light on seed germination of *Colchicum macrophyllum* BL Burtt. Propag Ornam Plants 2008; 8: 105-7.

[37]   Zencirkiran M, Tumsavas Z. Capacity of *Sternbergia lutea* (L.) Ker-Gawl. Ex Sprengel (Winter Daffodil). Pak J Biol Sci 2006; 9: 2366-8.
[http://dx.doi.org/10.3923/pjbs.2006.2366.2368]

[38]   Chong JA. Asexual propagation of *Anemone hupehensis* and *Anemone xhybrida* by a root-plug method. Michigan State University 2000.

[39]   Han SS. Flowering of three species of *Brodiaea* in relation to bulb size and source. Sci Hortic (Amsterdam) 2001; 91(3-4): 349-55.
[http://dx.doi.org/10.1016/S0304-4238(01)00261-8]

[40]   Shinoda K, Murata N. The effect of corm weight and low temperature treatment on the flowering of *Erythronium pagoda*. IX Int Symp Flower Bulbs. 673: 495-9.

[41]   Bakhshaie M, Khosravi S, Azadi P, Bagheri H, van Tuyl JM. Biotechnological advances in *Lilium*. Plant Cell Rep 2016; 35(9): 1799-826.
[http://dx.doi.org/10.1007/s00299-016-2017-8] [PMID: 27318470]

[42]   Seyidoğlu N. Propagation with chipping technique in *Leucojum aestivum* L. Bartin Orman Fak Derg 2009; 11(16): 7-11.

[43]   Hanks GR. Chips off the old bulb. Garden 1991; 116: 442-6.

[44]   Piskornik M, Klimek A, Kobyłko T, Surowka J. Production of adventitious bulblets in the snowflake (*Leucoium vernum* L.) as affected by division and circumference of mother bulbs. Folia Hortic 2000; 12(1): 107-13.

[45]   Seyidoglu N, Zencirkira M. Vegetative propagation of *Sternbergia lutea* (L.) Ker-Gawl. Ex Sprengel (winter daffodil) by chipping techniques. J Biol Sci (Faisalabad, Pak) 2008; 8(5): 966-9.
[http://dx.doi.org/10.3923/jbs.2008.966.969]

[46]   Dhiman MR. Effect of scale position and growing medium on bulblet formation and growth during scale propagation of *Lilium*. J Ornam Hortic 2007; 10(2): 119-21.

[47]   Yücel G. Değişik ekolojilerde Fritillaria imperialis Linn. soğanlarının farklı yöntemlerle yetiştirilmesi üzerinde bir araştırma. Doctoral dissertation, Bursa Uludag University, Turkey 1999.

[48] Uluğ BV, Korkut AB, Sısman EE, Muratozyavuz M. Research on propagation methods of Persian lily bulbs [*Fritillaria persica* Linn.] with various vegetative techniques. Pak J Bot 2010; 42: 2785-92.

[49] Le Nard M, De Hertogh AA. Plant breeding and genetics The Physiology of Flower Bulbs: A Comprehensive treatise on the physiology and utilization of ornamental flowering bulbous and tuberous plants. Amsterdam, the Netherlands: Elsevier 1993; pp. 161-9.

[50] De Klerk GJ. Micropropagation of bulbous crops: technology and present state. Floric Ornam Biotechnol 2012; 6(1): 1-8.

[51] Kim KW, De Hertogh AA. Tissue culture of ornamental flowering bulbs (geophytes). Hortic Rev (Am Soc Hortic Sci) 2010; 18: 87-169.

[52] Van Aartrijk J, Van der Linde PC. *in vitro* propagation of flower-bulb crops. Conference on Tissue Culture as a Plant Production System for Horticultural Crops. Beltsville, MD. Dordrecht: Springer Netherlands October 20–23, 1985; 317-31.

[53] Ulus A, Seyidoğlu N. Bazi doğal geofitlerin doku kültürü İle üretimi. Istanbul Üniv Orman Fak Derg 2006; 56(1): 71-80.

[54] Atay S. Soğanlı bitkiler, Türkiye'den İhracatı yapılan türlerin tanıtım ve üretim rehberi. İstanbul: Doğal Hayatı Koruma Derneği 1996.

[55] Steinegger D, Fech JC, Lindgren DT, Streich A. Ornamental grasses in Nebraska landscapes. Nebraska Coop Ext 1999.

[56] Dana MN, Pecknold P, Sadof C. Flowering Bulbs, Purdue University Cooperative Extension Service 2001. Available from: http://www.agoom.purdue.edu/AgCom/Pubs/menu.htm

[57] Fech JC, Rodie SN. How to: install bulbs. Grounds Maintanance 2002; 37(4): 49-53.

[58] Relf D, Ball EC. Flowering bulbs: Culture and maintenance Extension Publication Number 2004; 426-201. Available from: http://www.ext.vt.edu/pubs/envirohort/426-201/426-201.html

[59] Weaver SL, Beattie DJ, Holcomb EJ. Over-wintering spring bulbs in large containers. Bull Penn Flower Growers 1995; (432): 1-3.

[60] Duarte AR, Mendoza AB, Herrera LB, López AR, Maiti RK. Effect of light intensity on flower bud abortions in lily (*Lilium* spp.). Crop Res 2004; 28(1/3): 68-75.

[61] Tsai PeiFen TP. The responses of bulb emergence to temperatures in *Lilium* populations native in Taiwan. Zuowu, Huanjing Yu Shengwu Zixun 2004; 1(3): 215-24.

[62] Matsubara K, Inamoto K, Doi M, Imanishi H. Evaluation of cold hardiness of some geophytes for landscape planting. Sci Rep Grad Sch Agric Biol Sci. Osaka Prefecture University 2003; 55: pp. 37-41.

[63] Zimmer K, Girmen M. Temperature dependency of the development of *Anemone blanda* and *Eranthis hiemalis*. Gartenbauwissenschaft 1987; 52(6): 263-5.

[64] Odeny DA, Narina SS. In wild crop relatives: genomic and breeding resources: vegetables. Berlin, Heidelberg: Springer Berlin Heidelberg. 2011; pp. 1-10.

[65] Dirik H. Plantasyon (bitkilendirme ve dikim) teknikleri. İÜ Orman Fakültesi Yayın 2008; p. 490.

[66] Margaris HGNS, Vokou D, Vokou D. Effects of grazing pressure on succession process and productivity of old fields on Mediterranean islands. Environ Manage 1998; 22(4): 589-96. [http://dx.doi.org/10.1007/s002679900130] [PMID: 9582394]

[67] Škornik S, Vidrih M, Kaligarič M. The effect of grazing pressure on species richness, composition and productivity in North Adriatic Karst pastures. Plant Biosyst 2010; 144(2): 355-64. [http://dx.doi.org/10.1080/11263501003750250]

[68] Farahmand H, Nazari F. Environmental and anthropogenic pressures on geophytes of Iran and the possible protection strategies: a review. Int J Hortic Sci Technol 2015; 2(2): 111-32.

[69]   Ekici B. Some geophyte plants determined in Bartın/Turkey. Biological Diversity and Conservation 2017.

[70]   Fornal-Pieniak B, Ollik M, Schwerk A. Impact of different levels of anthropogenic pressure on the plant species composition in woodland sites. Urban For Urban Green 2019; 38: 295-304.
[http://dx.doi.org/10.1016/j.ufug.2019.01.013]

[71]   Younsi SE, Bouziane Z. Plant diversity in Mediterranean coastal dune systems subjected to anthropogenic disturbances. Biodivers Res Conserv 2023; 72(1): 25-38.
[http://dx.doi.org/10.14746/biorc.2023.72.4]

CHAPTER 2

Araceae

Gülşen Güçlü[1], Burak Tüzün[2,*] and Esra Uçar[2]

[1] *Department of Health Programmes, Health Services Vocational School, Sivas Cumhuriyet University, Sivas, Türkiye*

[2] *Department of Crop and Animal Production, Sivas Technical Sciences Vocational School, Sivas Cumhuriyet University, Sivas, Türkiye*

Abstract: The Araceae family comprises a diverse group of plants, the majority of which are found in tropical and subtropical regions. As of yet, 144 genera and 3,645 species have been identified. These plants often exhibit geophytic characteristics, with underground stems such as tubers and rhizomes.

The timing of flowering and fruiting varies among species and climates. Some species flower without leaves at the end of dry seasons, while others follow seasonal precipitation patterns. Although no Araceae species have been reported in true deserts, some, such as *Eminium spiculatum* subsp. *negevense*, are found in dry regions, demonstrating the family's adaptability. Despite the limited research conducted thus far, preliminary studies have indicated the potential anticancer properties of certain Araceae plants, including *Anthurium*, *Philodendron*, and *Dieffenbachia*. However, further research is necessary to confirm their efficacy and safety in cancer treatment.

The use of herbal medicine, which employs a variety of plant parts, has a long history in folk medicine. There is a growing interest in the biological effects of these plants. Phytochemicals derived from traditional medicinal plants, including those from the Araceae family, show promise in disease management, including cancer.

This chapter provides comprehensive information on the geophytic properties of plants in the Araceae family and their activity against cancer.

Keywords: Anticancer, Araceae, Breeding, Geophytes, *In silico* analyses.

INTRODUCTION

The Araceae family is a large family that includes plants with ground cover or climbing characteristics, mostly found in tropical and subtropical regions. There are 144 genera and 3,645 species reported so far [1 - 3]. The characteristic spathe

* **Corresponding author Burak Tüzün:** Department of Crop and Animal Production, Sivas Technical Sciences Vocational School, Sivas Cumhuriyet University, Sivas, Türkiye; E-mail: theburaktuzun@yahoo.com

Sibel Day (Ed.)

and spadix organs of the family member plants allow them to be easily distinguished in nature (Fig. **1**).

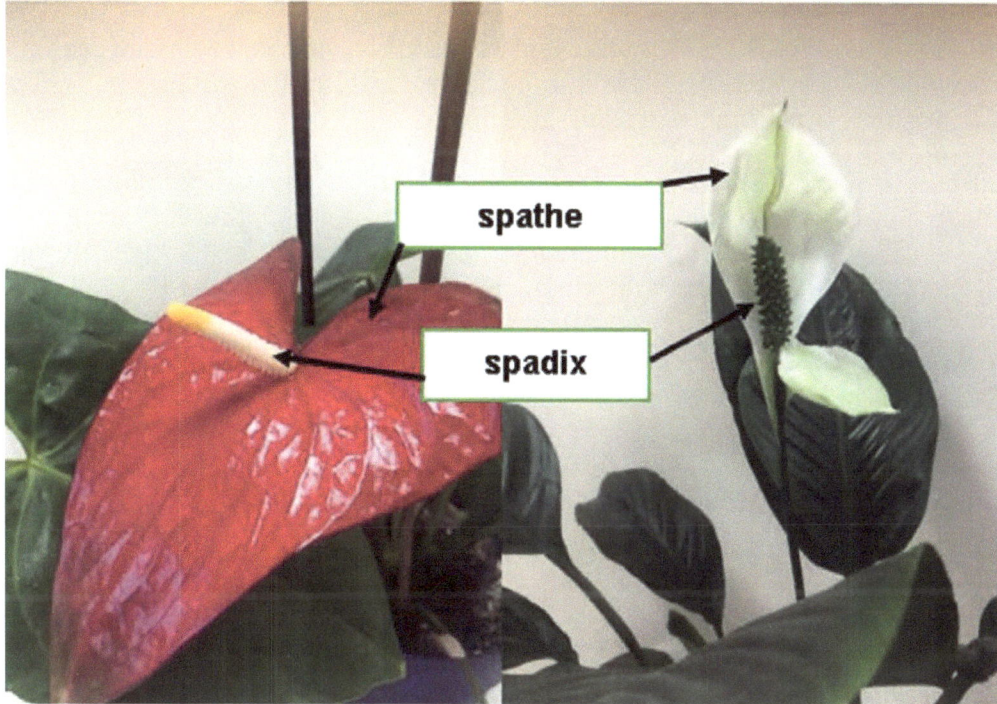

Fig. (1). Spathe and spadix organs in the Araceae family.

Araceae plants are commonly found in tropical humid regions. To a lesser extent, they also grow in temperate regions as halophytes or geophytes [4].

GEOPHYTES IN ARACEAE

Plants with underground stems, such as tubers and rhizomes, are classified as geophytes. In aroids, geophytic species are observed in arid regions or areas with intense winter seasons. However, there are also rainforest geophytes. Despite their climatic disparities, these species (*e.g.*, *Amorphophallus maculatus, Dracontium prancei, and Zomicarpella amazonica*) exhibit growth periodicity and dormancy.

A considerable number of genera are found in more than one climatic regime. In *Stylochaeton*, the rainforest species *S. zenkeri* has evergreen, unthickened roots, and the flower state occurs with the leaves. Other species, for example, *S. natalensis*, grow in regions with a pronounced dry season and are dormant during this period. This species has thick, fleshy roots and usually flowers before or just after the leaves appear. Similarly, the genera *Amorphophallus* and *Dracontium* exhibit considerable ecological diversity, occurring in rainforests or seasonally in green forests, deciduous forests, savannas, or grasslands (*A. abyssinicus* and *D. margaretae*).

Without leaves, geophytes from deciduous woods, savannas, or unique seasonal grasslands flower, usually at the end of the dry season after the first rains. The rainy season is when fruits and leaves develop.

Different species have different flowering and fruiting times depending on the climate. For instance, *Biarum ditschianum* (Türkiye) flowers in the spring after the end of the rainy season, while *Biarum davisii* (Crete and Türkiye) flowers early in the autumn, and fruit development continues all year long [5]. Native to the Mediterranean region, *Arum* species such as *A. dioscoridis* and *A. italicum* grow during the comparatively warm winter wet season, while *A. maculatum*, which is found further north, grows from spring to late summer and does not grow during the cold winter months [5]. *Arum* species native to the Mediterranean region (*e.g.*, *A. dioscoridis* and *A. italicum*) exhibit growth during the relatively warm winter wet season, whereas the more northerly *A. maculatum* demonstrates growth from spring to late summer and is dormant during the cold winter months [6].

No species of the Araceae family has been reported to occur in true deserts. However, *Eminium spiculatum* subsp. *negevense* has been observed to grow in the Najaf Desert [7]. However, some species are also known to grow in extremely dry areas. Examples of these species are *Arisaema* and *Sauromatum venosum* in the Arabian Peninsula and East Africa, *Arum* and *Eminium* in Central Asia, *Arum* and *Biarum* in North Africa and parts of Asia, and several *Stylochaeton* species in the African Sahel. These areas frequently have annual wet seasons during which the plants grow vegetatively, or they can be found in areas with subterranean water sources. Although it is more frequently found in savannas and evergreen forests, *Zamioculcas zamiifolia* is a succulent plant that can be found in settings with low moisture levels. It stores water in its thick petiole.

Morphogenesis and Flowering in Araceae Plants

Amorphophallus

Amorphophallus is an herbaceous perennial geophyte primarily distributed in Southeast Asia and Africa [8]. It is also a highly valuable economic crop, utilized across various industries such as food, pharmaceuticals, and chemicals, owing to the high content of glucomannan in its underground bulbs [9]. A notable characteristic of this genus is its morphology, characterized by a single leaf emerging from the tuber, consisting of a vertical petiole and a horizontal leaf layer (Fig. **2**) [10].

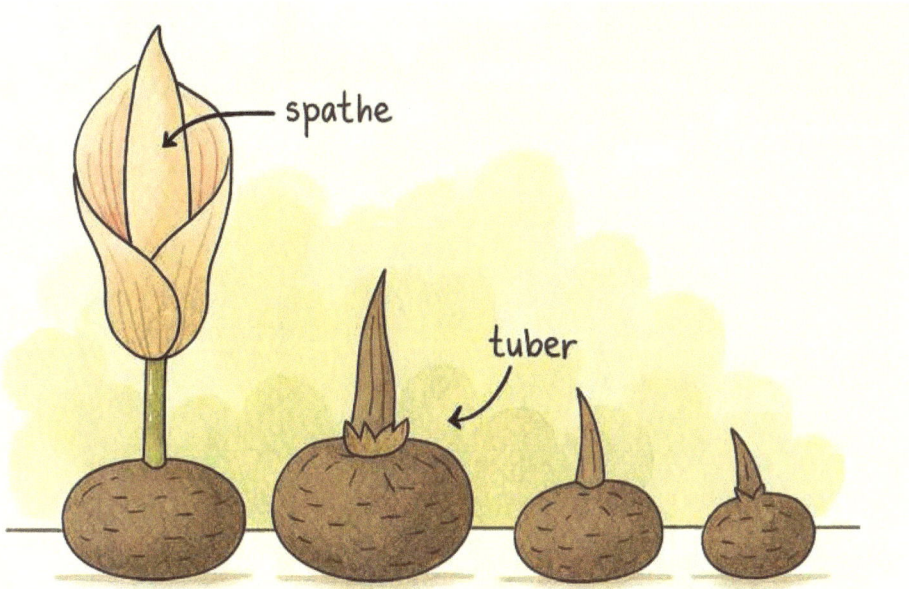

Fig. (2). Tuber and flower organs of *Amorphophallus* [11].

Some species of *Amorphophallus* have proven to be challenging to propagate due to their tendency to flower every 5-6 years and their low seed yield. Moreover, traditional asexual propagation methods yield only 6-10 rhizomes from a single bulb after more than 3 years of cultivation [12]. This limitation hampers large-scale cultivation of *Amorphophallus*.

Arum

Arum, a perennial herb characterized by an underground stem with tubers, is primarily found in Europe and Central Asia, typically thriving in temperate and warm temperate woodlands. The mature plant comprises a central axis and a terminal meristem. During development, this meristem produces a variety of structures, including leaves, petals, spathe, female and sterile female flowers, male flowers, and backward hairs [13]. An intriguing aspect of its growth is that the meristem ultimately forms a cylindrical, vascularized storage organ without lateral components (Fig. **3**).

In *Arum*, the onset of the flower state is known to occur in July or early August, with flowering occurring the following spring. The onset of the flower state has consistently been reported to occur in July, when the stem tuber reaches a minimum weight of 7.4 g and the bud first forms at least 6-10 leaf primordia at a specific position in the second leaf axil below the current year's spathe [15].

Fig. (3). Schematic view of the organs of the plant *Arum maculatum* [14].

Stylochaeton

Stylochaeton is a genus traditionally classified in the family Araceae [16]. The genus is native to and distributed in tropical and southeastern subtropical Africa in savanna and moist deciduous forests [17].

Members of *Stylochaeton* are geophytes characterized by a slender rhizome and often densely swollen fleshy roots (Fig. **4**). As is typical for the family Araceae, the genus has a spadix containing clusters of seated, unisexual flowers bearing a thickened, fleshy axis (spike) as the floral state. The small flowers are tightly packed along the erect spike, with the female flowers typically above the male flowers. The male flowers are composed of numerous filiform stamens clustered together, while the female flowers are comprised of numerous individual pistils covered by a tubular perigone with their protruding styles. The spadix emerges from a vase-shaped modified leaf (spathe), the base of which is completely closed [17].

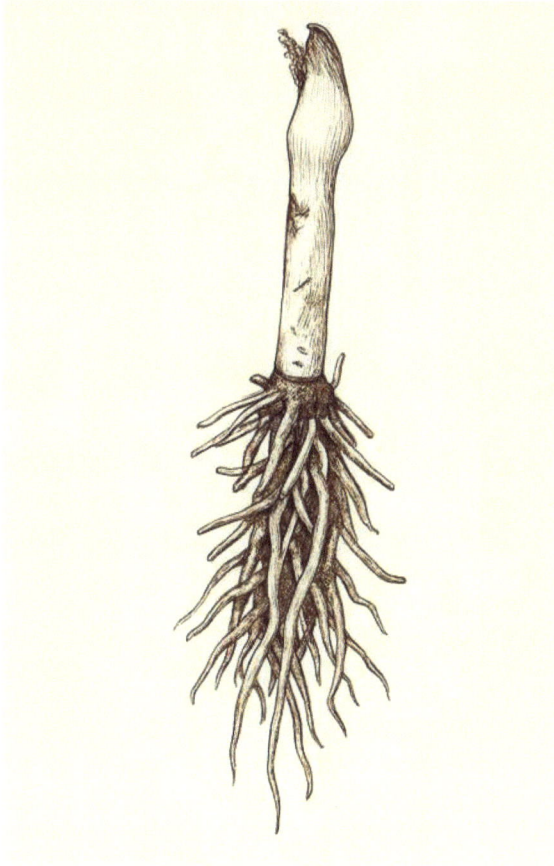

Fig. (4). Different root structures of *Stylochaeton hypogaeus* [18].

General Agronomic Aspects in Production

Suitable Habitats for Geophytes

The entirety of a region's genes, ecosystems, and biological processes is known as its biodiversity [19]. Natural plants are in mutual interaction with their surroundings in the areas they inhabit, contributing to the lives of organisms as shelters and food sources for wildlife [20, 21]. Wild species form the origin of essential food items necessary for our survival [22].

The stem structure of geophytes is in the form of underground organs, which undergo transformation into developed stems resembling roots. Some take the form of bulbs with detachable leaves. Some are hard tubers or corms, while others resemble elongated root structures called rhizomes [23]. Geophytes store reserve nutrients underground thanks to their bulbous or tuberous structures. When the underground part is separated from the main plant, it has the ability to generate a new plant. Bulbs planted in the fall, after completing their development underground, flower approximately five months later, thanks to reserve nutrients when appropriate conditions are provided [24]. Plants developing underground in this structure mostly require a soil texture in which they can comfortably thrive. Many Araceae grow well in humus-rich soils and in shady and semi-shaded areas. They can grow along with ferns and shade-loving plants. In the region where it grows, leaf residues on the soil surface protect the tubers or rhizomes from freezing in winter. They can easily grow in stony and rocky areas. Geophytes in the Mediterranean region are not cold-resistant. To protect them from frost in winter, it is necessary to remove the tubers from the soil and keep them dry in the sand. In contrast, some species can thrive in watery areas such as streams, swamps, and ponds [17]. The regions where geophytes show the best distribution are those with cold and rainy winters and hot and dry summers. In addition, geophytes are more commonly found in regions with dry and humid tropical climates. Geophytes grow in regions ranging from countries surrounding the Mediterranean to Central Asia, California and Chile, southwestern Africa, and western and southern Australia [24].

Uses of Geophytes

Because the stems of geophytes develop underground, they are resilient to adverse environmental conditions and can grow spontaneously in the mountains. The compounds they secrete, which contribute to their resistance to adverse environmental conditions, endow them with medicinal properties. In addition to their medicinal and aromatic values, these plants can also be used in landscaping applications, as well as in medians and roadside plantings, thanks to their showy and beautifully scented flowers [25]. In addition to their aesthetic beauty, geophytes are used in different areas, such as food, beverages, and herbal medicine. This family includes bulbous and rhizomatous plants. It is believed that due to climate change caused by global warming, there will be an increased demand for drought-resistant, low-water, and irrigation-independent plants. In this context, geophytes, which include rhizomatous and bulbous plants that are quite resilient, stand out [26]. Plants with bulbs, tubers, and rhizomes that grow naturally in nature can be used as breeding materials in terms of resistance to diseases and pests [27].

The Status of Geophytes

Geophytes contribute to the biological richness of a country. The cultivation of these plants ranks among the foremost protective factors for natural flora. Due to factors such as the opening of agricultural lands to transportation and urbanization, as well as technological and industrial developments, these spontaneously occurring natural populations can be adversely affected. At the same time, due to indiscriminate and uncontrolled harvesting, as well as consumption by animals, some plants may occasionally face the threat of extinction. Due to factors such as rehabilitation of wetlands and marshy areas, dams, herbicides applied to plants grown in cultural areas, and factory waste, these plants, which are damaged, can be preserved if they are cultivated. For these reasons, geophytes with known and perhaps yet-to-be-discovered phytochemicals, which are important for humans, may be at risk of extinction [26, 28]. These reasons contribute to the decrease in species diversity, and to ensure continuity, the preservation of habitat and ecosystem is necessary [29]. These plants need to be preserved, developed, and even ensured for their sustainability. In order to prevent the endangerment of geophytes and to ensure the availability of the desired quality and quantity of plants, they need to be cultivated.

The Reasons for Cultivating Geophytes

Thanks to the active substances they contain, some geophytes can possess medicinal and aromatic properties. Most medicinal and aromatic plants are supplied for consumption through direct harvesting from nature without cultivation. Gathering from nature not only endangers the survival of plant species but also results in low yields and more expensive products due to insufficient quantities of plants. Due to being collected by untrained individuals, sometimes the wrong plant or various chemical strains of that plant can be gathered during harvesting. The effective substances within these plants are at their highest levels during specific periods and should be harvested in a timely manner. If plants carrying active substances are harvested early in the morning after being watered, an increase in the amount of essential oil can be observed. However, since it is not possible to monitor the individuals collecting these plants, it may not be possible to determine when and how they were harvested. Additionally, if processes such as drying and storage are not carried out carefully after harvesting plants, disruptions in the quality of herbal drugs can occur. Such plants are recommended to be dried in the shade and ventilated on steel shelves. If drying is done in closed and unventilated areas, plants may experience decay, deterioration, and even carcinogenic fungal diseases. At the same time, plants should be cultivated in areas close to where they will be processed. Otherwise, disruptions may occur during transportation. The necessity of cultivating such plants is not limited only to these reasons. They are also threatened by many diseases in their natural habitats and by numerous pests feeding on these plants. Since the cultivation of such plants is not widely practiced, each plant may have its unique climate, soil, and care requirements, and there is limited information available about them. Preserving the natural habitats and genetic resources of plants, ensuring the continuity of species, and meeting the increasing demand for plant products may be possible through the cultivation of natural plant species. Solving problems in cultivation techniques through agronomic methods and breeding efforts is always the primary goal to increase yield and quality. Thus, biological resources are preserved and contribute to the economy [30, 31].

The content and quality of active ingredients in such plants with phytochemical compounds are also important. It is desired that the effective substances in these plants have minimal genetic heterogeneity due to pollination and fertilization.

There are two important factors in preserving plant species and diversity within species.

In situ **conservation**: The protection of plant genetic resources in their natural habitat, allowing for their evolution.

Ex situ **conservation:** Preservation in gene banks and cultured environments (such as collections and botanical gardens).

Many geophytes develop during dry summer days and cold winter days, spending their time underground in dormancy. They undergo rapid development with the arrival of spring rains and warm weather.

Production Methods of Geophytes

Geophytes can be produced by two methods

1- Generative (seed) method
2- Vegetative (division of baby bulbs, tubers, rhizomes and bulbous tubers, armpit baby bulbs, onion scales, particle and twin scales, cutting the onion base and tissue culture) method

Geophytes can be produced by both methods. However, generative production (seed production) has some disadvantages compared to vegetative production.

1- The resulting plants do not resemble the parent plant due to genetic variation.
2- Some species cannot produce enough seeds.
3- The time required to obtain a plant of sufficient size to produce flowers from seed planting is long [32].

For example, *Lysichiton, Orontium*, and *Symplocarpus*, which belong to the Araceae family, can propagate by seed, while *Acorus* and *Calla*, which cannot produce seeds and also belong to the Araceae family, are easily propagated by dividing rhizomes [17].

Some geophytes can also be propagated by seed. However, since cultivation of these plants is not widespread, obtaining seeds is not easy. In seed propagation, germination difficulties may occur. Seeds can be dispersed by insects, and if they are not seeded at the appropriate depth, they may rot due to improper burial. Even if everything goes well, the time from sowing the seed to flowering in bulbous plants is often very long, so the vegetative propagation method is preferred more [24].

Cancer Activities of some Plants in the Araceae Family

Information on cancer studies for plants in the Araceae family is quite limited, and generally, there is little research on the effects of these plants on cancer treatment. However, there are some preliminary studies and significant findings regarding the cancer-fighting potential of some plants belonging to the Araceae family [33 - 37].

For example, some studies suggest that components found in plants of the Araceae family, such as *Anthurium*, *Philodendron*, and *Dieffenbachia*, have antioxidant properties and that these properties may prevent the formation and spread of cancer cells [38 - 40]. However, more research is needed on the effectiveness and safety of these herbs in cancer treatment.

Herbal medicine, alternatively referred to as botanical medicine, entails the utilization of various parts of plants, including seeds, fruits, roots, leaves, bark, or flowers, for medicinal purposes [41]. In ancient times, medicinal plants, along with plant products and certain animal species, were extensively employed in folk medicine to address a wide spectrum of ailments. These plants serve as direct sources of therapeutic agents and raw materials for the synthesis of more complex compounds [42]. The extraction of these natural products is not only cost-effective but also deemed safe and readily available [43]. The demand for herbal remedies is increasing, leading to a rise in the use of plants in modern medicine. Due to the comparatively lower incidence of adverse effects associated with herbal medicines, there is a growing global interest in exploring the biological effects of traditional medicinal plants or isolating their phytochemical constituents for the treatment of various diseases. Phytochemicals, defined as naturally occurring chemical compounds in plants that exert biological effects in disease management, play a pivotal role in this regard. Certain key phytochemical components derived from traditional medicinal plants have demonstrated the capability to inhibit or attenuate specific types of cancer [44].

Laboratory studies and animal experiments continue to understand the potential of plants belonging to the Araceae family in fighting cancer. However, the results of these studies are not yet definitive, and more clinical research is needed before these plants can be used in cancer treatment.

It seems that there are a few studies on some important plants in the Araceae family with the potential to treat breast cancer. However, theoretical calculations have been made to determine the chemical that causes the activity of these plants from the Araceae family in breast cancer.

Anthurium

There is very little information about cancer-related research on the Anthurium plant, which is in the Araceae family. *Anthurium* plant is generally known as an indoor ornamental plant and is an important plant used for decorative purposes in various places. However, there is no scientifically verified evidence about the effects of this herb on cancer.

Cancer research generally continues at full speed, investigating whether plant extracts or components inhibit the growth of cancer cells, induce apoptosis (programmed cell death) of cells, or affect cancer cells in other ways [45, 46]. However, such studies on the *Anthurium* have not been widely conducted.

In the study conducted by Kuanprasert and his colleagues [47] on *Anthurium*, they performed GC/MS analysis for various species of *Anthurium*. With this analysis, they determined the chemistries within the plant. Based on the results of this analysis, all these chemicals were examined one by one, and their activities against breast cancer proteins were compared. The activities of these chemicals against Estrogen Receptor (PDB ID: 1A52) [48] and BRCT repeat region from the breast cancer-associated protein, BRCA1 (PDB ID: 1JNX) [49], were compared. The results obtained are detailed in Table **1**. The interaction of the molecule of beta-pinene and cis-sabinene hydrate, which has the highest activity, with these two proteins is given in Figs. (**5** and **6**).

Table 1. Numerical values of the docking parameters of molecules against proteins.

1A52	Docking Score	Glide Ligand Efficiency	Glide Hbond	Glide Evdw	Glide Ecoul	Glide Emodel	Glide Energy	Glide Einternal	Glide Posenum
beta pinene	-6.72	-0.67	0.00	-22.54	-0.02	-31.70	-22.56	0.00	120
1-8-cineole	-6.59	-0.60	0.00	-22.49	-0.04	-31.32	-22.52	0.00	238
cis-sabinene hydrate	-6.52	-0.59	-0.16	-14.92	-3.51	-23.25	-18.44	4.31	118
alfa pinene	-6.51	-0.65	0.00	-17.25	-0.10	-24.13	-17.35	0.00	374
limonene	-5.85	-0.59	0.00	-16.95	-0.07	-22.92	-17.02	0.38	390

(Table 1) cont.....

1JNX	Docking Score	Glide ligand efficiency	Glide hbond	Glide evdw	Glide ecoul	Glide emodel	Glide energy	Glide einternal	Glide posenum
cis-sabinene hydrate	-4.49	-0.41	-0.32	-11.09	-3.32	-18.27	-14.41	0.57	182
beta pinene	-4.00	-0.40	0.00	-15.46	0.13	-18.99	-15.33	0.00	265
alfa pinene	-3.82	-0.38	0.00	-12.47	0.39	-14.91	-12.08	0.00	111
1-8-cineole	-3.57	-0.32	0.00	-13.13	-0.48	-17.04	-13.61	0.00	224
limonene	-3.12	-0.31	0.00	-11.59	-1.14	-15.04	-12.73	0.20	374

Epipremnum aureum

There is no scientifically proven information about the direct effects of the plant known as *Epipremnum aureum* or popularly known as "Golden Pothos" [50] or "English ivy" on cancer. This plant is an indoor plant usually used for decorative purposes in homes.

However, some plants may contain compounds that can help fight cancer. However, such research and evidence regarding the plant *Epipremnum aureum* are limited, and more scientific research is needed to draw definitive conclusions.

When the study conducted by Patil and Wadkar [51] is examined, it is seen that good results are obtained against breast cancer. The MCF-7 cell lines were significantly cytotoxically affected by the chloroform extracts. Apoptotic bodies, which are tiny spherical pieces, and small nuclei with severe chromatin condensation, blebbing, and nuclear disintegration are the microscopic findings. The MCF-7 cell lines exhibit a substantial increase in apoptosis in response to the chloroform extract.

Ethanol at a 70–80% concentration is used to extract most chemical molecules. Using ethanol extract to draw a conclusion can be challenging. Therefore, the chloroform extract will be highlighted. Curiously, a large percentage of brine shrimp lethality is shown in the chloroform extract, and this is verified using MCF-7 cell lines. Due to their inherent complexity, many processes involving porous materials and micro-scale devices like MEMS demand significant CPU resources for effective simulation. Consequently, to make direct methods viable for micro-scale systems, mesoscopic approaches have been introduced, including Direct Monte Carlo Simulation (DSMC), Information Preservation (IP), and, more recently, Lattice Boltzmann (LB) methods. In this chapter, the discussion will explore certain aspects of macroscopic approaches, with a particular focus on DSMC and LB methods.

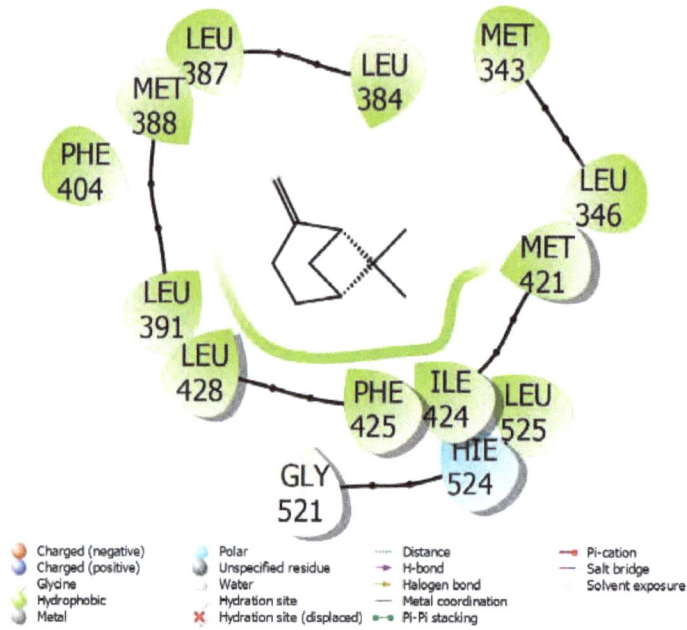

Fig. (5). Presentation interactions of beta-pinene with 1A52 protein.

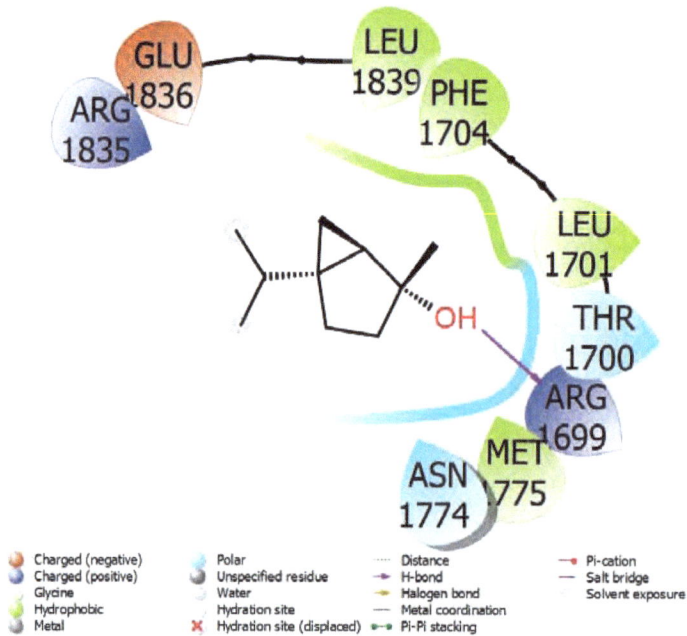

Fig. (6). Presentation interactions of cis-sabinene hydrate with 1JNx protein.

In the study conducted by Meshram [52] and his colleagues, GC/MS analysis was performed on *E. aureum*. With this analysis, they determined the chemistries within the plant. Based on the results of this analysis, all these chemicals were examined one by one, and their activities against breast cancer proteins were compared. The results obtained are detailed in Table **2**. The interaction of the molecule of 2-Ethoxycarbonyl-5-oxo pyrrolidine and (3S)-(-)-3-Acetamido-pyrrolidine, which has the highest activity, with these two proteins is given in Figs. (**7** and **8**).

Table 2. Numerical values of the docking parameters of molecules against proteins.

1A52	Docking Score	Glide Ligand Efficiency	Glide Hbond	Glide Evdw	Glide Ecoul	Glide Emodel	Glide Energy	Glide Einternal	Glide Posenum
2-Ethoxycarbonyl-5-oxo pyrrolidine	-7.38	-0.37	0.00	-37.10	0.08	-49.34	-37.02	3.96	113
3',5'-Diacetylthymidine	-7.29	-0.32	-0.02	-41.15	-1.02	-58.68	-42.18	7.64	246
Benzenemethanamine, N-(1,1-dimethylethyl)-	-6.52	-0.54	0.00	-22.23	-4.82	-38.08	-27.05	2.39	45
(3S)-(-)-3-Acetamidopyrrolidine	-6.43	-0.71	-0.18	-18.70	-8.40	-41.02	-27.10	0.16	396
1,2,4,5-Tetrazine, hexahydro-1,2,4,5-tetramethyl-	-5.90	-0.59	0.00	-17.57	0.07	-23.61	-17.50	0.00	255
1JNX	Docking Score	Glide ligand efficiency	Glide hbond	Glide evdw	Glide ecoul	Glide emodel	Glide energy	Glide einternal	Glide posenum
(3S)-(-)-3-Acetamidopyrrolidine	-5.34	-0.59	-0.61	-13.23	-8.20	-33.46	-21.43	0.01	223
5-Oxoproline	-4.92	-0.55	-0.45	-11.72	-5.81	-24.45	-17.54	0.59	85
Methyl 5-oxo-2-pyrrolidinecarboxylate	-4.89	-0.49	-0.41	-13.14	-4.96	-23.77	-18.10	0.10	373
1H-Tetrazole-1,5-diamine	-4.61	-0.66	-0.61	-8.08	-7.08	-19.93	-15.16	0.00	112
2-(Cyanoimino)oxazolidine	-4.46	-0.56	-0.19	-13.12	-4.09	-21.97	-17.21	0.00	375

Biarum bovei (Kardeh)

Biarum bovei is a plant belonging to the Araceae family and is commonly known as Kardeh. This plant is a plant native to the Mediterranean region, where it generally grows on limestone, hill slopes, and field edges and has traditional uses. In addition, four species have been reported so far in Iraq (Ruanduz and Haji Omeran) region at altitudes of 300-2750 m. These plants include *Biarum bovei, B. carduchrum, B. syriacum,* and *B. straussii* [53, 54]. While *B. carduchrum* and *B. straussii* are well-studied phytochemically and biologically, systematic studies have shown that *B. bovei* has no phytochemical profiling and cytotoxic effects [55 - 60]. Moreover, due to the wider geographical distribution of *B. straussii*, it has been extensively studied by numerous scientists [58, 59]. However, the number of studies on cancer is quite low.

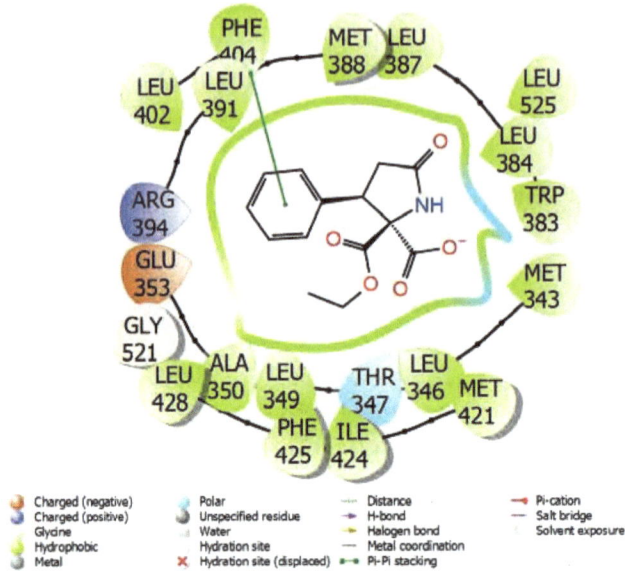

Fig. (7). Presentation interactions of 2-Ethoxycarbonyl-5-oxo pyrrolidine with 1A52 protein.

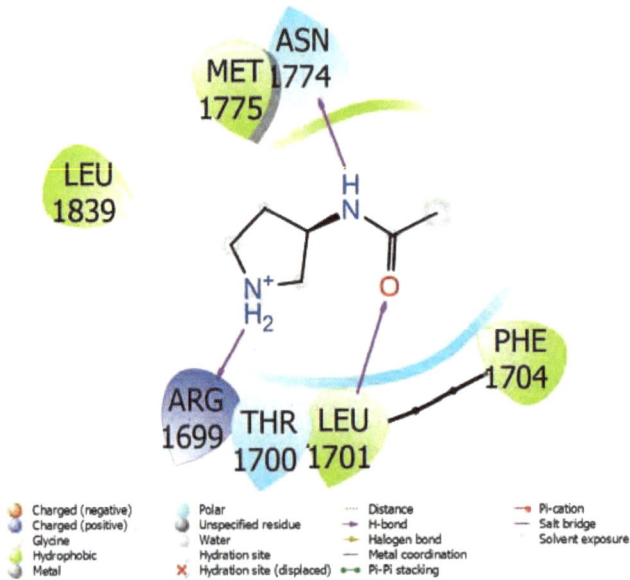

Fig. (8). Presentation interactions of (3S)-(-)-3-Acetamidopyrrolidine with 1JNx protein.

The subterranean portion (bulb) of *Biarum* species has long been used to cure hemorrhoids and diarrhea by drying, powdering, and then cooking it as a soup [61]. The phytochemical, antioxidant, and cytotoxic properties of *B. bovei*, an Iraqi native, have not yet been studied. Furthermore, *B. bovei* aqueous extract showed strong antioxidant, ACE enzyme reduction, antidiabetic, and antibacterial activities, which considerably enhanced the biofunctionality of produced gluten hydrolysates [62, 63]. Studies on the *Biarum* species in the literature have attested to the plant's efficacy against a range of oxidative stress-related ailments [64, 65].

Conventionally, *B. bovei*, known by its traditional name Kardin, is consumed as a soup known as Kardeh due to its edible properties. Moreover, its industrial utility as an enhancer for milk coagulation has been previously documented. Furthermore, studies have indicated the antibacterial potential of *B. bovei* against *Listeria monocytogenes*, *Salmonella enteritidis*, and *Pseudomonas aeruginosa* [66, 67].

Free radicals, also referred to as reactive oxygen or nitrogen species (ROS or RNS), are molecules possessing unpaired electrons, making them more reactive compared to paired molecules. Among the most significant ROS are hydroxyl radical, superoxide radical anion, nitric oxide, and peroxyl radicals, alongside hydrogen peroxide. Additionally, singlet oxygen is recognized as another important radical species [68]. ROS and RNS levels play a crucial role in cell physiology as beneficial or harmful factors. When their levels are in low to moderate amounts, they participate in many pathways of cell signaling. Free radicals can be harmful when too much is produced, and there are insufficient levels of antioxidant enzymes or reduced weight molecules [69, 70]. Oxidative/nitrosative stress can result from any disruption in ROS/RNS generation, which is necessary for redox regulators, the processes that keep cells functioning normally by balancing benefits and drawbacks. Reactive oxygen species (ROS) are hypothesized to contribute to the advancement of cancer by inducing carcinogenesis and enhancing tumor cell modification/proliferation or cell death [71]. This mechanism has been related to numerous health issues, including cancer. Alkaloids, flavonoids, tannins, terpenes, phenolics, saponins, anthraquinones, and phlobatannins are among the phytochemical constituents identified in *Biarum* species [55]. These phytochemicals can benefit or harm human health. Similarly, synthetic drugs can be therapeutic at one dosage and dangerous at another [72]. Therefore, some quality testing is done on herbs before they become available for consumers in order to avoid toxicity and find acceptable quantities of safe herbal products. One of the most used methods for determining the safe or harmful dosage of plant items and their phytochemicals is the acute toxicity test [73]. Previous studies on *B. carduchorum* and *B. straussi* have shown that they have non-toxic effects [54, 74], as evidenced by the absence of aberrant alterations in behavior or physiology when the extracts are used at varying dosages.

In the study conducted by Wahab and his colleagues [75], GC/MS analysis was performed on *B. bovei*. With this analysis, they determined the chemistries within the plant. Based on the results of this analysis, all these chemicals were examined one by one, and their activities against breast cancer proteins were compared. The results obtained are detailed in Table **3**. The interaction of the molecule of beta-pinene and cis-sabinene hydrate, which has the highest activity, with these two proteins is given in Figs. (**9** and **10**).

Table 3. Numerical values of the docking parameters of molecules against enzymes.

1A52	Docking Score	Glide Ligand Efficiency	Glide Hbond	Glide Evdw	Glide Ecoul	Glide Emodel	Glide Energy	Glide Einternal	Glide Posenum
beta pinene	-6.72	-0.67	0.00	-22.54	-0.02	-31.70	-22.56	0.00	120
cis-sabinene hydrate	-6.52	-0.59	-0.16	-14.92	-3.51	-23.25	-18.44	4.31	118
alfa pinene	-6.51	-0.65	0.00	-17.25	-0.10	-24.13	-17.35	0.00	374
limonene	-5.85	-0.59	0.00	-16.95	-0.07	-22.92	-17.02	0.38	390
myrcene	-3.53	-0.35	0.00	-18.63	-0.60	-22.82	-19.23	1.28	69
1JNX	Docking Score	Glide ligand efficiency	Glide hbond	Glide evdw	Glide ecoul	Glide emodel	Glide energy	Glide einternal	Glide posenum
cis-sabinene hydrate	-4.49	-0.41	-0.32	-11.09	-3.32	-18.27	-14.41	0.57	182
beta pinene	-4.00	-0.40	0.00	-15.46	0.13	-18.99	-15.33	0.00	265
alfa pinene	-3.82	-0.38	0.00	-12.47	0.39	-14.91	-12.08	0.00	111
1-8-cineole	-3.57	-0.32	0.00	-13.13	-0.48	-17.04	-13.61	0.00	224
limonene	-3.12	-0.31	0.00	-11.59	-1.14	-15.04	-12.73	0.20	374

Monstera deliciosa

There is no information about specific cancer-related research on the *Monstera deliciosa* plant. *M. deliciosa* is a tropical plant species belonging to the Araceae family and is a popular plant often used in indoor decoration. However, there are no cancer-related studies available on this herb.

In the study conducted by Peppard [76], GC/MS analysis was performed on *M. deliciosa*. With this analysis, they determined the chemistries within the plant.

Based on the results of this analysis, all these chemicals were examined one by one, and their activities against breast cancer proteins were compared. The results obtained are detailed in Table **4**.

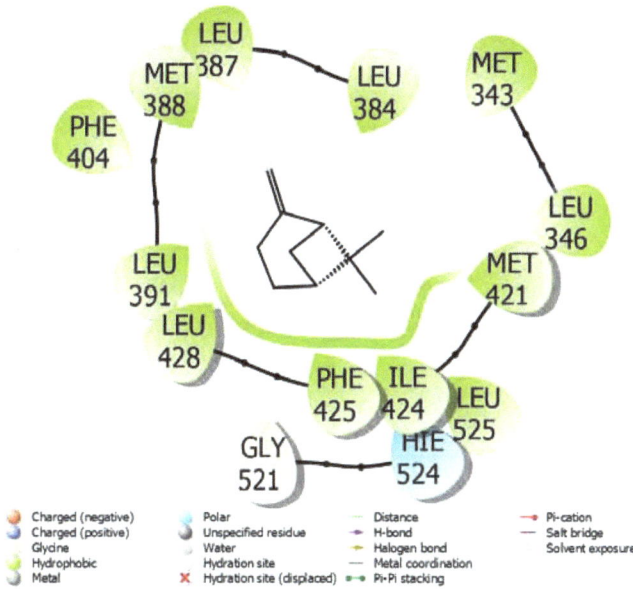

Fig. (9). Presentation interactions of beta-pinene with 1A52 protein.

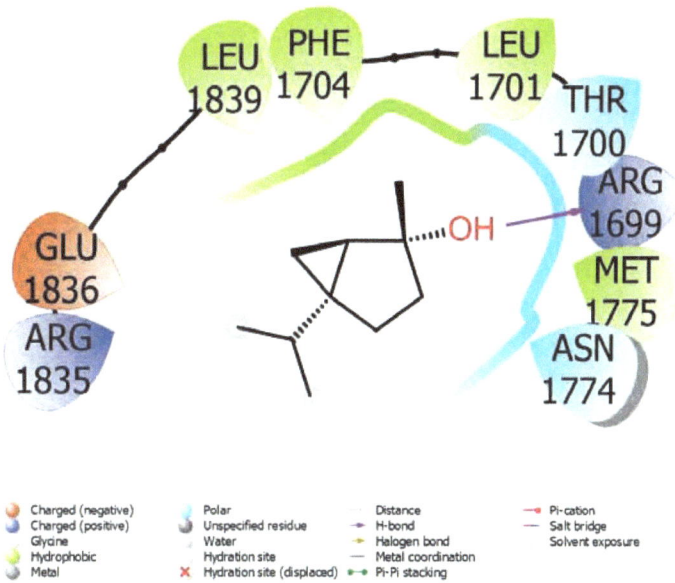

Fig. (10). Presentation interactions of cis-sabinene hydrate with 1JNX protein.

Table 4. Numerical values of the docking parameters of molecules against enzymes.

1A52	Docking Score	Glide Ligand Efficiency	Glide Hbond	Glide Evdw	Glide Ecoul	Glide Emodel	Glide Energy	Glide Einternal	Glide Posenum
3,4-dihydro-8-hydroxy-3-methyl-1H-2-benzopyran-1-one	-7.01	-0.54	0.00	-26.36	-3.20	-41.41	-29.56	0.04	73
delta-octalactone	-6.32	-0.63	0.00	-18.89	0.25	-26.30	-18.63	0.10	203
benzyl cyanide	-5.97	-0.66	0.00	-18.29	-1.17	-26.81	-19.45	0.22	366
trans-Iinalool oxide	-5.90	-0.49	-0.16	-24.38	-4.14	-38.34	-28.52	1.72	213
ethyl phenylacetate	-5.87	-0.49	0.00	-27.04	-0.75	-37.28	-27.79	0.97	184
1JNX	Docking Score	Glide ligand efficiency	Glide hbond	Glide evdw	Glide ecoul	Glide emodel	Glide energy	Glide einternal	Glide posenum
phenylacetaldehyde	-4.52	-0.50	-0.12	-14.78	-2.43	-21.80	-17.21	0.39	371
delta-octalactone	-4.48	-0.45	-0.30	-12.35	-3.49	-19.84	-15.84	0.93	349
acetoin	-4.47	-0.74	-0.24	-7.15	-8.49	-19.49	-15.64	2.20	355
acetoin	-4.21	-0.70	-0.32	-8.00	-5.05	-17.70	-13.05	1.05	395
4-vinylguaiacol	-4.12	-0.37	-0.16	-14.28	-4.95	-21.56	-19.24	6.37	129

The interaction of molecule 3,4-dihydro-8-hydroxy-3-methyl-1H-2-benzopyran-1-one and phenylacetaldehyde, which has the highest activity, with these two proteins is given in Figs. (**11** and **12**).

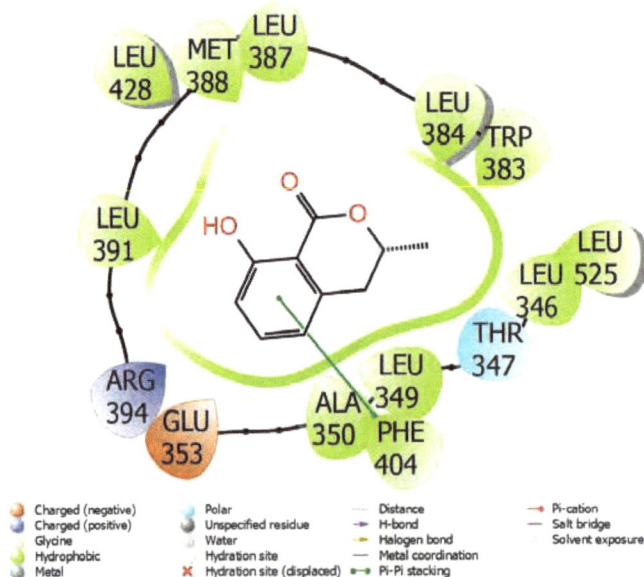

Fig. (11). Presentation interactions of 3,4-dihydro-8-hydroxy-3-methyl-1H-2-benzopyran- 1-one with 1A52 protein.

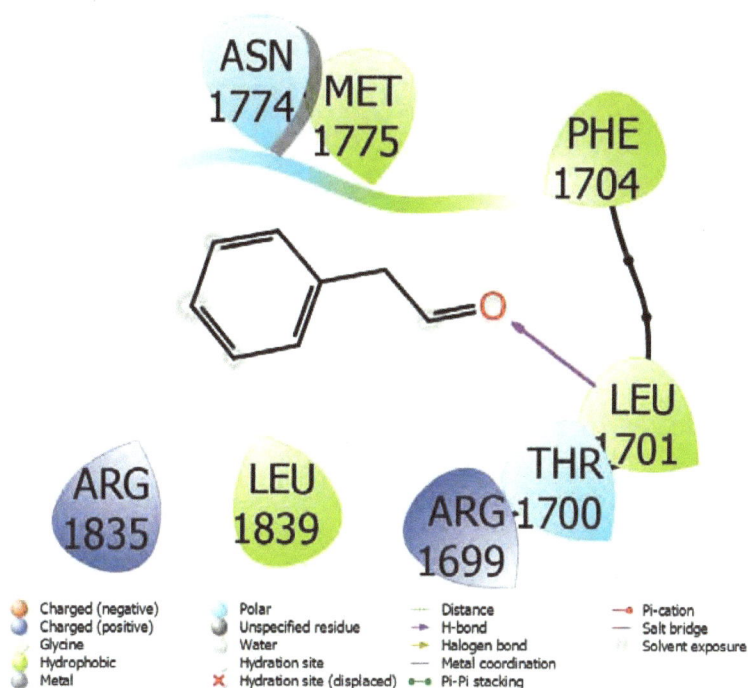

Fig. (12). Presentation interactions of phenylacetaldehyde with 1JNx protein.

Philodendron bipinnatifidum

The plant known in Brazil as guaimbé, banana-de-macaco, or imbé is an endemic species of South America called Philodendron bipinnatifidum Schott ex Endl. It is widely used in traditional medicine and possesses anesthetic, hemostatic, anti-inflammatory, and anthelmintic properties in addition to antitumor and anthelmintic properties [77]. Few scientific investigations have been conducted on this species despite its widespread usage in Brazilian popular medicine. The antioxidant capacity of the roots [78], the antiprotozoal activity of the branches and leaves [79], and the antiproliferative effect on liver cancer cells [80] have all been reported.

The pharmacological effect of the plant depends on the presence of secondary metabolites such as alkaloids, terpenes, flavonoids, and phytosterols. It modulates the immune system, and in addition to preventing cancer, it is also good for rheumatoid arthritis, cervical cancer, and benign prostatic hyperplasia [81, 82].

The process of encapsulating modifies the surface features of the utilized particles, modifies the release of compounds by directly affecting the rate of dissolution, and shields bioactive substances, hence decreasing contact with external elements like heat and light [83]. Supercritical fluid encapsulation techniques offer several benefits over conventional methods in the following areas: narrow size distribution of micro and/or nanoparticles formed, high encapsulation efficiency, control over crystal polymorphism, ability to process heat-sensitive compounds, and compound production [84].

The Solution Enhanced Dispersion with Supercritical Fluids (SEDS) technique is based on the fact that saturation with supercritical fluid causes solvent extraction and substrate precipitation, reducing the solubility of the active compound in an organic solvent. In addition to its antisolvent effect, supercritical fluid increases mass transfer by affecting solution dispersion and enables smaller particle sizes to be obtained [85].

In the study conducted by Scapinello and his colleagues [86], GC/MS analysis was performed on the plant *Philodendron bipinnatifidum*. With this analysis, they determined the chemistries within the plant. Based on the results of this analysis, all these chemicals were examined one by one, and their activities against breast cancer proteins were compared. The results obtained are detailed in Table **5**. The interaction of the molecule of D-asarinin and Alfa-Resorcinol, which has the highest activity, with these two proteins is given in Figs. (**13** and **14**).

Table 5. Numerical values of the docking parameters of molecules against enzymes.

1A52	Docking Score	Glide Ligand Efficiency	Glide Hbond	Glide Evdw	Glide Ecoul	Glide Emodel	Glide Energy	Glide Einternal	Glide Posenum
D-asarinin	-8.31	-0.32	0.00	-35.25	-0.56	-35.50	-35.80	5.97	273
Alfa-Resorcinol	-6.14	-0.77	-0.43	-15.00	-8.18	-33.68	-23.18	0.29	374
Glycerol 1-palmitate	-5.55	-0.24	0.00	-32.93	-8.96	-50.20	-41.89	13.60	320
Phytol acetate	-5.50	-0.23	-0.02	-31.75	-2.73	-42.35	-34.48	6.26	360
Phytol	-3.94	-0.19	-0.32	-28.33	-3.39	-28.40	-31.72	17.14	394
1JNX	Docking Score	Glide ligand efficiency	Glide hbond	Glide evdw	Glide ecoul	Glide emodel	Glide energy	Glide einternal	Glide posenum
Alfa-Resorcinol	-5.24	-0.66	-0.51	-6.20	-12.35	-24.96	-18.54	2.39	349
Ethyl iso-allocholate	-4.80	-0.15	-0.59	-16.64	-18.30	-45.22	-34.94	4.14	32
Betulin	-4.58	-0.14	-0.72	-13.45	-13.92	-32.80	-27.36	4.17	253
Ingol 12-acetate	-4.02	-0.14	-0.27	-11.50	-15.18	-34.17	-26.68	2.06	21
D-asarinin	-3.98	-0.15	-0.29	-27.40	-4.11	-37.64	-31.51	2.63	124

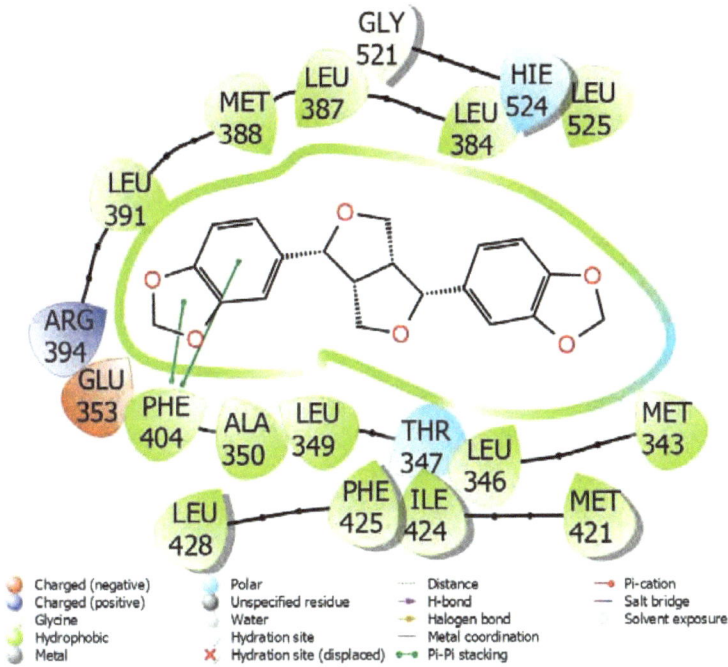

Fig. (13). Presentation interactions of D-asarinin with 1A52 protein.

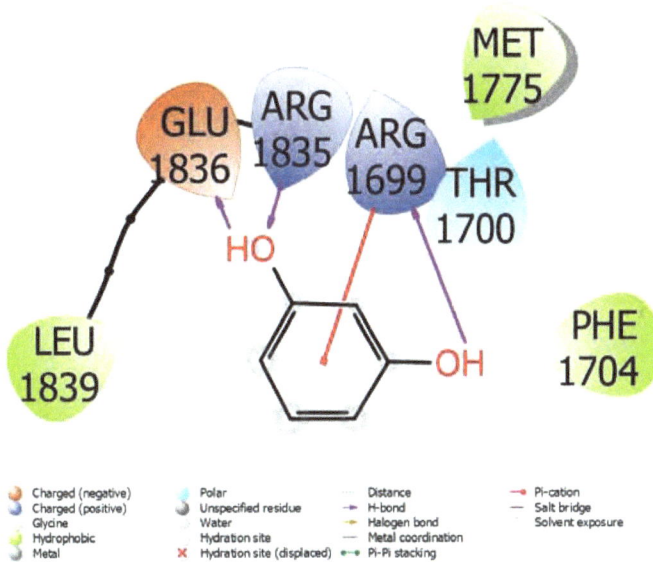

Fig. (14). Presentation interactions of Alfa-Resorcinol with 1JNX protein.

Arum palaestinum

It is well known that the leaves of *A. palaestinum* are edible only after cooking or roasting in oil, after drying in the sun, or soaking in salt water. It is most often boiled and then eaten by frying its leaves in olive oil. As *Arum* is considered a poisonous plant, its leaves and other plant parts show some side effects, such as vomiting, swelling of the mouth, and throat mucosa. This disorder can be stopped by using olive oil, as reported in Palestinian folklore [87, 88]. There are herbs commonly used for cancer patients [89]. It might be regarded as a potentially functional food for human consumption and a plant with prospective applications in drug discovery research.

Arum plants were screened phytochemically, which revealed that these plants had antimicrobial activities. Isoprenoids, also known as terpenoids, primarily comprise isoprene units and confer upon plant properties against bacteria, fungi, viruses, and protozoa [90]. A key constituent of *Arum* tubers is lectin, showing insecticidal effects tested against *Lipaphis erysimi* and *Aphis craccivor*, thus proving to be economically advantageous. It is well known that the polarity and molecular weight of these chemicals affect how well they extract into certain solvents. It was demonstrated that *A. palaestinum's* bioactive alkaloid Piperazirum exhibited considerable *in vitro* cytotoxic activity against a number of tumor cell lines [91, 92]. Another new diketopiperazine derivative was recently revealed to have modest cytotoxic action against cultivated multidrug-resistant human cells, according to a paper by El-Desouky and colleagues [93]. Furthermore, the flavonoid isoorientin (6-C glucoside of luteolin), which was isolated from *A. palaestinum*, was shown to have myolytic activity in animal smooth muscles by Afifi *et al.* [94]. However, *A. palaestinum* should be used with caution as it can have adverse effects. The methanol extract of *A. palaestinum* had the highest activity when Aboul-Enein *et al.* (2012) and Diab-Assaf *et al.* (2012) investigated the phenolic contents and antioxidant and anticancer properties of several organic solvent extracts of *A. palaestinum*. When compared to extracts of ethyl acetate and chloroform, it has been found to have higher phenolic and flavonoid concentrations. However, it has been demonstrated that there is a dose-dependent decrease in cell proliferation [95, 96]. Cole *et al.* investigated the *in vivo* and *in vitro* anti-cancer activity of *A. palaestinum* against aggressive androgen-independent prostate cancer models and found that *A. palaestinum* Bioss has the effect of suppressing prostate cancer cells through the activation of caspase 6 and prostate tumor [97].

In the study conducted by Farid and his colleagues [98], GC/MS analysis was performed on *A. palaestinum*. With this analysis, they determined the chemistries within the plant. Based on the results of this analysis, all these chemicals were examined one by one, and their activities against breast cancer proteins were compared. The results obtained are detailed in Table **6**. The interaction of the molecule of 1-monolinolenin and (-)-Loliolide, which has the highest activity, with these two proteins is given in Figs. (**15** and **16**).

Table 6. Numerical values of the docking parameters of molecules against enzymes.

1A52	Docking Score	Glide Ligand Efficiency	Glide Hbond	Glide Evdw	Glide Ecoul	Glide Emodel	Glide Energy	Glide Einternal	Glide Posenum
1-monolinolenin	-8.35	-0.33	0.00	-38.95	-12.45	-68.93	-51.41	14.52	203
(-)-Loliolide	-8.12	-0.58	-0.32	-30.11	-3.95	-50.43	-34.06	0.84	175
Butylated hydroxytoluene	-8.01	-0.50	0.00	-26.68	0.23	-34.20	-26.45	2.03	246
Dihydroactinidiolide	-7.44	-0.57	0.00	-28.79	-0.74	-42.95	-29.53	0.00	307
Phytol acetate	-5.50	-0.23	-0.02	-31.75	-2.73	-42.35	-34.48	6.26	360
1JNX	Docking Score	Glide ligand efficiency	Glide hbond	Glide evdw	Glide ecoul	Glide emodel	Glide energy	Glide einternal	Glide posenum
(-)-Loliolide	-4.69	-0.33	-0.16	-18.17	-4.99	-30.13	-23.16	0.02	399
Dihydroactinidiolide	-4.34	-0.33	-0.16	-16.54	-2.56	-24.51	-19.09	0.00	157
Dihydroactinidiolide	-4.04	-0.31	-0.07	-16.65	-2.12	-23.35	-18.77	0.00	213
1-monolinolenin	-3.51	-0.14	-0.32	-27.46	-15.50	-49.74	-42.96	7.84	237
Butylated hydroxytoluene	-3.49	-0.22	0.00	-14.78	-4.91	-24.14	-19.69	0.81	199

Keladi Candik (Alocasia longiloba)

Alocasia longiloba is a plant species belonging to the Araceae family and is usually found in tropical regions. There are studies on the cancer-fighting potential of some plants belonging to the Araceae family. For example, there are studies on the cancer-fighting potential of some Araceae family plants, such as *Anthurium*, *Philodendron* and *Dieffenbachia*. However, the number of similar studies conducted on the Keladi Candik plant is quite low.

Alocasia species with great commercial value are grown as houseplants. Some are grown outdoors, such as the Asian species of ethnobotanical significance, *A. cucullata* (Lour.) G. Don (Chinese taro), and the tropical decorative plant, *A. macrorrhizos* (Lour.) G. Don (Giant taro), which is grown for its leaves. These species' tubers are also fed to animals [99]. The *Alocasia* genus is used medicinally to cure a number of ailments, including cancer, diabetes, constipation, and diarrhea, in addition to being an attractive plant. Several phytochemicals found in *Alocasia* species, including flavonoids and phenolic compounds, have been linked to the traditional applications of these plants [100]. *Alocasia* species have been the subject of several *in vitro* and *in vivo* investigations, particularly on their antioxidant qualities as well as their anti-tumor and cytotoxic capabilities [101].

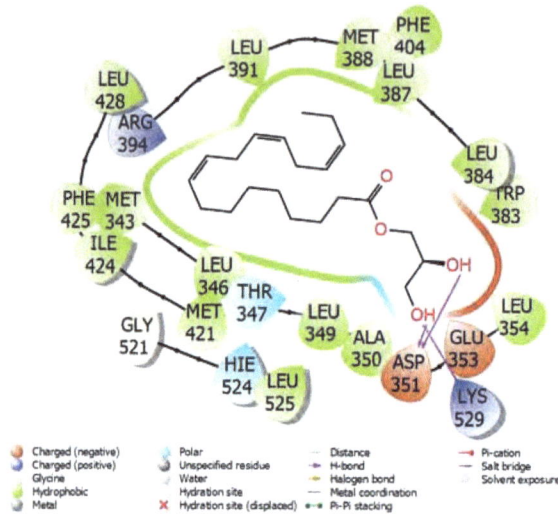

Fig. (15). Presentation interactions of 1-monolinolenin with 1A52 protein.

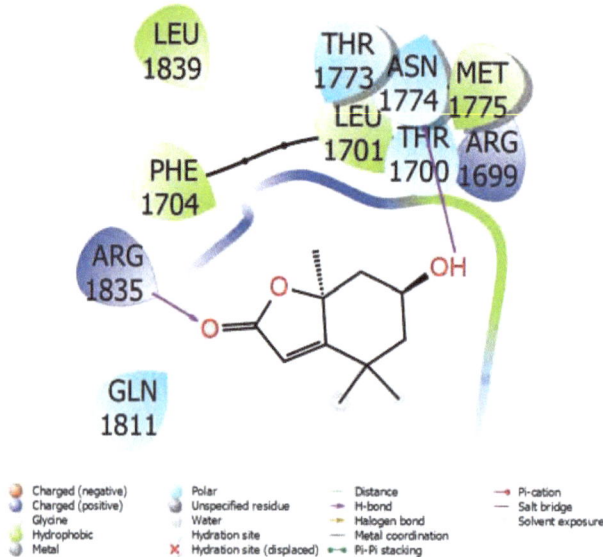

Fig. (16). Presentation interactions of (-)-Loliolide with 1JNx protein.

In the study conducted by Abdulhafiz and his colleagues [102], GC/MS analysis was conducted on *A. longiloba*. With this analysis, they determined the chemistries within the plant. Based on the results of this analysis, all these chemicals were examined one by one, and their activities against breast cancer proteins were compared. The results obtained are detailed in Table **7**. The interaction of the molecule of 2-Hydroxy-4,4,8-trimethyltricyclo- [6.3.1.0(1,5)] dodecan-9-one and Phen-1,4-diol, 2,3-dimethyl-5-trifluoromethyl-, which has the highest activity, with these two proteins is given in Figs. (**17** and **18**).

Table 7. Numerical values of the docking parameters of molecules against enzymes.

1A52	Docking Score	Glide Ligand Efficiency	Glide Hbond	Glide Evdw	Glide Ecoul	Glide Emodel	Glide Energy	Glide Einternal	Glide Posenum
2-Hydroxy-4,4,8-trimethyltricyclo-[6.3.1.0(1,5)]dodecan-9-one	-9.00	-0.53	-0.45	-29.76	-4.19	-49.01	-33.96	0.00	165
Cyclopropa[d]naphthalen-3-one,octahydro-2,4a,8,8-tetramethyl-,oxime	-8.62	-0.51	-0.16	-30.32	-3.94	-50.98	-34.26	0.02	217
Propanoic acid, 2-methyl-, (dodecahydro-6a-hydroxy-9a-methyl-3-methylene-2,9-dioxoazuleno [4,5-b]furan-6-yl)methyl ester	-8.07	-0.32	-0.32	-35.07	-4.51	-53.67	-39.58	2.98	221
2,6,10,10-Tetramethyl-1-oxaspiro[4.5] decan-6-ol	-8.04	-0.54	-0.17	-29.75	-1.81	-46.81	-31.56	0.46	344
5,5,8a-Trimethyl-3,5,6,7,8,8a-hexahydro-2H-chromene	-7.66	-0.59	0.00	-27.48	-0.31	-40.55	-27.78	0.00	289
1JNX	Docking Score	Glide ligand efficiency	Glide hbond	Glide evdw	Glide ecoul	Glide emodel	Glide energy	Glide einternal	Glide posenum
Phen-1,4-diol, 2,3-dimethyl-5-trifluoromethyl-	-5.67	-0.40	-0.52	-8.54	-14.19	-30.30	-22.73	3.26	389
Paromomycin	-5.51	-0.13	-0.58	-22.15	-32.26	-82.20	-54.41	12.49	10
5H-Cyclopropa [3, 4]benz [1,2-e]azulen-5-one	-4.83	-0.11	-0.52	-15.48	-25.76	-53.32	-41.24	6.00	268
2,6,10,10-Tetramethyl-1-oxaspiro[4.5] decan-6-ol	-4.60	-0.31	-0.32	-14.90	-5.63	-26.40	-20.53	0.12	115
Betulin	-4.58	-0.14	-0.72	-13.45	-13.92	-32.80	-27.36	4.17	253

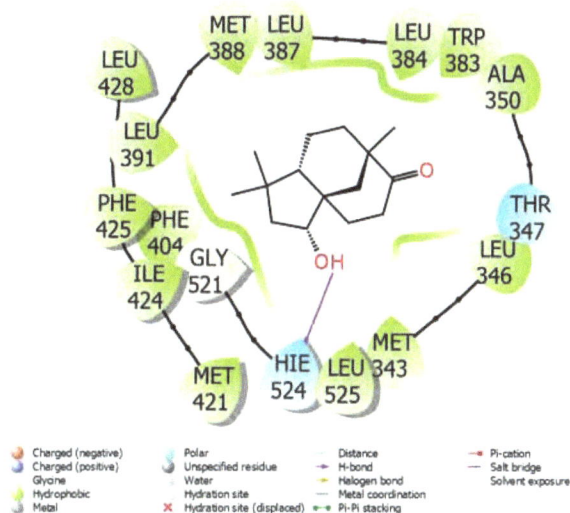

Fig. (17). Presentation interactions of 2-Hydroxy-4,4,8-trimethyltricyclo-[6.3.1.0(1,5)]dodecan-9-one with 1A52 protein.

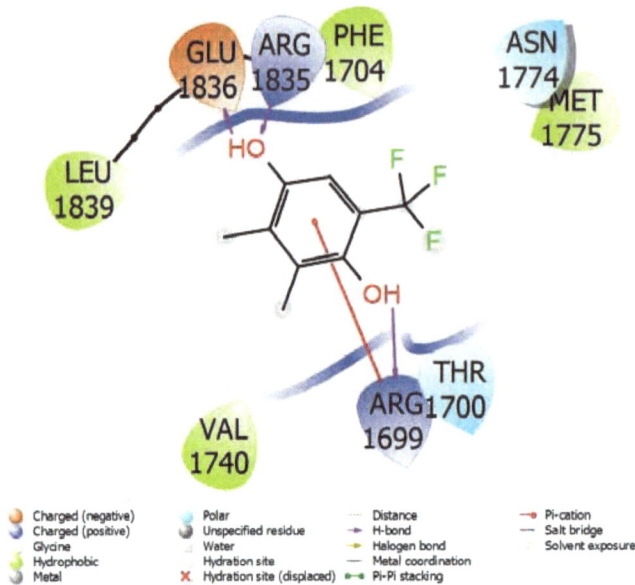

Fig. (18). Presentation interactions of Phen-1,4-diol, 2,3-dimethyl-5-trifluoromethyl- with 1JNx protein.

CONCLUSION

Araceae plants are known for their distinctive flower form and huge, colorful foliage. Many species are popular indoors and can be grown as ornamental plants. Certain species, though, may exhibit poisonous qualities; therefore, caution should be used when handling them. The Araceae family is significant in gardening and botany since they are vital to many habitats. Folk medicine has a long history of employing different plant components to make herbal remedies. The biological impacts of these plants are attracting increasing attention. Traditional medicinal plants, such as those in the Araceae family, contain phytochemicals that have shown promise in treating several diseases, including cancer.

The Araceae family may contain phytochemicals with antibacterial, anti-inflammatory, and antioxidant qualities. These characteristics make these plants useful in traditional medicine. Certain species, for instance, have long been used to cure respiratory conditions, wounds, and digestive issues. The medicinal potential of Araceae plants is revealed by contemporary scientific study, which also validates these ancient uses. These plants contain alkaloids, flavonoids, and other bioactive substances that may have benefits for the immune system and cancer cell growth inhibition. The future biodiversity and ecological significance of Araceae plants will rise even more as a result of their diverse range of uses.

REFERENCES

[1]   Arogundade OO, Adedeji O. Taxonomic significance of the vegetative anatomy of members of genera *Colocasia* (L.) Schott and *Xanthosoma* (L.) Schott in the family Araceae. Afr J Plant Sci 2019; 13(4): 92-106.
[http://dx.doi.org/10.5897/AJPS2019.1776]

[2]   Yıldırım H, Altıoğlu Y. Türkiye için yeni bir takson kaydı: Arum sintenisii (Engl.) P.C.Boyce (Araceae). Bağbahçe Bilim Dergisi 2016; 3(1): 47-54.

[3]   Croat TB, Ortiz OO. Distribution of araceae and the diversity of life forms. Acta Soc Bot Pol 2020; 89(3)
[http://dx.doi.org/10.5586/asbp.8939]

[4]   Mayo SJ, Bogner J, Boyce PC. Araceae. In: Kubitzki K, Flowering Plants Monocotyledons 1998; pp. 26-74.
[http://dx.doi.org/10.1007/978-3-662-03531-3_7]

[5]   Bogner J, Boyce P. A remarkable new *Biarum* (Araceae) from Turkey. Willdenowia 1989; 409-17.

[6]   Thomas W, Boyce P. The genus *arum*. Brittonia 1993; 45(4): 344.
[http://dx.doi.org/10.2307/2807613]

[7]   Lebot V. Aroids: taxonomy and botany. Trop Root Tuber Crops 2008; 285-300.
[http://dx.doi.org/10.1079/9781845934248.0285]

[8]   Kite GC, Hetterschieid WLA. Inflorescence odours of amorphophallus and pseudodracontium (Araceae). Phytochemistry 1997; 46(1): 71-5.
[http://dx.doi.org/10.1016/S0031-9422(97)00221-5]

[9]   Cescutti P, Campa C, Delben F, Rizzo R. Structure of the oligomers obtained by enzymatic hydrolysis of the glucomannan produced by the plant Amorphophallus konjac. Carbohydr Res 2002; 337(24): 2505-11.
[http://dx.doi.org/10.1016/S0008-6215(02)00332-4] [PMID: 12493237]

[10]   Hetterscheid WLA, Ittenbach S. Everything you always wanted to know about Amorphophallus, but were afraid to stick your nose into. Aroideana 1996; 19: 7-131.

[11]   Konjac Amorphophallus growth trees on nature foto stock 2305444277. Shutterstock 2024. Available from: https://www.shutterstock.com/it/image-photo/konjac-amorphophallus-growth-trees-on--ature-2305444277

[12]   Zhang SL, Liu PY, Zhang XG, Zhang YJ, Su CG. Resources of Chinese germplasms of Amorphophallus and proposal for its development and utilization. J Southwest Agric Univ 1999; 21: 515-9.

[13]   Anger EM, Weber M. Pollen-wall formation in *Arum alpinum.*. Ann Bot (Lond) 2006; 97(2): 239-44.
[http://dx.doi.org/10.1093/aob/mcj022] [PMID: 16299007]

[14]   *Arum maculatum* images: Free photos, PNG Stickers, wallpapers & backgrounds 2024. Available from: https://www.rawpixel.com/search/arum%20maculatum?page=1&path=_topics&sort=curated

[15]   Walton A. A morphogenetic study of *Arum maculatum* L. Ann Bot (Lond) 1964; 28(2): 271-82.
[http://dx.doi.org/10.1093/aob/28.2.271]

[16]   Kew science 2024. Available from: https://powo.science.kew.org/

[17]   Mayo SJ, Bogner J, Boyce PC. The genera of araceae. Royal Botanic Gardens Kew 1997; p. 370.

[18]   West African plants 2024. Available from: http://www.westafricanplants.senckenberg.de/root/index.php?page_id=14&id=1523#image=74656

[19]   Işık K. Biyolojik Çeşitlilik-Herkes İçin Okuma Parçaları ANG vakfı 2014; 2: 224.

[20]   Barış ME. Yeşil alan uygulamalarında doğal bitki örtüsünden yeterince yararlanıyormuyuz? II.

UlusalSüs Bitkileri Kongresi Antalya 2002; pp. 91-5.

[21] Eroğlu S, Cengiz YA. İstanbul metropolü dahilindeki çevre yollarının bitkisel tasarım açısından incelenmesi. Yüksek Lisans Tezi, İstanbul Teknik Üniversitesi. 2010.

[22] Arpa NY. Biyolojik çeşitliliğin korunmasında korunan alanların rolü ve önemi. Biyolojik Çeşitlilik Sempozyumu Bildiri Kitabı 2012; pp. 103-7.

[23] Bozkurt SG. Sivas ilinde Doğal Olarak yetişen bazı Geofitlerin Peyzaj Mimarlığında Kullanım olanaklarının incelenmesi. Atatürk Üniv Ziraat Fak Derg 2021.
[http://dx.doi.org/10.17097/ataunizfd.945878]

[24] Koyuncu M. Geofitler. Tübitak E-Derg Science and Technology Magazine 1994; 72-7.

[25] Seyidoğlu N. Bazı doğal geofitlerin peyzaj düzenlemelerinde kullanımı ve üretimi üzerine araştırmalar (Thesis). 2009.

[26] Kaya E. Geophytes of Turkey. Ataturk Central Horticultural Research Institute 2014; 96(1): 1-48.

[27] Asil H, Sarıhan EO. Türkiye'de Doğal Çiçek Soğanları Üretimi, Değerlendirilmesi ve Ticareti IV. Süs Bitkileri Kongresi 2010; p. 33.

[28] Erken K, Parlak S, Yılmaz M. Endemik taksonların korunması ve tür koruma eylem planları. Ağaç ve Orman 2022; 3(1): 33-46.

[29] Ekim T, Koyuncu M, Vural M, Duman H, Aytaç Z, Adıgüzel N. Türkiye Bitkileri Kırmızı Kitabı 2000.

[30] Ünal O. Antalya için endemik olan *Origanum* L. (Lamiaceae) türlerinin bazı biyolojik ve ekolojik özelliklerinin saptanması üzerine araştırmalar. Akdeniz Üniversitesi, Fen Bilimleri Enstitüsü, Biyoloji Anabilim Dalı. 2003; p. 173.

[31] Uçar E, Turgut K. Bazı dağ çayı (Sideritis) türlerinin *in vıtro* çoğaltımı. Akdeniz University Journal of the Faculty of Agriculture 2009; 22(1): 51-7.

[32] Ulus A, Seyidoğlu N. Bazı Dogal Geofitlerin Doku Kültürü İle Üretimi. Istanbul Üniv Orman Fak Derg 2006; 56(1): 71-80.

[33] Lai CS, Mas RHMH, Nair NK, Mansor SM, Navaratnam V. Chemical constituents and *in vitro* anticancer activity of *Typhonium flagelliforme* (Araceae). J Ethnopharmacol 2010; 127(2): 486-94.
[http://dx.doi.org/10.1016/j.jep.2009.10.009] [PMID: 19833183]

[34] Khalivulla SI, Mohammed A, Sirajudeen KNS, Shaik MI, Ye W, Korivi M. Novel phytochemical constituents and anticancer activities of the genus, *Typhonium*. Curr Drug Metab 2020; 20(12): 946-57.
[http://dx.doi.org/10.2174/1389200220666191118102616] [PMID: 31744445]

[35] Almaaty AHA, Keshk S, Galal A, Abbas OA, Hassan MK. Medicinal usage of some Arecaceae family members with potential anticancer effect. J Biotech Res 2022; 13: 55-63.

[36] Al-Dahmoshi HOM. Anticancer activity of some medicinal plants: mini review. Res Rev 2023.
[http://dx.doi.org/10.52845/JMRHS/2023-6-5-1]

[37] Van TH, Tran BN, Vo TTN, *et al.* Antioxidant capacity and flavoinoids, triterpenoids, polyphenol, polysaccharide content from tubers of two Amorphophallus species (Araceae). J Appl Biol Sci 2020; 14(1): 15-25.

[38] Viégas J, Rocha MTR, Ferreira-Moura I, *et al. Anthurium andraeanum* (Linden ex André) culture: *in vitro* and *ex vitro*. Floric Ornam Biotechnol 2007; 1(1): 61-5.

[39] Nur-Izzati M, Arifullah M, Nazahatul AA, *et al.* Elucidation of total phenolic content and antioxidant activity in medicinal Aroid, *Alocasia longiloba* Miq. IOP Conf Ser Earth Environ Sci 2021; 756(1): 012043.
[http://dx.doi.org/10.1088/1755-1315/756/1/012043]

[40] Donini LP, Ferreira-Moura I, Guisso AP, Souza JA, Viégas J. Preparo de Lâminas foliares de Aráceas Ornamentais: Desinfestação com diferentes concentrações de HIPOCLORITO de Sódio. Arq Inst Biol (Sao Paulo) 2005; 72(4): 517-22.
[http://dx.doi.org/10.1590/1808-1657v72p5172005]

[41] Rai M, Mares D. Plant-derived antimycotics: Current trends and future prospects. New York: Food Products Press 2003.

[42] Cragg GM, Newman DJ. Natural products: A continuing source of novel drug leads. Biochim Biophys Acta, Gen Subj 2013; 1830(6): 3670-95.
[http://dx.doi.org/10.1016/j.bbagen.2013.02.008] [PMID: 23428572]

[43] Saad B, Azaizeh H, Said O. Arab herbal medicine. Bot Med Clin Pract 2008; 31-9.
[http://dx.doi.org/10.1079/9781845934132.0031]

[44] Kunwar RM, Mahat L, Acharya RP, Bussmann RW. Medicinal plants, traditional medicine, markets and management in far-west Nepal. J Ethnobiol Ethnomed 2013; 9(1): 24.
[http://dx.doi.org/10.1186/1746-4269-9-24] [PMID: 23587109]

[45] Krupitza , Gridling M, Madlener S, *et al.* A polar extract of the Maya healing plant *Anthurium schlechtendalii* (Aracea) exhibits strong *in vitro* anticancer activity. Int J Mol Med 2009; 24(4): 513-21.
[http://dx.doi.org/10.3892/ijmm_00000260] [PMID: 19724892]

[46] Shukla A, Dubey S. A review: Traditionally used medicinal plants of family Arecaceae with phytoconstituents and therapeutic applications. Int J Biol Pharm Allied Sci 2022; 11(12)
[http://dx.doi.org/10.31032/IJBPAS/2022/11.12.6655]

[47] Kuanprasert N, Kuehnle AR, Tang CS. Floral fragrance compounds of some *anthurium* (ARACEAE) species and hybrids. Phytochemistry 1998; 49(2): 521-8.
[http://dx.doi.org/10.1016/S0031-9422(98)00088-0]

[48] Tanenbaum DM, Wang Y, Williams SP, Sigler PB. Crystallographic comparison of the estrogen and progesterone receptor's ligand binding domains. Proc Natl Acad Sci USA 1998; 95(11): 5998-6003.
[http://dx.doi.org/10.1073/pnas.95.11.5998] [PMID: 9600906]

[49] Williams RS, Green R, Glover JNM. Crystal structure of the BRCT repeat region from the breast cancer associated protein. BRCA1, Nat Struct Biol 2001; 8(10): 838-42.

[50] Khayyat M, Nazari F, Salehi H. Effects of different pot mixtures on pothos (*Epipremnum aureum* Lindl. and Andre 'Golden Pothos') growth and development. Am-Eurasian J Agric Environ Sci 2007; 2(4): 341-8.

[51] Patil SS, Wadkar KA. *in vitro* anti-cancer activity of *Epipremnum aureum.*. Bangladesh J Pharmacol 2024; 19(1): 23-8.

[52] Meshram A, Bhagyawant SS, Srivastava N. Characterization of pyrrolidine alkaloids of *Epipremnum aureum* for their antitermite activity against subterranean termites with sem studies. Proc Natl Acad Sci, India, Sect B Biol Sci 2019; 89(1): 53-62.
[http://dx.doi.org/10.1007/s40011-017-0893-5]

[53] Akan H, Çeçen C, Balos MM. Anatomical and morphological aspects of the taxa belonging to *Biarum schott* (Araceae Juss.) genus, which shows natural distribution in Şanlıurfa region. Kahramanmaraş Sütçü İmam Üniversitesi Tarım ve Doğa Dergisi 2019; 22: 69-83.
[http://dx.doi.org/10.18016/ksutarimdoga.vi.535514]

[54] Boyce PC. A taxonomic revision of *biarum*. Curtis's Bot Mag 2008; 25(1): 2-17.
[http://dx.doi.org/10.1111/j.1467-8748.2007.00607.x]

[55] Akbary P, Fereidouni MS, Hosseini AG. The effects of *Biarum carduchorum* and *Quercus infectoria* Gall extracts on percentage of hatching and survival rate in the early growth stage of *Oncorhynchus mykiss* larvae. J Vet Res 2016; 71(4): 403-7.

[56]   Tabatabaei-Yazdi F, Alizadeh-Behbahani B, Vasiee A, Mortazavi SA, Tabatabaei-Yazdi F. Antifungal activity of extracts *Biarum carduchorum* (kardeh) on *Aspergillus fumigatus* and *Penicillium expansum in vitro*. Zahedan J Res Med Sci 2016; 18(4): e6464.
[http://dx.doi.org/10.17795/zjrms-6464]

[57]   Ekradi S, Momeni-Isfahani T, Alimoradi M, Khanahmadi M. Histomorphological study of the effect of *Biarum straussiis*' rhizome extract on cutaneous wound healing in a rat model. J Med Herb 2021; 12(1): 19-26.

[58]   Dolatkhahi M, Dolatkhahi A, Nejad JB. Ethnobotanical study of medicinal plants used in Arjan - Parishan protected area in Fars Province of Iran. Avicenna J Phytomed 2014; 4(6): 402-12.
[PMID: 25386404]

[59]   Mordi A, Teimorian M, Shakiba B, Moudi E. Traditional botanical flora of medicinal plants in the treatment of kidney stones in Iran. J Biol Res Boll Soc Ital Biol Speriment 2021; 94: 2.
[http://dx.doi.org/10.4081/jbr.2021.9869]

[60]   Yeşil Y, İnal İ. Ethnomedicinal plants of Hasankeyf (Batman-Turkey). Front Pharmacol 2021; 11: 624710.
[http://dx.doi.org/10.3389/fphar.2020.624710] [PMID: 33776756]

[61]   Khosravi F, H M, Azizi , Rabani M, Nadoshan RM. Assessment of the biotechnological activity of wheat hydrolysates prepared with the *Biarum bovei* extract. J Food Meas Charact 2022; 16(4): 2738-48.
[http://dx.doi.org/10.1007/s11694-022-01379-1]

[62]   Pezeshkpour Vahid, Ghaedi M, Jannesar Ramin. Antibacterial effect of metal organic framework-3 and extract of *Biarum bovei* on standard and clinical strains of methicillin resistant *Staphylococcus aureus* (MRSA). 2016. Available from: https://sid.ir/paper/910517/en

[63]   Zanganehnejad Z, Setorki M. Effect of *Biarum carduchrum* extract on brain tissue thiol level in rat model of 6-hydroxydopamine-induced Parkinson's disease. J Herbmed Pharmacol 2018; 7(3): 136-40.
[http://dx.doi.org/10.15171/jhp.2018.23]

[64]   Valizadeh Z, Rafieirad M. Effects of hydro-alcoholic leaf extract of Kardeh (*Biarum bovei* Blume) on the blood glucose and lipid peroxidation in cerebral tissues and lipid profile in Streptozotocin induced diabetic rats. Iran J Diabetes Obes 2016; 8(1): 16-23.

[65]   Balos MM, Akan H, Durmaz EN, İlgaz FZ. Investigation of milk coagulation properties of some taxa belonging to the Araceae family. Int J Life Sci Biotechnol 2021; 4(3): 412-9.
[http://dx.doi.org/10.38001/ijlsb.889548]

[66]   Kordjazi A, Farahmandfar R. Antibacterial activity of hydroalcoholic extract of Cardin leaf on *Listeria monocytogenes*, *Salmonella enteritidis* and *Pseudomonas aeruginosa*.. Food Sci Technol (Campinas) 2020; 16(97): 29-35.
[http://dx.doi.org/10.29252/fsct.16.97.29]

[67]   Mustafa M, Abduljabbar A, Abduljabbar A. The effect of heat stress on oxidative stress and antioxidant status in local quail hens supplemented with onion and garlic oils. Tikrit J Agric Sci 2019; 19(1): 103-10.
[http://dx.doi.org/10.25130/tjas.19.1.11]

[68]   Abduljabbar AA, Ismail PA. Investigation of malondialdehyde (MDA), homocysteine (HCY) and C-reactive protein (CRP) in Sera of patients with angina pectoris. Al Mustansiriyah J Sci 2019; 30(1): 68-74.
[http://dx.doi.org/10.23851/mjs.v30i1.463]

[69]   Mojarradgandoukmolla S, Nanakali NM. Ab.Jabbar A. Hypolipidemic and anti-oxidative activities of *Terminalia arjuna* barks against induced hyperlipidemic albino rats. Plant Arch 2021; 21 (Suppl. 1): 2082-6.
[http://dx.doi.org/10.51470/PLANTARCHIVES.2021.v21.S1.343]

[70]   Aj.abduljabbar A, O.abdullah F, K.abdulrahman K, Galali Y, Sh.sardar A. *Papaver decaisnei*: gc-ms alkaloids profiling, *in vitro* antioxidant, and anticancer activity. 2022.
[http://dx.doi.org/10.21203/rs.3.rs-1207324/v3]

[71]   Windolf H, Chamberlain R, Quodbach J. Dose-independent drug release from 3D printed oral medicines for patient-specific dosing to improve therapy safety. Int J Pharm 2022; 616: 121555.
[http://dx.doi.org/10.1016/j.ijpharm.2022.121555] [PMID: 35131358]

[72]   Oloya B, Namukobe J, Ssengooba W, Afayoa M, Byamukama R. Phytochemical screening, antimycobacterial activity and acute toxicity of crude extracts of selected medicinal plant species used locally in the treatment of tuberculosis in Uganda. Trop Med Health 2022; 50(1): 16.
[http://dx.doi.org/10.1186/s41182-022-00406-7] [PMID: 35177126]

[73]   Ekradi S, Momeni-Isfahani T, Alimoradi M, Khanahmadi M. Histomorphological study of the effect of *Biarum straussiis'* rhizome extract on cutaneous wound healing in a rat model. Journal of Medicinal Herbs 2021; 12(1): 19-26.

[74]   Mašković PZ, Diamanto LD, Vujic JM, *et al.* Onosma aucheriana: A source of biologically active molecules for novel food ingredients and pharmaceuticals. J Funct Foods 2015; 19: 479-86.
[http://dx.doi.org/10.1016/j.jff.2015.09.054]

[75]   Wahab BA, Alamri ZZ. Phytochemistry, antioxidant, anticancer, and acute toxicity of traditional medicinal food Biarum bovei (kardeh). BMC Complement Med Ther 2023; 23(1)
[http://dx.doi.org/10.1186/s12906-023-04080-y]

[76]   Peppard TL. Volatile flavor constituents of Monstera deliciosa. J Agric Food Chem 1992; 40(2): 257-62.
[http://dx.doi.org/10.1021/jf00014a018]

[77]   Lorenzi H. Plantas Medicinais no Brasil Nativas E Exóticas. Nova Odessa: Instituto Plantarum 2008.

[78]   Menezes PR, Schwarz EA, Santos CAM. *in vitro* antioxidant activity of species collected in Paraná. Fitoterapia 2004; 75(3-4): 398-400.
[http://dx.doi.org/10.1016/j.fitote.2004.01.014] [PMID: 15159006]

[79]   Muelas-Serrano S, Nogal JJ, Martínez-Díaz RA, Escario JA, Martínez-Fernández AR, Gómez-Barrio A. *in vitro* screening of American plant extracts on *Trypanosoma cruzi* and *Trichomonas vaginalis.*. J Ethnopharmacol 2000; 71(1-2): 101-7.
[http://dx.doi.org/10.1016/S0378-8741(99)00185-3] [PMID: 10904152]

[80]   El-Deeb AN, Abdel-Aleem IM, El-Amin SM, Refahy LA, El-Shazly MA. Antiproliferative effect of phenolic glucosides isolated from Philodendron bipinnatifidum on HepG2 cells. Phytopharmacology 2012; 3: 351-8.

[81]   Saeidnia S. The story of beta-sitosterol- A Review. European J Med Plants 2014; 4(5): 590-609.
[http://dx.doi.org/10.9734/EJMP/2014/7764]

[82]   Ulbricht C. An evidence-based systematic review of beta-glucan by the natural standard research collaboration. J Diet Suppl 2014; 11(4): 361-475.
[http://dx.doi.org/10.3109/09286586.2014.975066] [PMID: 25361467]

[83]   Ezhilarasi PN, Karthik P, Chhanwal N, Anandharamakrishnan C. Nanoencapsulation techniques for food bioactive components: A Review. Food Bioprocess Technol 2013; 6(3): 628-47.
[http://dx.doi.org/10.1007/s11947-012-0944-0]

[84]   Sheth P, Sandhu H, Singhal D, Malick W, Shah N, Serpil Kislalioglu M. Nanoparticles in the pharmaceutical industry and the use of supercritical fluid technologies for nanoparticle production. Curr Drug Deliv 2012; 9(3): 269-84.
[http://dx.doi.org/10.2174/156720112800389052] [PMID: 22283656]

[85]   Jung J, Perrut M. Particle design using supercritical fluids: Literature and patent survey. J Supercrit Fluids 2001; 20(3): 179-219.

[http://dx.doi.org/10.1016/S0896-8446(01)00064-X]

[86]   Scapinello J, Aguiar GPS, Dal Magro C, *et al.* Extraction of bioactive compounds from Philodendron bipinnatifidum Schott ex Endl and encapsulation in PHBV by SEDS technique. Ind Crops Prod 2018; 125: 65-71.
       [http://dx.doi.org/10.1016/j.indcrop.2018.08.079]

[87]   Mayer-Chissick U, Lev E. Wild edible plants in Israel tradition versus cultivation. Medicinal and Aromatic Plants of the World 2014; pp. 9-26.
       [http://dx.doi.org/10.1007/978-94-017-9276-9_2]

[88]   Abu-Rabia A. Palestinian plant medicines for treating renal disorders: an inventory and brief history. Altern Complement Ther 2005; 11(6): 295-300.
       [http://dx.doi.org/10.1089/act.2005.11.295]

[89]   Sawsan ASO. Selected wild plant species with exotic flowers from Jordan. Int J Biodivers Conserv 2015; 7(5): 308-20.
       [http://dx.doi.org/10.5897/IJBC2014.0797]

[90]   Parshikov IA, Sutherland JB. The use of *Aspergillus niger* cultures for biotransformation of terpenoids. Process Biochem 2014; 49(12): 2086-100.
       [http://dx.doi.org/10.1016/j.procbio.2014.09.005]

[91]   El-Desouky SK, Kim KH, Ryu SY, Eweas AF, Gamal-Eldeen AM, Kim YK. A new pyrrole alkaloid isolated *fromArum palaestinum* Boiss. and its biological activities. Arch Pharm Res 2007; 30(8): 927-31.
       [http://dx.doi.org/10.1007/BF02993958] [PMID: 17879743]

[92]   El-Desouky SK, Ryu SY, Kim YK. Piperazirum, a novel bioactive alkaloid from *Arum palaestinum* boiss. ChemInform 2007; 38(38): chin.200738193.
       [http://dx.doi.org/10.1002/chin.200738193]

[93]   El-Desouky SK, Hawas UW, Kim YK. Two new diketopiperazines from *Arum palaestinum.*. Chem Nat Compd 2014; 50(6): 1075-8.
       [http://dx.doi.org/10.1007/s10600-014-1162-y]

[94]   Afifi FU, Khalil E, Abdalla S. Effect of isoorientin isolated from *Arum palaestinum* on uterine smooth muscle of rats and guinea pigs. J Ethnopharmacol 1999; 65(2): 173-7.
       [http://dx.doi.org/10.1016/S0378-8741(98)00147-0] [PMID: 10465658]

[95]   Aboul-Enein AM, El-Ela FA, Shalaby EA, El-Shemy HA. Traditional medicinal plants research in Egypt: Studies of antioxidant and anticancer activities. J Med Plants Res 2012; 6(5): 689-703.

[96]   Diab-Assaf M, Taleb RI, Shebaby W, *et al.* Antioxidant and anticancer activities of methanolic, ethyl acetate and chloroform extracts of *Arum Palaestinum.*. Planta Med 2012; 78(11)
       [http://dx.doi.org/10.1055/s-0032-1321076]

[97]   Cole C, Burgoyne T, Lee A, Stehno-Bittel L, Zaid G. *Arum Palaestinum* with isovanillin, linolenic acid and β-sitosterol inhibits prostate cancer spheroids and reduces the growth rate of prostate tumors in mice. BMC Complement Altern Med 2015; 15(1): 264.
       [http://dx.doi.org/10.1186/s12906-015-0774-5] [PMID: 26243305]

[98]   Farid MM, Hussein SR, Ibrahim LF, *et al.* Cytotoxic activity and phytochemical analysis of *Arum palaestinum* Boiss. Asian Pac J Trop Biomed 2015; 5(11): 944-7.
       [http://dx.doi.org/10.1016/j.apjtb.2015.07.019]

[99]   Nauheimer L, Boyce PC, Renner SS. Giant taro and its relatives: A phylogeny of the large genus Alocasia (Araceae) sheds light on Miocene floristic exchange in the Malesian region. Mol Phylogenet Evol 2012; 63(1): 43-51.
       [http://dx.doi.org/10.1016/j.ympev.2011.12.011] [PMID: 22209857]

[100] Nabis B. Karyomorphological studies in three species of Alocasia (Schott.) g.don.- an ethno-medicinally and economically important genus. International Journal of Life-Sciences Scientific

Research 2018; 4(6): 2116-21.
[http://dx.doi.org/10.21276/ijlssr.2018.4.6.8]

[101] Ongpoy RC Jr. The Medicinal Properties of the Alocasia Genus: A Systematic Review. JAASP 2017; 6(1): 25-33.

[102] Abdulhafiz F, Mohammed A, Kayat F, *et al.* Xanthine oxidase inhibitory activity, chemical composition, antioxidant properties and GC-MS analysis of Keladi Candik (*Alocasia longiloba* Miq). Molecules 2020; 25(11): 2658.
[http://dx.doi.org/10.3390/molecules25112658] [PMID: 32521624]

CHAPTER 3

Amaryllidaceae Family

Sibel Day[1,*]

[1] *Department of Field Crops, Faculty of Agriculture, Ankara University, Ankara, Türkiye*

Abstract: The Amaryllidaceae family is significant, as it includes ornamental and medicinal species. The most common genera found in the Mediterranean are *Allium, Galanthus, Leucojum, Narcissus, Pancratium*, and *Sternbergia*. *Allium*, the largest genus in the Amaryllidaceae family, is distributed in the Mediterranean, Asia, Europe, and North America. The genus *Galanthus* comprises 19 species native to Europe and Asia. Both *Allium* and *Galanthus* are rich in alkaloids and are economically important worldwide. In conclusion, this chapter emphasises the importance of cultivating these species and their endemism rate in Türkiye.

Keywords: *Allium, Galanthus, Leucojum, Narcissus, Pancratium, Sternbergia.*

INTRODUCTION

The Amaryllidaceae family, commonly referred to as the Amaryllis family, is a diverse and economically significant group of flowering plants that includes numerous ornamental and medicinal species. This botanical family is known for its characteristic features, which include showy, trumpet-shaped flowers, typically with six petal-like tepals and a variety of growth habits. Amaryllidaceae is a taxonomically well-defined group of monocots encompassing over 75 genera and approximately 1600 species [1].

The Amaryllidaceae family is indeed present in the Mediterranean region, and it includes several genera and species that are native to or have naturalised in this area. Some of the notable genera within the Amaryllidaceae family found in the Mediterranean are *Allium, Galanthus, Leucojum, Narcissus, Pancratium*, and *Sternbergia*. *Allium* covers a wide variety of plants commonly known as onions, garlic, and chives. These genera are distributed across the Mediterranean region and are known for their culinary, medicinal, and ornamental uses [2].

[*] **Corresponding author Sibel Day:** Department of Field Crops, Faculty of Agriculture, Ankara University, Ankara, Türkiye; E-mail: day@ankara.edu.tr

The Amaryllidaceae family is of considerable economic and ecological importance. Many species within the family are cultivated for their ornamental value. Amaryllis (*Hippeastrum*), daffodils (*Narcissus*), and snowdrops (*Galanthus*) are popular garden plants prized for their striking flowers.

These plants have become horticultural staples. They are grown for both indoor and outdoor decoration. Medicinally, some members of the Amaryllidaceae family are used in traditional medicine. For example, the bulbs of plants like *Crinum* and *Galanthus* contain compounds with potential pharmaceutical applications, including the treatment of Alzheimer's disease, cancer, and neurodegenerative disorders. In addition, several species of Amaryllidaceae produce alkaloids with pesticidal properties [3].

More than 500 alkaloids have been identified and extracted from the Amaryllidaceae family of plants. The alkaloids of the Amaryllidaceae have been structurally classified into nine subgroups, namely lycorine, crinine, haemanthamine, narciclasine, galanthamine, tazettine, homolycorine, montanine, and norbelladine [4].

Ecologically, Amaryllidaceae plants play a role in various ecosystems as a food source for herbivores and pollinators. They can be important nectar sources for insects and are essential for the survival of specific pollinator species.

ALLIUM GENUS

Taxonomy and Properties

Regnum: Plantae

Divisio: Magnoliophyta

Subclassis: Magnoliidae

Familia: Amaryllidaceae

Genus: *Allium*

Allium is the largest genus in the family Amaryllidaceae, involving 1100 accepted taxa and distributed in the Mediterranean, Asia, Europe, and North America [5 - 8]. The Mediterranean region is one of the centres of species diversity of the genus *Allium*. This genus is rich in Türkiye and is represented by 255 taxa in Türkiye, of which 100 are endemic. The endemic taxa found in Türkiye are listed in Table **1**.

Table 1. Endemic taxa found in Türkiye [32].

1	*Allium alpinarii* Özhatay & Kollmann	Endemic
2	*Allium anatolicum* Özhatay & B.Mathew	Endemic
3	*Allium antalyense* Eren, Çinbilgel &Parolly	Endemic
4	*Allium armenum* Boiss. & Kotschy	Endemic
5	*Allium armerioides* Boiss.	Endemic
6	*Allium arzusense* Eker & Koyuncu	Endemic
7	*Allium asperiflorum* Miscz.	Endemic
8	*Allium balansae* Boiss.	Endemic
9	*Allium baytopiorum* Kollmann & Özhatay	Endemic
10	*Allium brevicaule* Boiss. & Balansa	Endemic
11	*Allium cappadocicum* Boiss.	Endemic
12	*Allium circinatum subsp. evae* R.M.Burton	Endemic
13	*Allium colchicifolium* Boiss.	Endemic
14	*Allium czelghauricum* Bordz.	Endemic
15	*Allium deciduum subsp. deciduum*	Endemic
16	*Allium djimilense* Boiss. ex Regel	Endemic
17	*Allium eginense* Freyn	Endemic
18	*Allium elmaliense* Deniz & Sümbül	Endemic
19	*Allium enginii* Özhatay & B.Mathew	Endemic
20	*Allium ertugrulii* Demir. & Uysal	Endemic
21	*Allium fethiyense* Özhatay & B.Mathew	Endemic
22	*Allium flavum subsp. flavum var. minus* Boiss.	Endemic
23	*Allium flavum subsp. tauricum var. pilosum* Kollman & Koyuncu	Endemic
24	*Allium gayi* Boiss.	Endemic
25	*Allium glumaceum* Boiss. & Hausskn.	Endemic
26	*Allium goekyigitii* Ekim, H.Duman & Güner	Endemic
27	*Allium gorumsense* (*Regel*) Boiss.	Endemic
28	*Allium huber-morathii* Kollmann, Özhatay & Koyuncu	Endemic
29	*Allium ilgazense* Özhatay	Endemic
30	*Allium isauricum* Hub.-Mor. & Wendelbo dağ	Endemic
31	*Allium junceum subsp. tridentatum* Kollmann, Özhatay & Koyuncu	Endemic
32	*Allium karamanoglui* Koyuncu & Kollmann	Endemic
33	*Allium kastambulense* Kollmann	Endemic
34	*Allium koenigianum* Grossh.	Endemic

(Table 1) cont.....

35	*Allium koyuncui* H.Duman & Özhatay	Endemic
36	*Allium kurtzianum* Ascherson & Sint. ex Kollmann	Endemic
37	*Allium maraschicum* M.Koçyiğit & Özhatay	Endemic
38	*Allium microspathum* Ekberg	Endemic
39	*Allium nemrutdaghense* Kit Tan & Sorger	Endemic
40	*Allium nevsehirense* Koyuncu & Kollmann	Endemic
41	*Allium oltense* Grossh.	Endemic
42	*Allium olympicum* Boiss.	Endemic
43	*Allium peroninianum* Aznav.	Endemic
44	*Allium phanerantherum subsp. deciduum* Kollmann & Koyuncu	Endemic
45	*Allium phrygium* Boiss.	Endemic
46	*Allium pictistamineum* O.Schwarz	Endemic
47	*Allium proponticum* Stearn & Özhatay	Endemic
48	*Allium proponticum subsp. proponticum*	Endemic
49	*Allium pseudoalbidum* N.Friesen & Özhatay	Endemic
50	*Allium purpureoviride* Koyuncu & İ.Genç	Endemic
51	*Allium retrorsum* (Özhatay & Kollmann) Brullo, Guglielmo, Pavone & Salmeri	Endemic
52	*Allium rhetoreanum* Nab.	Endemic
53	*Allium rhodopeum subsp. turcicum* Brullo, Guglielmo & Terrasi	Endemic
54	*Allium robertianum* Kollmann	Endemic
55	*Allium roseum subsp. gulekense* Koyuncu & Eker	Endemic
56	*Allium rumelicum* M.Koçyiğit & Özhatay	Endemic
57	*Allium sandrasicum* Kollmann, Özhatay & Bothmersandras	Endemic
58	*Allium scabriflorum* Boiss.	Endemic
59	*Allium shatakiense* Rech.f.	Endemic
60	*Allium sibthorpianum* Schult. & Schult.f.	Endemic
61	*Allium sieheanum* Kollmann	Endemic
62	*Allium sintenisii* Freyn	Endemic
63	*Allium sivasicum* Özhatay & Kollmann	Endemic
64	*Allium stearnianum subsp. stearnianum*	Endemic
65	*Allium stearnianum subsp. vanense* Kollmann & Koyuncu	Endemic
66	*Allium stenopetalum* Boiss. & Kotschy ex Regel	Endemic
67	*Allium stylosum* O.Schwarz	Endemic
68	*Allium tauricola* Boiss.	Endemic
69	*Allium tchihatschewii* Boiss.	Endemic

70	*Allium tubergenii* Freyn	Endemic
71	*Allium tuncelianum* (Kollmann) Özhatay, B.Mathew & Şiraneci	Endemic
72	*Allium turcicum* Özhatay & Cowley	Endemic
73	*Allium variegatum* Boiss.	Endemic
74	*Allium wendelboanum* Kollmann	Endemic
75	*Allium proponticum subsp. parviflorum* (Kollmann) Koyuncu	Endemic
76	*Allium shirnakiense* L.Behçet & Rüstemoğlu	Endemic
77	*Allium eldivanense* Özhatay	Endemic
78	*Allium aksekiense* Özhatay, Koyuncu & E.Kaya	Endemic
79	*Allium aybukeae* H.Duman & Ekşi	Endemic
80	*Allium bilgeae* Yıld.	Endemic
81	*Allium bilgilii* H.Duman & Ekşi	Endemic
82	*Allium bingoelense* Yıld. & Kılıç	Endemic
83	*Allium efeae* Özhatay & İ.Genç	Endemic
84	*Allium ekeri* E.Kaya & Koçyiğit	Endemic
85	*Allium ekimianum* Ekşi, Koyuncu & Özkan	Endemic
86	*Allium erzincanicum* Özhatay & Kandemir	Endemic
87	*Allium gabardaghense* Fırat	Endemic
88	*Allium gemiciana* Yıld. & Kılıç	Endemic
89	*Allium hoshabicum* Fırat	Endemic
90	*Allium istanbulense* Özhatay, Koçyiğit, Brullo & Salmeri	Endemic
91	*Allium kandemirii* İ.Genç & Özhatay	Endemic
92	*Allium kayae* Özhatay & Koyuncu	Endemic
93	*Allium lazikkiyense* Koçyiğit, Özhatay & E.Kaya	Endemic
94	*Allium liliputianum* Koçyiğit, Özhatay & E.Kaya	Endemic
95	*Allium perpendiculum* Koçyiğit, Özhatay & E.Kaya	Endemic
96	*Allium pervariensis* Fırat & Koyuncu	Endemic
97	*Allium serpentinicum* İ.Genç & Özhatay	Endemic
98	*Allium undulatipetalum* İ.Genç & Özhatay	Endemic
99	*Allium urusakiorum* Özhatay, Seregin & N.Friesen	Endemic
100	*Allium yilandaghense* Yıld. & Kılıç	Endemic

Allium species are used as spices, vegetables, ornamentals, and medicinal plants. Some are of worldwide importance for human consumption; others are collected in the wild or cultivated regionally. *Allium cepa* is the most widely consumed, and the other important species *are Allium sativum, Allium ampeloprasum, Allium fistulosum, Allium tuberosum, Allium schoenoprasum, and Allium tuncelianum.* Chemical compounds found in *Allium* plants are polysaccharides, polyphenols, saponins, and many compounds of the sulphur-containing amino acid cysteine [9].

The distinctive aroma and taste of alliums contribute to their widespread use in various domains. In the culinary arts, they are popular ingredients, often employed as vegetables or spices. They are also used in medicinal and folk remedies for a wide range of health problems. In general, all parts of Allium plants are edible, although the specific part consumed varies from species to species. Some authors have raised questions about the consumption of seeds, but in modern cuisine, the seeds are germinated and the young plants are incorporated into the diet. The edible components can be prepared in various ways, such as raw, cooked, frozen, pickled, canned, dehydrated, or processed into various products. They play a significant role in the daily diets of people in different cultural regions. Spring onions, shallots, or green onions, for example, are popular for fresh salads and are often cultivated in home gardens. Meanwhile, dry bulbs, primarily from onions and garlic, are essential condiments and can be found in local markets. Alimardanova *et al.* [10] conducted a study on the use of dried *A. odorum* in cheese production to enhance the taste and nutritional qualities of cheese. Onion rings, dried onions, garlic powder, and similar products are also market favourites in processed forms. In addition, many wild allium species are used for food and medicinal purposes, particularly the common alliums [11].

The use of alliums in both official and traditional medicine is closely linked to their rich nutritional composition, characterised by a high content of phytochemicals with significant therapeutic potential.

Numerous studies have shown the effectiveness of Alliaceae in addressing various health conditions. For instance, *A. cepa* is used to manage high blood pressure, bronchitis, migraines, coronary heart disease, hypercholesterolaemia, cataracts, hypertension, and diabetes. *A. sativum* is recognised as a carminative, stimulant, and antiseptic and is used to relieve stomach discomfort and respiratory infections while also demonstrating preventive and therapeutic effects in heart disease and asthma. *A. fistulosum* is a common remedy for headaches, diarrhoea, abdominal pain, heart disease, and cold symptoms. *A. ampeloprasum* is traditionally used to relieve symptoms associated with various inflammatory conditions and as a digestive stimulant for hypertension. *A. schoenoprasum* is employed to treat high blood pressure and colds and to stimulate appetite and digestion. Wild species like *A. ursinum, A. vinale*, and *A. scorodoprasum* also exhibit a wide range of medicinal properties that are consistent with the therapeutic effects of common alliums. In general, *Allium* species are noted for their antioxidant activity, making them valuable in combating diseases in which reactive oxygen species (ROS) play a significant role [11, 12]. *Allium* plants are a significant source of dietary antioxidants. Antioxidants help prevent cell and DNA damage by scavenging free radicals such as ROS or RNS, inhibiting their production, or activating antioxidant enzymes such as SOD2, CAT, and GPX. The analysis of the antioxidant activity of Allium species is crucial due to the proven link between oxidative stress and the development of diseases such as atherosclerosis, cancer, and ageing. The first study on the antioxidant properties was conducted with crude extracts, which led investigators to conclude that organosulphur compounds were mainly responsible for the observed antioxidant effects [13]. Yin and Cheng [14] and Benkeblia [15] found that the antioxidant activity of onions is not only related to organosulphur compounds but also to phenolic compounds.

Dietary supplements containing garlic are highly regarded for their ability to boost the immune system, lower serum lipids, and prevent atherosclerosis. These supplements come in various forms, including garlic oil, garlic oil maceration, garlic powder, and aged garlic extract [16]. Garlic has also been used in the cosmetics industry as an ingredient in skin and hair care products [17]. The beneficial effects of alliums have been attributed primarily to their chemical composition, with particular emphasis on the sulphurous compounds that are the most abundant constituents of Allium species [18].

Morphology of *Allium* Species

Allium species exhibit a comprehensive set of morphological characteristics that encompass underground components (consisting of a true stem, bulb structure, and pseudostem), leaves, flower stalks, flowers, inflorescences, fruits, and seeds. While there is a notable commonality in these characteristics across Allium species, each species also has distinct morphological features. These plants are typically characterised as biennial or perennial, relying on various underground storage organs, such as rhizomes, tunicate bulbs, or swollen roots [19].

The bulb of an Allium plant is made up of discrete elements, including the basal plate, which serves as the true stem, fresh thickened leaves, dry coated leaves, and buds that give rise to the development of a flower stalk. These bulbs may exist as individual units, as in true bulbs such as onions or pseudobulbs such as leeks, or they may clustered, as in garlic, where multiple cloves surround the basal plate densely. In some cases, certain species produce smaller bulbs, called daughter bulbs, around the older bulbs as a means of propagation [19].

Allium leaves exhibit a diverse range of shapes, some tubular, as in onions, and others flat, as in garlic. The lower part of these leaves together form a pseudostem. Inflorescences are typically organised in umbellate or head-like clusters at the apex of a flower stalk devoid of leaves. In their early stages, these inflorescences are often surrounded by protective leaves called spathe. Allium flowers consist of six tepals, which are either free or almost free and arranged in two whorls. There are also six stamens, sometimes fused at their base, and the ovary is trilocular and superior. Notably, certain Allium species can produce bulbils instead of some or all of the flowers in the inflorescence, which can be employed for propagation purposes. The fruits are in the form of capsules, and the seeds inside are characteristically black, with either a rhomboid or spheroid shape [19].

Climate and Soil Requirements

The ideal pH range for cultivating alliums is between 6.5 and 7.5. Maintaining the correct soil pH is crucial for optimum nutrient uptake and overall plant health.

Alliums have varying climate requirements depending on the specific species, but many have similar preferences. Here are the general climate requirements for Allium species:

Alliums typically thrive in temperate climates. They are adapted to a wide range of temperatures. Most alliums prefer cool to moderate temperatures during the growing season. Adequate temperature fluctuations between day and night are often beneficial for bulb development. In general, alliums are not well-suited to extremely hot or tropical climates [20].

Many allium species require a period of cold exposure, known as winter chilling, to break dormancy and promote bulb formation. Without sufficient winter chilling, some alliums may not produce bulbs or flower properly. The duration and intensity of chilling varies from species to species.

Alliums prefer well-drained soils and do not tolerate waterlogged conditions. They are often grown in regions with moderate rainfall. Some alliums, such as onions, are somewhat drought-tolerant but still require adequate moisture for bulb development. Alliums thrive in well-drained soils that are light and sandy in texture. Good drainage is essential to prevent waterlogging, which can be detrimental to these plants [21].

Alliums generally require full sun to thrive. They should receive at least 6 to 8 hours of direct sunlight a day for optimum growth and bulb formation.

The length of the growing season depends on the type of allium. Some species are suitable for both spring and autumn planting, while others have a longer growing season and can be planted in autumn for a summer harvest.

Alliums are often tolerant of light frosts, and some even require a period of cold weather to trigger bulb development. However, they can be sensitive to hard freezes, which can damage the foliage and bulbs. Protection from severe frost may be necessary in colder regions [22].

Alliums can be grown in a wide range of climates, depending on the species. For example, the common onion (*Allium cepa*) is adaptable to a broad range of zones, while some ornamental alliums, like *Allium giganteum*, are suitable for specific climates.

It is important to note that certain types of allium may have unique climatic requirements, so growers should consider the specific needs of the species they are cultivating. Local climatic conditions and microclimates can also influence the success of allium cultivation in a particular region. It is, therefore, advisable to consult local agricultural extension services or experts for advice on growing alliums in your specific climate and location [23].

Diseases and Pests

Alliums are susceptible to various diseases and insects, including:

Sclerotium cepivorum (white root): This pathogen can cause root loss, wilting, and chlorotic (yellowing) foliage in alliums. Good soil management and sanitation practices are essential to reduce the risk of white root disease [24].

Rusts: Rust diseases can affect various Allium species. Fungicides and disease-resistant cultivars may be used to control rust infections [25].

Penicillium: This fungus can affect most allium bulbs and should be controlled by good storage and handling practices [26].

Viruses: Alliums are susceptible to several viruses, including the Onion Yellow Dwarf Virus (OYDV) and the Tobacco Rattle Virus (TRV). These viruses can cause symptoms like mosaic patterns and chlorosis. Disease control measures and the use of virus-free plant material can help prevent the spread of viruses [27].

Aphids: Aphids can damage alliums by feeding on the sap and spreading disease. Insecticidal sprays or biological control methods can be employed to manage aphid infestations [28].

Thrips: Thrips can cause damage by feeding on plant tissue and spreading disease. Integrated pest management (IPM) practices are often used to control thrips in allium crops [29].

Onion fly: The onion fly can lay eggs on allium plants, resulting in maggot infestations in the bulbs. Practices such as crop rotation and protective covers can help mitigate onion fly damage [30].

Successful allium cultivation requires addressing these agronomic requirements and implementing appropriate disease and pest management strategies to ensure healthy and productive crops.

Breeding

There are several key characteristics that breeders need to consider when selecting alliums. One of the most important is the ability of the foliage to remain green until after the flowers have withered. Another important trait to evaluate is the fragrance of the plant. While some species may have a typical garlic or onion scent, *Allium karataviense* has a sweet and pleasant fragrance. In addition, breeders should prioritise traits such as tolerance or resistance to viruses, as well as resistance to leaf diseases and nematodes [23].

In general, the juvenile period for alliums typically spans 2 to 3 years, depending on the species. For cut flower varieties, flowers, it is essential that the scapes are more than 60 cm long. In addition, the flowers should have a vase life of more than 10 days and be able to withstand storage and transport after cutting [23, 31].

Breeding selections that are easy to cultivate in the greenhouse, whether for use as cut flowers or pot plants, are also highly desirable in the selection process [23].

Endemic Taxa in Türkiye

The studies showed that there are 100 endemic taxa found in Türkiye (Table **1**). Among *Allium* species, apart from *Allium cepa* and *Allium sativum*, which are the most cultivated, *Allium tuncelianum* (Tunceli garlic) is one of the endemic taxa that has started to be cultivated in Türkiye. In this chapter, *Allium tuncelianum* is highlighted for its unique properties.

Morphology of *Allium tuncelianum*

Allium tuncelianum, also known as "Tunceli garlic" because of its mild garlic odour and flavour, is a species native to Eastern Anatolia. It shares several intriguing similarities with the common cultivated garlic (*Allium sativum*), leading to the suggestion that A. *tuncelianum* may be the wild progenitor of garlic.

Here are some of the key features and characteristics of *Allium tuncelianum*:

Allium tuncelianum is native to Eastern Anatolia, which includes parts of Türkiye. Its natural habitat and distribution are specific to this area.

A. tuncelianum bears a striking resemblance to cultivated garlic (*A. sativum*) in terms of its plant architecture. This resemblance extends to its mild garlic odour and flavour, which has contributed to its local name, 'garlic'.

One of the most striking similarities between *A. tuncelianum* and garlic is the number of chromosomes. Both species have a diploid genome with 16 chromosomes (2n=16). This shared chromosome number is an interesting point of comparison, as it is consistent with most cultivated edible Allium species [33].

Allium tuncelianum has a unique fringed root structure. This feature enables it to thrive in stony and gravelly habitats. The plant's robust root development allows it to anchor itself firmly and absorb nutrients from difficult soil conditions.

While *A. tuncelianum* typically produces single-clove white bulbs, garlic is known to produce bulbs with multiple cloves. This difference in bulb formation is an important distinction between the two species. *Allium tuncelianum* typically produces 4-8 very long, green leaves (Fig. **1**). These leaves are hairless and are arranged in a spiral pattern. The presence of spirally arranged leaves is a notable botanical feature, contributing to the plant's distinctive appearance (Fig. **2**). Unlike garlic, which often produces bulbils (small bulbous structures) in addition to flowers in its inflorescences, *A. tuncelianum* produces non-bulbiferous inflorescences with fertile flowers (Fig. **1**). This difference in inflorescence structure is significant when comparing the two species [34].

Allium tuncelianum, like many Allium species, produces fertile seeds in its umbels (Fig. **1**). These seeds are distinctive, being black, wrinkled, and triangular, similar to onion seeds. The weight of 1000 seeds is 3-3.4 grams. Seed ripening occurs in August and marks an important stage in the life cycle of the plant [35].

The possibility that *A. tuncelianum* serves as the wild progenitor of garlic is an intriguing avenue of study, and further research is required to establish this relationship definitively. Both species are valuable for their culinary and potential medicinal uses, making them of interest to botanists and horticulturists. Understanding the genetic and morphological links between these plants may provide insights into the domestication of garlic and its genetic diversity.

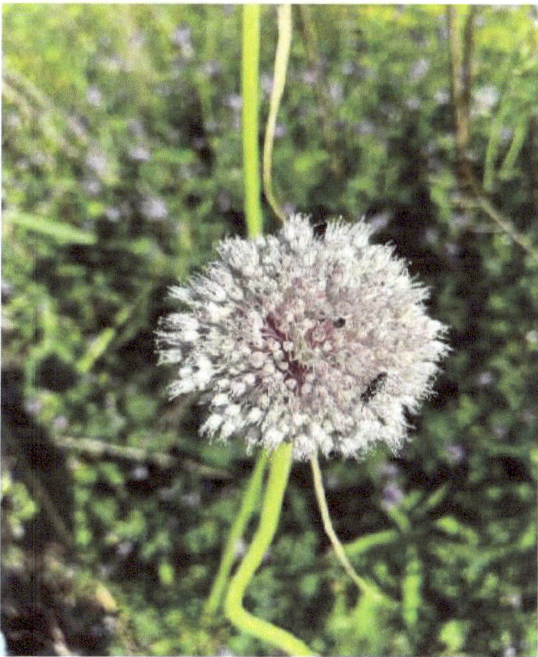

Fig. (1). The inflorescence of *Allium tuncelianum*.

Fig. (2). The plant morphology of *Allium tuncelianum*.

It is worth noting that the number and genetic characteristics of chromosomes often play a crucial role in the study of plant evolution and domestication. While there has been a historical debate about the alleged sterility of garlic due to bulbil formation, this idea has been refuted by studies demonstrating the production of true seeds in garlic. Cytological studies have confirmed that the diploid genome of *A. tuncelianum* is similar to that of many other edible Allium species, further highlighting its potential importance in the evolutionary history of garlic [36].

Cultivation of Tunceli Garlic

Selection of Field

For successful garlic production, it is important to choose a field rich in organic matter, with a humus content of at least 4-5%. Garlic thrives in neutral soils, but the use of commercial fertilisers can alter the pH. It is, therefore, advisable to use fertilisers based on a soil analysis [33].

Planting Material

Garlic cloves are used as the planting material. They are selected for their characteristics and graded by size, and damaged cloves are discarded.

Planting

The cloves are planted by hand or with mechanised equipment. The tips of the cloves (growth tips) should be visible at ground level. They are planted 10-12 cm apart in weed-free fields. In weed-prone areas, the distance between rows is 25-30 cm to facilitate weed control. Within rows, the spacing should be 6-8 cm [37].

Irrigation

Garlic growth coincides with the period of intense rainfall, so irrigation is often unnecessary. Where necessary, sprinkler irrigation is most effective. Timely irrigation during the initial growth stages promotes healthy plant development and clove formation. As maturity approaches and leaves turn yellow and dry, reducing irrigation allows the field to dry before harvest. This also helps to prevent root and head rot, increasing market value [38].

Soil Preparation and Fertilization

The garlic field is fertilised with organic material (3-5 tonnes da^{-1}) at least three months before planting. The organic fertiliser is worked into the soil to a depth of 25 cm. In regions where conditions permit, the soil is ploughed again during the winter to a depth of 20-25 cm. Before planting, inorganic fertilisers should be applied according to soil structure and needs, typically 10-15 kg da^{-1} nitrogen (N), 20-25 kg da^{-1} phosphorus (P$_2$O$_5$), and 20-25 kg da^{-1} potassium (K$_2$O). Some of these fertilisers should be added to the soil before planting, with the remainder applied as needed throughout the growing cycle [38].

GALANTHUS GENUS

Taxonomy and Properties

Regnum: Plantae

Divisio: Magnoliophyta

Subclassis: Magnoliidae

Familia: Amaryllidaceae

Genus: Galanthus

The genus Galanthus is well-defined within the Amaryllidaceae family. The name "Galanthus" is derived from the Greek words "gala," meaning milk, and "anthos," meaning flower, alluding to the white, milky appearance of the flowers. There are about 19 distinct species within the genus. These species often have subtle variations in characteristics, making them popular with plant enthusiasts and collectors.

The genus *Galanthus*, commonly known as snowdrops, originated in Europe and Asia. These delicate, early-flowering bulbous plants are thought to be native to a broad geographical area encompassing parts of Europe and Asia [39].

Various *Galanthus* species can be found in European countries, from Spain in the West to Ukraine in the East, and in countries such as Albania, Armenia, Austria, Bosnia, Bulgaria, Croatia, the Czech Republic, France, Georgia, Germany, Greece, Hungary, Italy, Poland, Macedonia, Moldova, Montenegro, Romania, Serbia, Slovakia, Slovenia, Switzerland, and Türkiye. Türkiye is important with 5 endemic taxa (Table **2**). While Europe is the primary centre of diversity for snowdrops, some *Galanthus* species also occur in parts of Asia, including countries such as Armenia and Georgia. The exact origin of the *Galanthus* may be difficult to determine due to its wide distribution and the complex history of plant migrations and distributions. However, snowdrops have been cherished for centuries for their early spring blooms and resilience in cold climates. They have become a beloved and iconic symbol of hope and renewal as they push through the snow and cold to herald the arrival of spring [40].

Table 2. Galanthus taxa found in Türkiye [32, 41].

1	*Galanthus alpinus Sosn.*	-
	Galanthus alpinus var. alpinus Sosn.	-
	Galanthus alpinus var. bortkewitschianus (Koss)	-
2	*Galanthus angustifolius Koss*	-
3	*Galanthus cilicicus Baker*	Endemic in Türkiye
4	*Galanthus elwesii Hook.f.*	-
	Galanthus elwesii var. elwesii Hook.f.	-
	Galanthus elwesii var. monostictus P.D.Sell	Endemic in Türkiye
5	*Galanthus fosteri Baker*	-
6	*Galanthus gracilis Čelak.*	-
7	*Galanthus ikariae Baker*	-
8	*Galanthus koenenianus Lobin, C.D.Brickell & A.P.Davis*	Endemic in Türkiye
9	*Galanthus krasnovii Khokhr*	-
10	*Galanthus lagodechianus Kem-Nath.*	-
11	*Galanthus nivalis L.*	-
12	*Galanthus peshmeni A.P. Davis & C.D. Brickell*	-
13	*Galanthus plathyphyllus Traub & Moldenke*	-
14	*Galanthus plicatus M.Bieb.*	-
	Galanthus plicatus subsp. byzantinus (Baker) D.A.Webb	Endemic in Türkiye
	Galanthus plicatus subsp. plicatus	-
15	*Galanthus reginae-olgae Orph.*	-
	Galanthus reginae-olgae subsp. reginae-olgae	-
	Galanthus reginae-olgae subsp. vernalis Kamari	-
16	*Galanthus rizehensis Stern*	-
	Galanthus transcaucasicus Fomin	-
17	*Galanthus trojanus A.P.Davis & N.Özhatay*	Endemic in Türkiye
18	*Galanthus x valentinei Beck*	-
19	*Galanthus woronowii Losinsk.*	-
20	*Galanthus x valentinei nothosubsp. subplicatus (N.Zeybek) A.P.Davis*	-
21	*Galanthus x valenthinei Beck*	-

One of the primary reasons for the economic importance of *Galanthus* species is their ornamental potential. Their delicate, nodding, white flowers, often adorned with green markings, make them highly desirable for gardens and landscaping.

They are particularly appreciated as early spring bloomers, bringing beauty to the garden after the winter season.

Wild bulbs are exported annually from Türkiye in large numbers each year, particularly *Galanthus elwesii* bulbs, which have been exported by the millions *via* the Netherlands since the early 1980s. This practice raised concerns about the sustainability of collecting bulbs in such large numbers. As a result, Galanthus was listed in CITES Appendix II in 1990. Today, the collecting of *G. elwesii* bulbs from nature is closely monitored and controlled, with export quotas set annually. Most countries now prohibit the collection of bulbs from the wild, as some snowdrop species are endangered in their natural habitats. CITES regulations make it illegal to trade in any quantity of *Galanthus*, including hybrids, cultivars, and species, without a CITES permit. However, limited trade in wild-collected bulbs of only three species (*G. nivalis*, *G. elwesii*, and *G. woronowii*) from Türkiye is permitted under CITES guidelines [41].

Galanthus species are also noteworthy for their alkaloid content. These alkaloids have demonstrated pharmacological activity and are of interest in the field of medicinal chemistry [41]. The study of these alkaloids may have implications for their potential use in pharmaceuticals or other applications. Ninety alkaloids have been identified from the *Galanthus,* and some of them are tyramine, methyltyramine, hordenine, N-feruloyltyramine, O-methylnorbelladine, ismine, N-formylismine, trisphaeridine, 5,6-dihydrobicolorine, arolycoricidine, narciprimine, galanthamine, 3-epigalanthamine, narwedine, buphanisine, flexinine, 11-deoxytazettine, tazettine, anhydrolycorine, lycorine, homolycorine, graciline, plicamine, and bulbocapnine [41].

Morphology of *Galanthus* Species

All *Galanthus* species are perennial, herbaceous, bulbous plants. During flowering, the 5-25 cm above-ground part consists of the inflorescence stem, flowers, and leaves. During this period, the leaves are erect or open to the side and may curl into a corkscrew shape. This condition is common in *G. gracilis* populations. The curl is in the form of 2-3 turns around the main axis. After flowering, during fruit development, the leaves develop and become flat. In some populations of *G. elwesii var. elwesii,* there are individuals that stand upright with corkscrew curled leaves. The fruit that develops after flowering matures lying on the soil [42].

The bulb is ovoid and globular, and the outside is covered with dead leaves, which may be light yellow or light to dark brown. Although the shape and size of the bulb may vary slightly between species, it is generally thought that it would not be appropriate to use it to differentiate species. However, field studies have shown that bulb shape can be used as an auxiliary character to distinguish *G. elwesii* from *G. gracilis*. During flowering, the bulb of *G. gracilis* is generally globular, whereas that of *G. elwesii* is ovoid. The size of the bulb generally depends on the age of the plant, and its shape may vary during the flowering and dormant periods. In autumn flowering *G. peshmenii*, root development was observed, and although the bulb shape was ovoid in the flowering samples, it was observed that the bulb shape was globose in the flowering samples without root development [43].

The leaves arise from the centre of the bulb, near the base. Each bulb normally develops 3 leaves, one of which differentiates into a transparent, membranous sheath surrounding the other two assimilating leaves. The sheath is a transformed leaf and serves to protect young leaves and flower buds. This tubular membranous structure often shows colour as green stripes towards the top and is usually split on one side during flowering. When the leaves appear above the ground, they lie opposite each other, with their upper surfaces facing each other [43].

The inflorescence, which rises from the bulb between two leaves, has a round or oval structure in cross-section. The evaluation made by Yüzbaşıoğlu [43] showed that two floral states are very common in some species (*Galanthus rizehensis, Galanthus gracilis, Galanthus plicatus, Galanthus* x *valentinei*). In addition to the species that always have a single inflorescence (*Galanthus peshmenii, Galanthus cilicicus, Galanthus koenenianus, Galanthus alpinus, Galanthus woronowii, Galanthus krasnovii*), there are also species that rarely have two inflorescences (*Galanthus trojanus, Galanthus elwesii var. elwesii*) [43].

The inflorescence consists of three tepals arranged in two circles. The outer tepals are about twice as long as the inner tepals. The outer tepals have a 3-dimensional structure and are bowl-spoon shaped, which can be 2.5-5 mm deep. Their general shape varies between ± elliptic and obovate. Towards the base, the three-dimensional structure disappears and becomes narrower, and this narrowed part is called the nail. There are papillae on the outer surface.

The male organs are arranged in groups of three in two circles around the female organ. The bag-shaped anthers first open with pores from the tip towards the style; then, the anther splits downwards. They have awns (arista) at their ends, either straight or pointing outwards.

The style can be thin, thick, short, or long. It has been observed that stigma features vary even within the same population. Capitate and acapitate stigma structures can be seen in the same population [43].

The fruit, which ripens about 2 months after fertilization, is a fleshy locust capsule. The ripening process continues even after the leaves have completely dried. The capsule continues its development process by maintaining its connection to the bulb through the scapula. The shape of the capsule, which can be globular, ovoid, ellipsoid, or pyriform, varies even within the species. The number of seeds produced also depends on the fruit size. Fruits with between 4 and 54 seeds have been observed [43].

While *Galanthus* has its own characteristics, it is closely related to the genus *Leucojum* (snowflakes). One primary distinguishing feature is that *Leucojum* flowers have six equal tepals. In addition, *Leucojum* typically produces 2 to 6-7 flowers on a single scape and has several leaves [2].

The simple elegance of *Galanthus* flowers, with their white petals and green markings (Fig. **3**), has endeared them to gardeners and enthusiasts. Their early spring bloom is a welcome sight, and their unique ecological relationship with ants for seed dispersal adds an extra layer of fascination to these graceful plants.

Fig. (3). Galanthus plant.

Climate and Soil Requirements

Snowdrops (*Galanthus*) are known for their early spring blooms, typically appearing in February and March. They are well adapted to growing at altitudes up to 2000 metres above sea level and are particularly cold-resistant [44].

Snowdrops are well known for their ability to withstand cold temperatures. They are one of the earliest flowering bulbs, often breaking through snow and frost to herald the arrival of spring [45].

Snowdrops thrive in cool, moist soils that are rich in organic matter (humus). These conditions mimic their natural woodland habitat, where they often grow under deciduous trees. Partial shade provides the ideal conditions for their growth and flowering.

Snowdrops prefer soils with a slightly alkaline pH in the range of 6.5 to 7. Soils within this pH range provide the optimum environment for their growth. Snowdrops grow best in well-drained soils with a loose and friable structure.

Heavy or compacted soils can hinder their root development and drainage. Adequate soil moisture is essential for snowdrop growth and bulb development. The soil should maintain a high level of moisture without becoming waterlogged.

Snowdrop bulbs mature better on dry and light soils, especially if there is no autumn rainfall, indicating the importance of well-drained soil conditions for bulb development. Excessive moisture during the dormant season can lead to bulb rot [46].

Cultivation of Snowdrops

It is well known that snowdrops grow very poorly in the field for commercial purposes. Arslan *et al*. [46] demonstrated that its cultivation is suitable for small family farms in Türkiye due to the lack of suitable mechanisation systems. Snowdrops can be propagated by various production methods, such as *in vitro* bulb production, seed, bulb, bulb chipping, or twin scaling [47]. Seed is sown in well-prepared beds, which are kept moist and shaded in summer. Bulbs produced from seeds take four to five years to bulbs produced by seeds to flower [48].

Chipping was found to be superior to the use of offsets in *G. elwesii* in the Netherlands, and the best yields were obtained by chipping [49].

Pre-emergence (in early winter) and post-emergence applications of suitable herbicides can be used to control weeds [50].

Fungal diseases (*Botrytis galanthina* and *Stagonospora curtisii*), nematodes (*Ditylenchus dipsaci, Pratylenchus penetrans*), large narcissus fly, and aphids are the most important pests and diseases [44]. Fungal diseases can be controlled by hot water treatment for 1 hour at 42 °C with added fungicide [51, 52].

Harvest and Bulb Storage

It is well known that snowdrops perform best when transplanted 'in the green' soon after flowering rather than when the bulbs are stored dry and planted in the autumn. While potted plants in growth are attractive, there are situations where selling dry bulbs would be more convenient [53]. It is currently recommended to store snowdrop bulbs in peat or silver sand at 17 °C to prevent desiccation, although this method is only partially successful and rapid replanting is necessary [44, 48].

Rees [53] suggested that transplanting snowdrop bulbs while they are still green before leaf senescence occurs would reduce the bulking that typically occurs at this time. He also recommended research into ways of improving dry storage, as snowdrop bulbs can dry out quickly due to their high surface-to-volume ratio, low scale, and underdeveloped skin. Studies have shown that the best emergence occurs after storage at 13 °C in silver sand. However, conventional storage of snowdrop bulbs has been found to result in low success rates [48]. The best flowering rate achieved was 50% when potted bulbs (5-6 cm class) were grown in a heated greenhouse, although 95% had started to flower. Storage, particularly at low temperatures (9 °C), can cause bud shrinkage. Some attempts have been made to retard snowdrops in a similar way to ice tulips.

CONCLUSION

The Amaryllidacea family, with 75 genera and approximately 1600 species, is an important ornamental and medicinal plant family. The most important genera are found in the Mediterranean region. In particular, *Allium* and *Galanthus* are of considerable economic importance. More than 500 alkaloids have been identified and extracted from the Amaryllidaceae. *Allium* is the largest genus in the Amaryllidaceae family. This genus is rich in Türkiye and represented by 255 taxa in Türkiye with 100 endemic species. The genus *Galanthus*, commonly known as snowdrop, originated in Europe and Asia. *Galanthus* species are also noteworthy for their alkaloid content. The studies related to the cultivation and the alkaloid content of these genera are increasing with the demand.

REFERENCES

[1]   Xu Z, Chang L, Xu Z, Chang L. Amaryllidaceae. Identif Control Common Weeds 2017; 877-89.

[2]   Meerow AW, Snijman DA. Amaryllidaceae. Flowering Plants Monocotyledons: Lilianae (except Orchidaceae). Berlin, Heidelberg: Springer Berlin Heidelberg 1998; pp. 83-110.
[http://dx.doi.org/10.1007/978-3-662-03533-7_11]

[3]   Meerow AW. Taxonomy and phylogeny In ornamental geophytes: from basic science to sustainable production Boca Raton. Edited, FL: CRC Taylor and Francis Group 2012; pp. 17-56.
[http://dx.doi.org/10.1201/b12881-3]

[4]   Berkov S, Atanasova M, Georgiev B, Bastida J, Doytchinova I. The Amaryllidaceae alkaloids: An untapped source of acetylcholinesterase inhibitors. Phytochem Rev 2021; 1-29.

[5]   Stearn WT. How many species of Allium are known?. Curtis's Bot Mag 1992; 9(4): 180-2.
[http://dx.doi.org/10.1111/j.1467-8748.1992.tb00096.x]

[6]   Rahn K. Alliaceae In Flowering Plants Monocotyledons: Lilianae (except Orchidaceae). Berlin, Heidelberg: Springer Berlin Heidelberg 1998; pp. 70-8.

[7]   Koyuncu M, Eker İ. *Allium arsuzense* sp. nov. and *A. roseum* subsp. *gulekense* subsp. nov. from Turkey. Nord J Bot 2011; 29(4): 391-6.
[http://dx.doi.org/10.1111/j.1756-1051.2011.00879.x]

[8]   Koçyiğit M, Salmeri C, Özhatay N, Kaya E, Brullo S. *Allium sphaeronixum* (Amaryllidaceae), a new species from Turkey. Plants 2023; 12(11): 2074.
[http://dx.doi.org/10.3390/plants12112074] [PMID: 37299055]

[9]   Bastaki SMA, Ojha S, Kalasz H, Adeghate E. Chemical constituents and medicinal properties of Allium species. Mol Cell Biochem 2021; 476(12): 4301-21.
[http://dx.doi.org/10.1007/s11010-021-04213-2] [PMID: 34420186]

[10]   Alimardanova M, Tlevlessova D, Bakiyeva V, Akpanov Z. Revealing the features of the formation of the properties of processed cheese with wild onions. Eastern-European Journal of Enterprise Technologies 2021; 4(11(112)): 73-81.
[http://dx.doi.org/10.15587/1729-4061.2021.239120]

[11]   Voća S, Šic Žlabur J, Fabek Uher S, Peša M, Opačić N, Radman S. Neglected potential of wild garlic (*Allium ursinum* L.). Specialized metabolites content and antioxidant capacity of wild populations in relation to location and plant phenophase. Horticulturae 2021; 8(1): 24.
[http://dx.doi.org/10.3390/horticulturae8010024]

[12]   Kurnia D, Ajiati D, Heliawati L, Sumiarsa D. Antioxidant properties and structure-antioxidant activity relationship of Allium species leaves. Molecules 2021; 26(23): 7175.
[http://dx.doi.org/10.3390/molecules26237175] [PMID: 34885755]

[13]   Fredotović Ž, Puizina J. Edible Allium species: Chemical composition, biological activity and health effects. Ital J Food Sci 2019; 31: 1.

[14]   Yin M, Cheng W. Antioxidant activity of several Allium members. J Agric Food Chem 1998; 46(10): 4097-101.
[http://dx.doi.org/10.1021/jf980344x]

[15]   Benkeblia N. Antimicrobial activity of essential oil extracts of various onions (Allium cepa) and garlic (Allium sativum). Lebensm Wiss Technol 2004; 37(2): 263-8.
[http://dx.doi.org/10.1016/j.lwt.2003.09.001]

[16]   Mathew B, Biju R. Neuroprotective effects of garlic a review. Libyan J Med 2008; 3(1): 23-33.
[PMID: 21499478]

[17]   Aburjai T, Natsheh FM. Plants used in cosmetics. Phytother Res 2003; 17(9): 987-1000.
[http://dx.doi.org/10.1002/ptr.1363]

[18]   Patel NR, Mohite SA, Shaha RR. Formulation and evaluation of onion hair nourishing shampoo. J Drug Deliv Ther 2018; 8(4): 335-7.
[http://dx.doi.org/10.22270/jddt.v8i4.1810]

[19]   Vuković S, Popović-Djordjević JB, Kostić AŽ, *et al.* Allium species in the Balkan region—Major metabolites, antioxidant and antimicrobial properties. Horticulturae 2023; 9(3): 408.
[http://dx.doi.org/10.3390/horticulturae9030408]

[20]   Pérez Ortolá M, Knox JW. Water relations and irrigation requirements of onion (*Allium cepa* L.): A review of yield and quality impacts. Exp Agric 2015; 51(2): 210-31.
[http://dx.doi.org/10.1017/S0014479714000234]

[21]   Atif MJ, Amin B, Ghani MI, *et al.* Influence of different photoperiod and temperature regimes on growth and bulb quality of garlic (*Allium sativum* L.) cultivars. Agronomy (Basel) 2019; 9(12): 879.
[http://dx.doi.org/10.3390/agronomy9120879]

[22]   Howard TM. Bulbs for warm climates 2001.

[23]   De Hertogh AA, Zimmer K. Allium—ornamental species. Handbook of flowering. CRC Press 2019; 22-33.

[24]   Gonzales M, Mattos L. Cultural, biological and chemical control of the white rot fungus (Sclerotium cepivorum, Berk) in onions (Allium cepa) in Arequipa´s countryside. Peruvian Journal of Agronomy 2018; 2(3): 27-34.
[http://dx.doi.org/10.21704/pja.v2i3.1230]

[25]   Lupien SL, Hellier BC, Dugan FM. First report of onion rust caused by *Puccinia allii* on *Allium pskemense* and *A. altaicum.*. Plant Dis 2004; 88(1): 83.
[http://dx.doi.org/10.1094/PDIS.2004.88.1.83D] [PMID: 30812465]

[26]   Dugan FM, Hellier BC, Lupien SL. Resistance to *Penicillium allii* in accessions from a national plant germplasm system Allium collection. Crop Prot 2011; 30(4): 483-8.
[http://dx.doi.org/10.1016/j.cropro.2010.12.021]

[27]   Walkey DG. Virus diseases. Onions and allied crops. CRC Press 2018; 191-212.
[http://dx.doi.org/10.1201/9781351075152-9]

[28]   Hori M. Onion aphid (*Neotoxoptera formosana*) attractants, in the headspace of *Allium fistulosum* and *A. tuberosum* leaves. J Appl Entomol 2007; 131(1): 8-12.
[http://dx.doi.org/10.1111/j.1439-0418.2006.01130.x]

[29]   Yadav M, Prasad R, Kumar P, Pandey C, Kumar P, Kumar U. A review on onion thrips and their management of bulb crops. J Pharmacogn Phytochem 2018; 7(1S): 891-6.

[30]   Erdogan P, Mustafa Z. Harmful Diptera pests in garlic and onion and their management. Adv Diptera-Insight, Challenges Manag Tools. IntechOpen. 2022.
[http://dx.doi.org/10.5772/intechopen.106862]

[31]   Krzymińska A, Gawłowska M, Wolko B, Bocianowski J. Genetic diversity of ornamental Allium species and cultivars assessed with isozymes. J Appl Genet 2008; 49(3): 213-20.
[http://dx.doi.org/10.1007/BF03195616] [PMID: 18670056]

[32]   Bizimbitkiler Available from: www.bizimbitkiler.org.tr Access date: 25.24.2024

[33]   Arslan N, İpek A, Sarıhan EO. Farklı ortamların Tunceli sarımsağı (Allium tuncelianum) tohumlarına çıkış ve fide gelişimine etkisi. Türkiye VII. Tarla Bitkileri Kongresi 2007; 25-7.

[34]   Karakaya S, Eksi G, Koca M, *et al.* Chemical and morphological characterization of Allium tuncelianum (Amaryllidaceae) and its antioxidant and anticholinesterase potentials. Anales Jardín Bot Madrid 2019; 76(2): e085-5.

[35]   Yıldız H, Binici S, Şan B, Yıldırım F, Telci İ. Tunceli sarımsağı (*Allium Tuncelianum*) tohumlarının *in vitro* koşullarda çimlendirilmesi ve bitki gelişimi üzerine GA₃ uygulamalarının etkisi. Türk Tarım ve

Doğa Bilimleri Dergisi 2022; 9(3): 689-95.
[http://dx.doi.org/10.30910/turkjans.1121404]

[36]   Ipek M, Ipek A, Simon PW. Genetic characterization of *Allium tuncelianum*: An endemic edible Allium species with garlic odor. Sci Hortic (Amsterdam) 2008; 115(4): 409-15.
[http://dx.doi.org/10.1016/j.scienta.2007.11.002]

[37]   Yanmaz R, Beşirli G, Uzun Y, *et al.* Tunceli sarımsağını (Allium tuncelianum (Kollman) Özhatay, Matthew, Siraneci) kültüre alma çalışmaları. VI Sebze Tarımı Sempozyumu. Eylül, Kahramanmaraş, 2006; pp. 29-33.

[38]   Peker S. Diyarbakır koşularında sarımsak yetiştiriciliğinde farklı dikim tarihlerinin hasat, verim ve kalite üzerine etkisi 2019.

[39]   Rønsted N, Zubov D, Bruun-Lund S, Davis AP. Snowdrops falling slowly into place: An improved phylogeny for Galanthus (Amaryllidaceae). Mol Phylogenet Evol 2013; 69(1): 205-17.
[http://dx.doi.org/10.1016/j.ympev.2013.05.019] [PMID: 23747523]

[40]   Semerdjieva I, Sidjimova B, Yankova-Tsvetkova E, Kostova M, Zheljazkov VD. Study on *Galanthus* species in the Bulgarian flora. Heliyon 2019; 5(12): e03021.
[http://dx.doi.org/10.1016/j.heliyon.2019.e03021] [PMID: 32373724]

[41]   Berkov S, Codina Mahrer C, Bastida Armengol J. The genus Galanthus: a source of bioactive compounds. Chapter 11 in: Rao, Venketeshwer 2012 Phytochemicals: A Global Perspective of Their Role in Nutrition and Health IntechOpen 2012; 235-54.
[http://dx.doi.org/10.5772/28798]

[42]   Yüzbaşıoğlu S. The development of non-detriment findings for *Galanthus elwesii* Hook. f. Turkey NDF Workshop Case Studies Mexico 2008; 1-13.

[43]   Yüzbaşıoğlu IS. Revision of snowdrops (Galanthus) taxa in Turkey. PhD Dissertation, İstanbul Üniversitesi Fen Bilimleri Enstitüsü 2010; 189.

[44]   Langeslag JJ. Teelt en gebruiksmogelijkheden van Bijgoedgewassen. Tweede Uitgave. Ministerie van Landbouw, Natuurbeheer en Visserij en Consulentschap Algemene Dienst Bloembollenteelt, Lisse, The Netherlands 1989; 273: 231-4.

[45]   Sakai A, Yoshie F. Freezing tolerance of ornamental bulbs and corms. Engei Gakkai Zasshi 1984; 52(4): 445-9. [in Japanese].
[http://dx.doi.org/10.2503/jjshs.52.445]

[46]   Arslan N, Koyuncu M, Ekim T. Commercial propagation of snowdrops (Galanthus elwesii Hook.) in different environments. VII Int Symp Flower Bulbs. 430: 743-6.

[47]   Aksu E, Çelikel FG. The effect of initial bulb size on snowdrop (*Galanthus elwesii* Hook. f.) bulb propagation by chipping. Acta Hortic 2003; (598): 69-71.
[http://dx.doi.org/10.17660/ActaHortic.2003.598.9]

[48]   De Hertogh AA, le Nard M. The physiology of flower bulbs: A Comprehensive Treatise on the Physiology and Utilization of Ornamental Flowering Bulbous and Tuberous Plants. Amsterdam, The Netherlands: Elsevier Science Publishers 1993; 812.

[49]   Van Leeuwen PJ, van Der Weijden JA. Propagation of specialty bulbs by chipping. VII Int Symp Flower Bulbs. 430: 351-4.

[50]   Wallis LW. Weed control in miscellaneous bulbs. ADAS Experiments and Development in the Eastern Region. 1975; 403-4.

[51]   Moore WC, Brunt AA, Price D, Rees AR, Dickens JSW. Diseases of bulbs. 2nd edition, Her Majesty's Stationery Office, London 1979.

[52]   Lane A. Bulb pests. 7th edition, Her Majesty's Stationery Office, London. 1984.

[53]   Rees AR. Galanthus "in the green". Plantsman (Lond, Engl) 1989; 10: 243-4.

CHAPTER 4

Colchicaceae

Nilüfer Koçak Şahin[1,*]

[1] *Department of Field Crops, Faculty of Agriculture, Ankara University, Ankara, Türkiye*

Abstract: Colchicaceae is a family of angiosperm plants with 16 genera and 161 accepted species, widely distributed in temperate and Mediterranean climates. It has a basal leaf aggregation, reproducing by corms or rhizomes, parallel vein leaves, sessile, petiolate, lamina with stomata, and mesophyll cells with calcium oxalate crystals. *Colchicum* spp. is a non-cyanogenic plant with toxic alkaloids that are active against gout, have anti-inflammatory and anti-cancer properties, and are used in folk medicines. Corms of all species are nutritive due to low alkaloids and high starch/carbohydrates. Colchicine is a pseudocrocus that is biosynthetically extracted through condensation of tyrosine and phenylalanine to a phenethylisoquinoline precursor. Gloriosa is a perennial climbing tuberous herb that grows in tropical, sub-tropical areas and Himalayan foothills. It is used to extract colchicine and to treat cancer neuralgic pains, rheumatism, and other diseases. It is also used in horticulture as a cut and garden flower. Chapter 4 reviews the taxonomy of two species and the general characteristics of the plants in this family.

Keywords: Angiosperm plants, *Colchicum*, *Gloriosa*.

INTRODUCTION

Colchicaceae are a family of angiosperm plants containing 16 genera (Table **1**), 161 accepted species in the genus *Colchicum,* and 11 species in the genus *Gloriosa* (Table **2**) [1 - 5]. The genera *Gloriosa* and *Colchicum* (Çiğdemgiller in Turkish, Sorenjan in Persian, Urdu, and Baluchi) are the two most important groups of plants in this family. This chapter will discuss the Colchicaceae family as a whole, including multiplication agronomy of the genera *Colchicum* and *Gloriosa* spp.

Distribution and Habitat

This family is widely distributed in almost all areas of the world with a temperate or Mediterranean type of climate or pockets in the tropical areas of New Zealand,

* **Corresponding author Nilüfer Koçak Şahin:** Department of Field Crops, Faculty of Agriculture, Ankara University, Ankara, Türkiye; E-mail: nkocak@ankara.edu.tr

Sibel Day (Ed.)

Australia, Africa, Asia, Europe, and North America, with several common seasonal similarities with rain in winter (Figs. **1** and **2**) [2, 8 - 10].

Table 1. Genera of *Colchicaceae* (Desai C. (2016)) [6].

No.	Latin name	English name
1	*Androcymbium*	(Men in a Boat)
2	*Anguillaria*	(Anguillaria)
3	*Burchardia*	(Milkmaids)
4	*Camptorrhiza*	(Camptorrhiza)
5	*Colchicum*	(Naked Lady)
6	*Disporum*	(Fairy Bells)
7	*Gloriosa*	(Glory Lily)
8	*Iphigenia*	(Iphigenia)
9	*Kuntheria*	(Kuntheria)
10	*Littonia*	(Climbing Lily)
11	*Merendera*	(Merendera)
12	*Neodregea*	(Neodregea)
13	*Ornithoglossum*	(Bird's Tongue)
14	*Sandersonia*	(Christmas Bells)
15	*Uvularia*	(Bellwort)
16	*Wurmbea*	(Early Nancy)

Table 2. A list of accepted species in the genus *Colchicum* spp. (Source: https://www.worldfloraonline.org/ accessed date: 20.12.2023) [7].

No.	Species
1	*C. zahnii* Heldr.
2	*C. worsonense* (U.Müll.-Doblies & D.Müll.-Doblies) J.C.Manning & Vinn.
3	*C. woronowii* Bokeriya
4	*C. walteri* (Pedrola, Membrives & J.M.Monts.) J.C.Manning & Vinn.
5	*C. wendelboi* K.Perss.
6	*C. volutare* (Burch.) J.C.Manning & Vinn.
7	*C. villosum* (U.Müll.-Doblies & D.Müll.-Doblies) J.C.Manning & Vinn.
8	*C. variegatum* L.
9	*C. varians* (Freyn & Bornm.) Dyer
10	*C. vanjaarsveldii* (U.Müll.-Doblies, Hähnl., U.U.Müll.-Doblies & D.Müll.-Doblies) J.C.Manning & Vinn.

(Table 2) cont.....

No.	Species
11	*C. undulatum* (U.Müll.-Doblies & D.Müll.-Doblies) J.C.Manning & Vinn.
12	*C. umbrosum* Steven
13	*C. tuviae* Feinbrun
14	*C. turcicum* Janka
15	*C. tunicatum* Feinbrun
16	*C. tulakii* Giannakis, Tsiftsis & Elefth
17	*C. troodi* Kotschy
18	*C. triphyllum* Kunze
19	*C. trigynum* (Steven ex Adams) Stearn
20	*C. szovitsii* Fisch. & C.A.Mey.
21	*C. swazicum* (U.Müll.-Doblies & D.Müll.-Doblies) J.C.Manning & Vinn.
22	*C. striatum* (Hochst. ex A.Rich.) J.C.Manning & Vinn.
23	*C. stirtonii* (U.Müll.-Doblies, Raus, Weiglin & D.Müll.-Doblies) J.C.Manning & Vinn.
24	*C. stevenii* Kunth
25	*C. speciosum* Steven
26	*C. soboliferum* (C.A.Mey.) Stef.
27	*C. sieheanum* Hausskn. ex Stef.
28	*C. sfikasianum* Kit Tan & Iatroú
29	*C. serpentinum* Woronow ex Miscz.
30	*C. schimperianum* (Hochst.) C.Archer
31	*C. schimperi* Janka ex Stef.
32	*C. scabromarginatum* (Schltr. & K.Krause) J.C.Manning & Vinn.
33	*C. roseum* (Engl.) J.C.Manning & Vinn.C. sanguicolle K.Perss.
34	*C. robustum* (Bunge) Stef.
35	*C. ritchii* R.Br.
36	*C. rechingeri* (Greuter) J.C.Manning & Vinn.
37	*C. rausii* K.Perss.
38	*C. raddeanum* (Regel) K.Perss.
39	*C. pusillum* Sieber
40	*C. pulchellum* K.Perss.
41	*C. psammophilum* (Svent.) J.C.Manning & Vinn
42	*C. praeirroratum* (U.Müll.-Doblies & D.Müll.-Doblies) J.C.Manning & Vinn.
43	*C. polyphyllum* Boiss. & Heldr.
44	*C. poeltianum* (U.Müll.-Doblies & D.Müll.-Doblies) J.C.Manning & Vinn.

(Table 2) cont.....

No.	Species
45	*C. persicum* Baker.
46	*C. peloponnesiacum* Rech.f. & P.H.Davis
47	*C. paschei* K.Perss.
48	*C. parnassicum* Sart., Orph. & Heldr.
49	*C. parlatoris* Orph.
50	*C. palaestinum* (Baker) C.Archer
51	*C. orienticapense* (U.Müll.-Doblies & D.Müll.-Doblies) J.C.Manning & Vinn.
52	*C. neapolitanum* (Ten.) Ten.
53	*C. natalense* (Baker) J.C.Manning & Vinn.
54	*C. nanum* K.Perss.
55	*C. munzurense* K.Perss.
56	*C. multiflorum* Brot.
57	*C. montanum* L.
58	*C. minutum* K.Perss.
59	*C. micranthum* Boiss.
60	*C. micaceum* K.Perss.
61	*C. melanthioides* (Willd.) J.C.Manning & Vinn.
62	*C. maraschicum* E.Kaya & Özhatay
63	*C. manissadjianii* (Azn.) K.Perss.
64	*C. macrophyllum* B.L.Burtt
65	*C. macedonicum* Košanin
66	*C. luteum* Baker
67	*C. lusitanum* Brot.
68	*C. longipes* (Baker) J.C.Manning & Vinn.
69	*C. longifolium* Castagne
70	*C. lingulatum* Boiss. & Spruner
71	*C. leistneri* (U.Müll.-Doblies & D.Müll.-Doblies) C.Archer
72	*C. lagotum* K.Perss.
73	*C. laetum* Steven
74	*C. kurdicum* (Bornm.) Stef.
75	*C. kunkelianum* (U.Müll.-Doblies, P.Hirsch, Stearn & D.Müll.-Doblies) J.C.Manning & Vinn.
76	*C. kotschyi* Boiss.
77	*C. knersvlaktense* (U.Müll.-Doblies & D.Müll.-Doblies) J.C.Manning & Vinn.
78	*C. kesselringii* Regel

(Table 2) cont.....

No.	Species
79	*C. karooparkense* (U.Müll.-Doblies, Daber, J.M.Anderson & D.Müll.-Doblies) J.C.Manning & Vinn.
80	*C. kackarense* Rukšāns & Zubov
81	*C. irroratum* (Schltr. & K.Krause) J.C.Manning & Vinn.
82	*C. inundatum* K.Perss.
83	*C. imperatoris*-friderici Siehe ex K.Perss.
84	*C. huntleyi* (Pedrola, Membrives, J.M.Monts. & Caujapé) J.C.Manning & Vinn.
85	*C. hungaricum* Janka
86	*C. hughocymbion* (U.Müll.-Doblies & D.Müll.-Doblies) J.C.Manning & Vinn.
87	*C. hirsutum* Stef.
88	*C. hierrense* (A.Santos) J.C.Manning & Vinn.
89	*C. hierosolymitanum* Feinbrun
90	*C. henssenianum* (U.Müll.-Doblies & D.Müll.-Doblies) J.C.Manning & Vinn.
91	*C. heldreichii* K.Perss.
92	*C. haynaldii* Heuff.
93	*C. hantamense* (Engl. ex Diels) J.C.Manning & Vinn.
94	*C. guessfeldtianum* Asch. & Schweinf.
95	*C. greuterocymbium* (U.Müll.-Doblies, Raus & D.Müll.-Doblies) J.C.Manning & Vinn.
96	*C. gramineum* (Cav.) J.C.Manning & Vinn.
97	*C. graecum* K.Perss.
98	*C. gracile* K.Perss.
99	*C. gonarei* Camarda
100	*C. freynii* Bornm.
101	*C. filifolium (Cambess.) Stef.*
102	*C. figlalii* (Varol) Parolly & Eren
103	*C. fharii* Fridl.
104	*C. feinbruniae* K.Perss.
105	*C. fasciculare* (L.) R.Br.
106	*C. exiguum* (Roessler) J.C.Manning & Vinn.
107	*C. europaeum* (Lange) J.C.Manning & Vinn.
108	*C. eucomoides* (Jacq.) J.C.Manning & Vinn.
109	*C. euboeum* (Boiss.) K.Perss.
110	*C. etesionamibense* (U.Müll.-Doblies & D.Müll.-Doblies) J.C.Manning & Vinn.
111	*C. etesionamibense* (U.Müll.-Doblies & D.Müll.-Doblies) J.C.Manning & Vinn.
112	*C. eghimocymbion* (U.Müll.-Doblies & D.Müll.-Doblies) J.C.Manning & Vinn.

(Table 2) cont.....

No.	Species
113	*C. dregei* (C.Presl) J.C.Manning & Vinn.
114	*C. dolichantherum* K.Perss.
115	*C. doerfleri* Halácsy
116	*C. decipiens* (N.E.Br.) J.C.Manning & Vinn.
117	*C. decaisnei* Boiss.
118	*C. davisii* C.D.Brickell
119	*C. cuspidatum* (Baker) J.C.Manning & Vinn.
120	*C. cupanii* Guss.
121	*C. cruciatum* (U.Müll.-Doblies & D.Müll.-Doblies) J.C.Manning & Vinn.
122	*C. crocifolium* Boiss.
123	*C. crispum* (Schinz) J.C.Manning & Vinn.
124	*C. cretense* Greuter
125	*C. crenulatu*m (U.Müll.-Doblies, *e.g.*H.Oliv. & D.Müll.-Doblies) J.C.Manning & Vinn.
126	*C. corsicum* Baker
127	*C. confusum* K.Perss.
128	*C. clanwilliamense* (Pedrola, Membrives & J.M.Monts.) J.C.Manning & Vinn.
129	*C. circinatum* (Baker) J.C.Manning & Vinn.
130	*C. cilicicum* (Boiss.) Dammer
131	*C. chlorobasis* K.Perss.
132	*C. chimonanthum* K.Perss.
133	*C. chalcedonicum* Azn.
134	*C. cedarbergense* (U.Müll.-Doblies, Hähnl., U.U.Müll.-Doblies & D.Müll.-Doblies) J.C.Manning & Vinn.
135	*C. capense* (L.) J.C.Manning & Vinn.
136	*C. burt*ii Meikle
137	*C. buchubergense* (U.Müll.-Doblies & D.Müll.-Doblies) J.C.Manning & Vinn.
138	*C. bulbocodium* Ker Gawl.
139	*C. burchellii* (Baker) Ined.
140	*C. burkei* (Baker) J.C.Manning & Vinn.
141	*C. boissieri* Orph.
142	*C. bivonae* Guss.
143	*C. bellum* (Schltr. & K.Krause) J.C.Manning & Vinn.
144	*C. baytopiorum* C.D.Brickell
145	*C. balansae* Planch.

(Table 2) cont.....

No.	Species
146	*C. autumnale* L
147	*C. austrocapense* (U.Müll.-Doblies & D.Müll.-Doblies) J.C.Manning & Vinn.
148	*C. atticum* Spruner ex Tommas.
149	*C. asteroides* (J.C.Manning & Goldblatt) J.C.Manning & Vinn.
150	*C. asteranthum* Vassiliades & K.M.Perss.
151	*C. arenasii* Fridl.
152	*C. arenarium* Waldst. & Kit.
153	*C. antilibanoticum* Gomb.
154	*C. antepense* K.Perss.
155	*C. androcymbioides* (Valdés) K.Perss.
156	C. amphigaripense (U.Müll.-Doblies, Weiglin, M.Gottlieb & D.Müll.-Doblies) J.C.Manning & Vinn
157	*C. amphigaripense* (U.Müll.-Doblies, Weiglin, M.Gottlieb & D.Müll.-Doblies) J.C.Manning & Vinn.
158	*C. alpinum* DC.
159	*C. albomarginatum* (Schinz) J.C.Manning & Vinn.
160	Colchicum. × alberti Regel
161	*C. albanense* (Schönland) J.C.Manning & Vinn.
162	*C. actupii* Fridl.

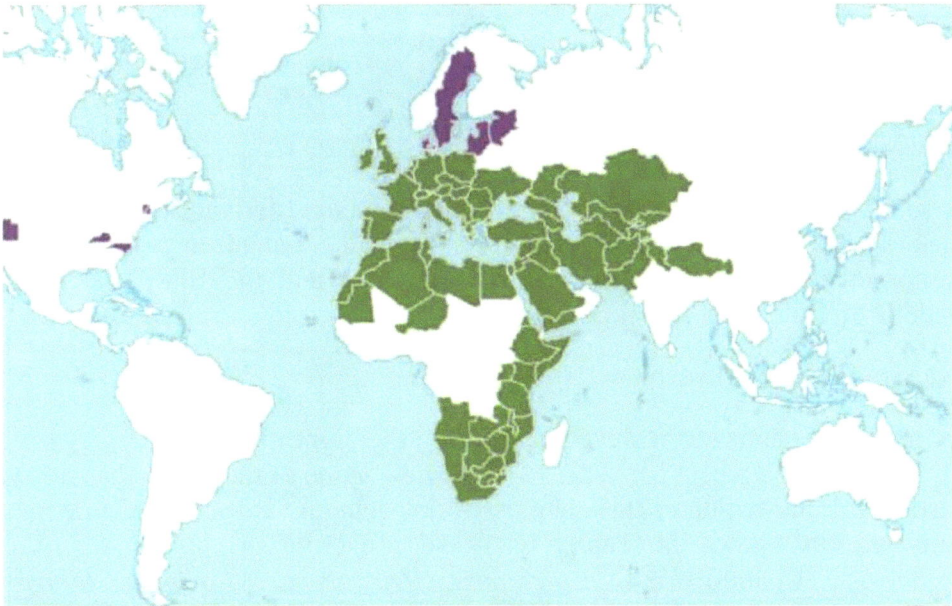

Fig. (1). *Colchicum* species are Native to Zimbabwe, Zambia, Yugoslavia, Yemen, Western Sahara, West Himalaya (Azad Kashmir and Indian occupied Kashmir), Uzbekistan, Ukraine, Uganda, Turkmenistan,

Türkiye-in-Europe, Türkiye Tunisia, Transcaucasus, Tibet, Tanzania, Tadzhikistan, Syria, Switzerland, Swaziland, Spain, South European Russi, Somalia, Sinai, Sicilia, Saudi Arabia, Sardegna, Romania, Portugal, Poland, Palestine, Pakistan, Northern Provinces, Niger, North Caucasus, Netherlands, Namibia, Mozambique, Morocco, Mauritania, Malawi, Libya, Lesotho, Lebanon, KwaZulu-Natal, Krym, Kriti, Kirgizstan, Kenya, Kazakhstan, Italy, Ireland, Iraq, Iran, Hungary, Greece, Great Britain, Germany, Free State, France, Ethiopia, Eritrea, Egypt, East Aegean Is., Czechoslovakia, Cyprus, Corse, Caprivi Strip, Cape Provinces, Canary Is., Bulgaria, Botswana, Belgium, Baleares, Austria, Angola, Algeria, Albania, and Afghanistan as shown by green colors in the map. They are introduced or naturalized to Vermont, Utah, Sweden, Oregon, Northwest European R, North Carolina, New Zealand South, New Hampshire, Kentucky, Denmark, and the Baltic States.

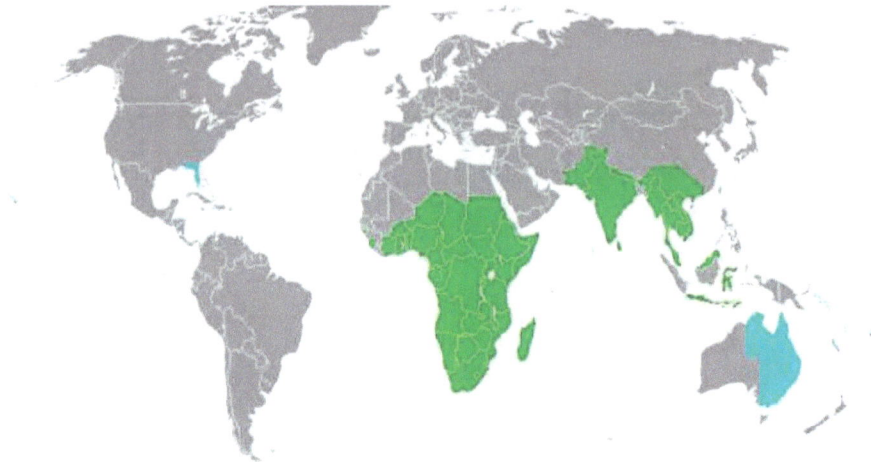

Fig. (2). Distribution map of *Gloriosa superba* as shown by green color on the map. They are introduced or naturalized in areas as shown by blue color. (*Gloriosa_superba*_distribution.png#/media/File:*Gloriosa_superba*_distribution.png accessed 20.12.2023) Access Date: 20.11.2023 [5].

Etymology

The family takes its name from the genus *Colchicum* (derived from the ancient Greek word "Kolchikòn") and is etymologically linked to a geographical transcontinental region between the Caspian Sea and the Black Sea ancient kingdom of Colchis [11, 12].

Taxonomy

This family of plants has received or suffered the highest segregations by several taxonomists in the recent past [13, 14]. The new name of the family has not been revised until the writing of this chapter. Major general names of the Colchiaceae family are as shown in Table **1**. These are *Androcymbium, Anguillaria, Burchardia, Camptorrhiza, Colchicum, Disporum, Gloriosa, Iphigenia, Kuntheria, Littonia, Merendera, Neodregea, Ornithoglossum, Sandersonia, Uvularia,* and *Wurmbea* [6, 15, 16].

Morphological Description

The vast majority of species are herbaceous, including some perennial plants. They may or may not have a basal aggregation of leaves. They reproduce by corms (*e.g.*, *Colchicum*) or rhizomes (*e.g.*, *Gloriosa*). They have alternate, whorled (usually spiral or distichous) leaf arrangements on the stem, form a basal rosette, have parallel vein leaves, are sheathed at the base, and end "in a tendril"(sometimes). The leaves do not have stipules and are sessile, rarely petiolate. The lamina is entire, linear, or lanceolate with a normocytic stomata, and the lamina is dorsiventral with mesophyll cells containing crystals of calcium oxalate [13, 17 - 19].

The inflorescence is pentacyclic, hermaphrodite, actinoform, and trimerous. The perigonium has six U-shaped tepals bent around each stamen, with different colors and/or stipplings; the androecium has six stamens, having separate filaments. The gynoecium has three carpels. The ovary is superior, with multiple ovules (with 1 or 2 integuments and a single megasporangium). They have three petals (truncated or elongated). They have nectaries (nectar-producing glands) with secretion from the perianth (mostly) or androecium. They could be arranged or solitary, forming several types of terminal or axillary inflorescences in umbels or clusters. Fruit is indehiscent, dry, with a capsule shape. The seeds have very varied (globose, angular, *etc.*) shapes, with red or brown color containing an oily endosperm, which is entomophile and can be dispersed easily [20, 21].

Medicinal Uses

Phytochemistry

Non-cyanogenic, with toxic alkaloids (generally colchicine) that are active against gout, as an anti-inflammation agent or anti-cancer agent, may or may not cause diarrhea or vomiting, they are also used to treat jaundice, osteoarthritis, inflammations, and sexual impotence in folk medicines.

The seeds and corms of *Colchicum* are very important pharmaceutically and are used to extract bioactive compounds, like alkaloids, including tropolone and isoquinoline [22]. They are also used to obtain carbohydrates, flavonoids, tannins, and phenolic compounds. Their concentration and amounts vary depending on the season and growth cycles of the plants [23, 24]. Tropolone is a compound isolated from Colchicum, which is used to treat cancers and gout. Tubulin and anti-tubulin inhibition bioactivities are mainly checked by colchicine, demecolcine, and colchicine, obtained from the species in Colchicum. They have a narrow therapeutic index with potential toxicity. Corms of all species of *Colchicum* are nutritive due to low alkaloids and high starch or carbohydrates [25]. These species are also known for their compounds like isoquinoline, having anticholinesterase inhibitory bioactivities due to the presence of 4, 6-dimethoxy-3, 7- luteolin, apigenin, 2-hydroxybenzoic acid, vanillic acid, caffeic acid, ferulic acid, and coumaric acid. Phenolic acids, flavonoids, and tropolone alkaloids are examples of bioactive compounds. *Colchicum autumnale* L. and other species of *Colchicum* are used to treat inflammations and osteoarthritis [26, 27]. They are well established in human and animal cell lines with <5% hemolytic activity, with LC90 and LC50 of > 450 and 1700μg/mL, respectively. Furthermore, they have cytotoxic IC50 of >13 μg/mL and LD50 of > 6 mg/kg [28].

Colchicine is commercially isolated from *Colchicum autumnale* L. and *Gloriosa superba* L. However, it is detected in almost all species of the expanded Colchicaceae family [29 - 31] (like Disporum, Salisb, Uvularia L., Kuntheria Conran & Clifford, Schelhammera R.Br. and Tripladenia D.Don) previously placed in other families, and a new classification has been adopted (see Table **1**).

Alkaloid Diversity

Although colchicine has been reported in several families, the scope of this chapter is to review alkaloids found in the species belonging to the Colchicaceae family with about 150 metabolites [32], which is biosynthesized by condensation of tyrosine and phenylalanine to a phenethylisoquinoline precursor, which has been shown in many feeding experiments to explain colchicine synthesis [33 - 40]. Autumn crocus *Colchicum autumnale* (a pseudocrocus) is rich in colchicine and several other alkaloids. All species in the genus Gloriosa, Merendera, and others also contain colchicine, including *Androcymbium* species, *Iphigenia* species, and *Wurmbea* species. Iphigenia, indica (shan cigu) is used in the conventional Chinese system of herbal medicines [41].

Cultivation

There are no in-cultivation methods for these plants under *in vitro* or ex vitro conditions. Most of the time, they are collected from the natural flora and grow under wild conditions. Some techniques to grow and multiply the two most important species in the family, namely *Colchicum* and *Gloriosa* spp., are described in the following sections.

COLCHICUM

The genus *Colchicum* spp. has been known for > 2000 years [42] and grows naturally in many parts of the world. Generally, they grow rarely at very altitudes with limited growth. They can be cultivated and survive in a large range of climates. However, they grow best in well-drained soils in full or partially shaded areas. They bloom well in gardens in the late summer to autumn season [43]. The most important cultivars include the amethyst-purple "Atrorubens" and white "Album" 2023). *Colchicum speciosum* has another cultivar popularly known as Atrorubens (AGM Plants - Ornamental 2023).

In Vitro Culture Studies

Several studies have reported tissue cultures based on callus induction from peduncles of *C. autumnale* using MS (Murashige & Skoog 1962) medium modified with 2,4-D. Hayashi *et al*. [44] produced colchicine from these tissues on an MS medium modified with IBA and kinetin. Daradkeh *et al*. [45] induced callus on *C. hierosolymitanum* using MS medium corrected with 0.45 µM 2, 4-D under darkness. They induced colchicine through callus after their subcultures of 27 days on liquid MS medium modified with 0.54 µM 1- NAA. They noted higher cell fresh weight on 9 µM 6-BAP - 0.45 µM 2, 4- D. They noted a maximum amount of 0.090 mg g^{-1} DW on 0.1 M tissue culture grade sucrose after a delay of 4 weeks [45]. Different explants of endemic *C. chalcedonicum* and *C. micranthum* Boiss were investigated for cytotoxic activities. They isolated N-diacetyl-Nformylcolchicine, demecolcine, 4-hydroxy colchicine colchicine, 2-demethylcolchicine, and colchifoline, which were highly cytotoxic. The major alkaloids were colchifoline and colchicine. Maximum diversity in tropolone alkaloids was noted in the seeds of *C. chalcedonicum* [46, 47].

Genus *Gloriosa*

Habitat

Gloriosa is a perennial climbing tuberous herb that grows on several types of soil and climatic conditions in tropical and sub-tropical areas and Himalayan foothills [48]. *G. superba* is also a recognized national flower of Zimbabwe [49] (Fig. **2**). *G. superba* is a climbing woody herbaceous 5 meters tall plant.

Some Important Species

G. superba naturally grows in tropical Africa, Tropical Asia, Myanmar, Malaysia, Sri Lanka, Karnataka, Asam (India), and Bangladesh [40]. *G. lutea, G. superba, G. sudanica, G. plantii, G. virescens, G. simplex, G. longifolia, G. lipolidii, G. superba, G. Rothschildiana,* and *G. grandiflora are the most important species.*

Whole plant is used to extract colchicine and colchicine and to treat cancer and diseases like scrofula, piles, and ulcers [50].

Medicinal Uses

It is noted that the plant can grow on nutrient-poor sandy-loam soils under the sunny deciduous forests or foothills in thickets and forest edges up to 2530 m above sea level [51]. The extracts are also used to kill hair lice. The tubers contain gloriosine and superbine and gloriosine, which are used in medicine as purgative, anti-abortive, and tonic or stimulant in low doses. It is also used to treat neuralgic pains, rheumatism [52], and gout.

Agronomy

They are generally multiplied using corms. Multiplication through seeds is poor and very restricted.

In Vitro Regeneration

All *Gloriosa* spp. is another important source to obtain and extract colchicine [53], inhibit cell division, and multiply chromosomes in liquid, agar, gelrite, phytagel, lanolin paste, or cotton swabs applied to leaf axils. Khan *et al.* (2007) [54] mentioned their enzyme inhibition activities on the rhizomes by acetylcholinesterase lipoxygenase, urease, butyrylcholinesterase urease, and lipoxygenase activity. Khan *et al.* (2008) [55] also noted antimicrobial and antifungal activities against *Candida albicans*, *Staphylococcus aureus*, *Trichophyton longifusus,* and *Microsporum canis*.

Phytochemistry

Gloriosa superba produces some important alkaloids, such as colchicine, N-formyl deacetylcolchcine, and 3-demethyl-N-deformyl-N-deacetylcolchicine [56]. Suri *et al.* (2001) [56] also extracted colchicine glycoside and 3--demethylcolchicine-3-O-alpha-D-glucopyranoside from the *G. superba* seeds and also discussed the extraction of 3-monomeric monocot mannose-binding tryptophan, lysine, tyrosine, lectins phenylalanine, and ornithine.

Kala *et al.* [57] studied the folk and ethno-medicinal uses of medicinal plants in the Indian state of Uttaranchal with the documentation of *G. superba*. Custers and Bergervoet [58] and Hassan and Roy [59] mentioned plant shoot regeneration from axillary and apical buds. Custers and Bergervoet [57] also mentioned micropropagation on pedicels, flowers, tubers leaves, shoot cuttings, and internodes using *G. rothschildiana* × *G. rothschildiana* (new accession) and *G. rothschildiana* × *G. Superba, which* were cultured on MS nutrient medium rectified with 3% (w/v) sucrose, 0-10 mg L^{-1} BAP (BA), and 0.1 mg indole acetic acid (IAA) and kept for a 16 h photoperiod. Modifying the medium with 1 mg L^{-1}

had a positive effect, and 10 mg l^{-1} BAP induced negative effects on rhizome meristems and regeneration after 136 d of culture. They mentioned the propagation of *G. superba* from apical bud and node segment of shoot tip on 8 g l^{-1}of Gamborg's B$_5$ medium gelled with 2,4-D, IBA, Kinetin, IAA, BA, and NAA, or at 26 ± 1°C. Shoot proliferation took place in 28-56 d.

Somani *et al.* [60] mentioned micropropagation of *G. superba* on MS medium corrected with 30 g l^{-1} sucrose and 6 g l^{-1} agar in 30 d. Sivakumar and Krishnamurthy [61] induced indirect organogenetic on *G. superba* using MS medium BAP.

The yield of colchicine from Gloriosa superba is generally higher than that from *Colchicum autumnale*. Specifically, *G. superba* produces colchicine at a rate of 0.7-0.9%, while *C. autumnale* yields 0.18-0.9%. *G. superba* also produces other colchicine-related compounds like dimethyl-3-colchicine (0.19%), colchicoside (0.82%), and their formyl derivatives. Sivakumar and Krishnamurthy [61, 62] mentioned *G. superba* for the induction of isopentyldene on 2,4-D. Jha *et al.* [63] mentioned the production of colchicine, withanolides, tylophorine, and forskolin.

Phytopathology and Entomology

All species in all genera of the family Colchicaceae are counted among minor industrial plants and are neglected as far as their cultivation is concerned. No study related to their phytopathology, entomology, virology, and mycology is available.

CONCLUSION

All species in any genera of Colchicaceae are of significant economic importance and are/can be used in diverse ways. They are important for the duplication of chromosomes and plant breeding. These plants can also be used as ornamental plants, pot plants, cut flowers, and in rock gardens. Non-careful exploitation of the plants can endanger their existence at the local or national level, as affirmed by IUCN. Therefore, there is a need for their conservation by developing *in vitro*, *in situ*, or *ex situ* multiplication techniques and teaching these to rural people with the creation of an increased sense of responsibility among them to guarantee their survival and their economic production for the diverse industries. Their participation in the conservation of these plants will also be very useful and beneficial.

The wide diversity and restricted distribution of species in genus require the establishment of protocols for them.

REFERENCES

[1]   Croft J, Cross N, Hinchcliffe S, *et al*. Plant names for the 21st century: the International Plant Names Index, a distributed data source of general accessibility. Taxon 1999; 48(2): 317-24.
[http://dx.doi.org/10.2307/1224436]

[2]   Manning J, Forest F, Vinnersten A. The genus *Colchicum* L. redefined to include *Androcymbium* Willd. based on molecular evidence. Taxon 2007; 56(3): 872-82.
[http://dx.doi.org/10.2307/25065868]

[3]   Christenhusz MJM, Byng JW. The number of known plants species in the world and its annual increase. Phytotaxa 2016; 261(3): 201-17.
[http://dx.doi.org/10.11646/phytotaxa.261.3.1]

[4]   WFO and IPNI 2023. Available from: https://www.ipni.org/n/urn:lsid:ipni.org:names:77126743-1

[5]   Gloriosa. World Checklist of Selected Plant Families 2018.

[6]   Desai C. Meyler's side effects of drugs: The international encyclopedia of adverse drug reactions and interactions. Indian J Pharmacol 2016; 48(2): 224.
[http://dx.doi.org/10.4103/0253-7613.178821]

[7]   The World Flora. Available from: https://www.worldfloraonline.org/

[8]   Chacón J, Renner SS. Assessing model sensitivity in ancestral area reconstruction using L AGRANGE : a case study using the Colchicaceae family. J Biogeogr 2014; 41(7): 1414-27.
[http://dx.doi.org/10.1111/jbi.12301]

[9]   Nordenstam B. Colchicaceae. In: Kubitzki K. Flowering Plants· Monocotyledons: Lilianae (except Orchidaceae). Berlin, Heidelberg: Springer Berlin Heidelberg 1998; 175-85.
[http://dx.doi.org/10.1007/978-3-662-03533-7_24]

[10]   Vinnersten A, Manning J. A new classification of Colchicaceae. Taxon 2007; 56(1): 171-8.

[11]   Kahraman A, Celep F. Anatomical properties of *Colchicum kurdicum* (Bornm.) Stef. (Colchicaceae). Aust J Crop Sci 2010; 4(5): 369-71.

[12]   Boboev S, Makhkamov T, Bussmann RW, Zafar M, Yuldashev A. Anatomical and phytochemical studies and ethnomedicinal uses of *Colchicum autumnale* L. Ethnobot Res Appl 2023; 25: 1-9.
[http://dx.doi.org/10.32859/era.25.6.1-9]

[13]   Panda SP, Saha T, Dasgupta S, *et al. Gloriosa simplex* L. (Colchicaceae): a new distributional record for India. Vegetos 2023; 37(5): 1843-6.
[http://dx.doi.org/10.1007/s42535-023-00671-9]

[14]   Verloove F. The seventh edition of the Nouvelle Flore de la Belgique: nomenclatural and taxonomic remarks. 2012.

[15]   Dehgan B. Garden Plants Taxonomy: Volume 2: Angiosperms (Eudicots). Springer Nature 2023.

[16]   Mosoh DA, Khandel AK, Verma SK, Vendrame WA. Effects of sterilization methods and plant growth regulators on *in vitro* regeneration and tuberization in *Gloriosa superba* (L.). Cell Dev Biol Plant 2023; 59(6): 792-807.
[http://dx.doi.org/10.1007/s11627-023-10387-9]

[17]   Babaie Naeij M, Peyvandi M, Abbaspour H, Noormohammadi Z, Arbabian S. Responses of *Colchicum speciosum* L. populations to conventional and nano-fertilizers of nitrogen through changes in morphological and biochemical attributes. Not Bot Horti Agrobot Cluj-Napoca 2023; 51(1): 12827.
[http://dx.doi.org/10.15835/nbha51112827]

[18]   Singh A, Rai G, Kumar A, Gautam DN. Pharmacognostical assessment, antioxidant ability and determination of phytomolecules using GC-MS in *Gloriosa superba* Linn. J Plant Sci Res 2023; 39(2): 219-28.
[http://dx.doi.org/10.32381/JPSR.2023.39.02.23]

[19]   Tribble CM, May MR, Jackson-Gain A, Zenil-Ferguson R, Specht CD, Rothfels CJ. Unearthing modes of climatic adaptation in underground storage organs across Liliales. Syst Biol 2023; 72(1): 198-212.
[http://dx.doi.org/10.1093/sysbio/syac070] [PMID: 36380514]

[20]   Rajasekar C, Anurag PS, Kottaimuthu R. Distributional note on magnificent grass lilly, Iphigenia magnifica (Colchicaceae) in Tamil Nadu. Flora and Fauna 2023; 29(2): 276-8.

[21]   Remizowa MV, Shipunov AB, Sokoloff DD. When asymmetry mimics zygomorphy: flower development in Chamaelirium japonicum (Melanthiaceae, Liliales). Bot Pac 2023; 12: 3-14.
[http://dx.doi.org/10.17581/bp.2023.12s01]

[22]   Baczyński J, Claßen-Bockhoff R. Pseudanthia in angiosperms: a review. Ann Bot (Lond) 2023; 132(2): 179-202.
[http://dx.doi.org/10.1093/aob/mcad103] [PMID: 37478306]

[23]   Gulsoy-Toplan G, Goger F, Yildiz-Pekoz A, Gibbons S, Sariyar G, Mat A. Chemical constituents of the different parts of Colchicum micranthum and C. chalcedonicum and their cytotoxic activities. Nat Prod Commun 2018; 13(5): 1934578X1801300506.

[24]   Alali FQ, El-Alali A, Tawaha K, El-Elimat T. Seasonal variation of colchicine content in *Colchicum brachyphyllum* and *Colchicum tunicatum* (Colchicaceae). Nat Prod Res 2006; 20(12): 1121-8.
[http://dx.doi.org/10.1080/14786410600857504] [PMID: 17127666]

[25]   Al-Fayyad M, Alali F, Alkofahi A, Tell A. Determination of colchicine content in *Colchicum hierosolymitanum* and *Colchicum tunicatum* under cultivation. Nat Prod Lett 2002; 16(6): 395-400.
[http://dx.doi.org/10.1080/10575630290033178] [PMID: 12462344]

[26]   Chaldakov GN. Colchicine, a microtubule-disassembling drug, in the therapy of cardiovascular diseases. Cell Biol Int 2018; 42(8): 1079-84.
[http://dx.doi.org/10.1002/cbin.10988] [PMID: 29762881]

[27]   Alkadi H, Khubeiz MJ, Jbeily R. Colchicine: a review on chemical structure and clinical usage. Infect Disord Drug Targets 2018; 18(2): 105-21.
[http://dx.doi.org/10.2174/1871526517666171017114901]

[28]   Azadbakht M, Davoodi A, Hosseinimehr SJ, *et al.* Tropolone alkaloids from *Colchicum kurdicum* (Bornm.) Stef. (Colchicaceae) as the potent novel antileishmanial compounds; purification, structure elucidation, antileishmanial activities and molecular docking studies. Exp Parasitol 2020; 213: 107902.
[http://dx.doi.org/10.1016/j.exppara.2020.107902] [PMID: 32353376]

[29]   Dahlgren RM, Clifford HT, Yeo FT. The Families of the monocotyledons Springer Verlag. Berlin, Heidelberg, New York, Tokyo 1985; 193.
[http://dx.doi.org/10.1007/978-3-642-61663-1]

[30]   Vinnersten A, Reeves G. Phylogenetic relationships within Colchicaceae. Am J Bot 2003; 90(10): 1455-62.
[http://dx.doi.org/10.3732/ajb.90.10.1455] [PMID: 21659097]

[31]   Vinnersten A, Larsson S. Colchicine is still a chemical marker for the expanded Colchicaceae. Biochem Syst Ecol 2010; 38(6): 1193-8.
[http://dx.doi.org/10.1016/j.bse.2010.12.004]

[32]   Larsson S, Rønsted N. Reviewing Colchicaceae alkaloids - perspectives of evolution on medicinal chemistry. Curr Top Med Chem 2013; 14(2): 274-89.
[http://dx.doi.org/10.2174/1568026613666131216110417] [PMID: 24359194]

[33]   Leete E. The biosynthesis of the alkaloids of Colchicum. III. The incorporation of phenylalanine-2- C^{14} into colchicine and demecolcine. J Am Chem Soc 1963; 85(22): 3666-9.
[http://dx.doi.org/10.1021/ja00905a030]

[34]   Battersby AR, Böhler P, Munro MHG, Ramage R. Biosynthesis of homoaporphines. J Chem Soc D

1969; 0(18): 1066-7.
[http://dx.doi.org/10.1039/C29690001066]

[35]   Battersby AR, Herbert RB, McDonald E, Ramage R, Clements JH. Alkaloid biosynthesis. Part XVIII.
        Biosynthesis of colchicine from the 1-phenethylisoquinoline system. J Chem Soc, Perkin Trans 1
        1972; 14: 1741-6.
        [http://dx.doi.org/10.1039/p19720001741] [PMID: 4672436]

[36]   Trozyan AA, Yusupov MK, Aslanov KA, Sadykov AS. A study of the biosynthesis of colchicine and
        merenderine in *Merendera raddeana*. Chem Nat Compd 1972; 8(6): 746-50.
        [http://dx.doi.org/10.1007/BF00564601]

[37]   McDonald E, Ramage R, Woodhouse RN, Underhill EW, Wetter LR, Battersby AR. Biosynthesis.
        Part 27.1,2 Colchicine: studies of the phenolic oxidative coupling and ring-expansion processes based
        on incorporation of multiply labelled 1-phenethylisoquinolines. J Chem Soc, Perkin Trans 1 1998;
        (18): 2979-88.
        [http://dx.doi.org/10.1039/a803850c]

[38]   Barker AC, Julian DR, Ramage R, *et al.* Biosynthesis. Part 28.1,2 Colchicine: definition of
        intermediates between O-methylandrocymbine and colchicine and studies on speciosine. J Chem Soc,
        Perkin Trans 1 1998; (18): 2989-94.
        [http://dx.doi.org/10.1039/a803851a]

[39]   Sheldrake PW, Suckling KE, Woodhouse RN, *et al.* Biosynthesis. Part 30.1 Colchicine: studies on the
        ring expansion step focusing on the fate of the hydrogens at C-4 of autumnaline. J Chem Soc, Perkin
        Trans 1 1998; (18): 3003-10.
        [http://dx.doi.org/10.1039/a803853h]

[40]   Sivakumar G, Krishnamurthy KV, Hao J, Paek KY. Colchicine production in *Gloriosa superba*
        calluses by feeding precursors. Chem Nat Compd 2004; 40(5): 499-502.
        [http://dx.doi.org/10.1007/s10600-005-0020-3]

[41]   De Smet PAGM. Health risks of herbal remedies. Drug Saf 1995; 13(2): 81-93.
        [http://dx.doi.org/10.2165/00002018-199513020-00003] [PMID: 7576267]

[42]   Brickell CD. Colchicum L. In: Davis PH, Ed. Flora of Turkey and the East Aegean Islands.
        Edinburgh: University Press 1984; Vol. 8.

[43]   RHS. Colchicum speciosum 'Atrorubens'|giant meadow saffron 'Atrorubens'/RHS Gardening.

[44]   AGM Plants - Ornamental (PDF). Royal Horticultural Society. 2017 Available from:
        https://www.rhs.org.uk/plants/pdfs/agm-lists/agm-ornamentals.pdf

[45]   Hayashi T, Yoshida K, Sano K. Formation of alkaloids in suspension-cultured *Colchicum autumnale*..
        Phytochemistry 1988; 27(5): 1371-4.
        [http://dx.doi.org/10.1016/0031-9422(88)80196-1]

[46]   Daradkeh NQ, Shibli RA, Makhadmeh IM, Alali F, Al-Qudah TS. Cell suspension and *in vitro*
        production of colchicine in wild *Colchicum hierosolymitanum* Feib. Open Conf Proc J. 2012; 3.(1)

[47]   Gulsoy-Toplan G, Goger F, Yildiz-Pekoz A, Gibbons S, Sariyar G, Mat A. Chemical constituents of
        the different parts of *Colchicum micranthum* and *C. chalcedonicum* and their cytotoxic activities. Nat
        Prod Commun 2018; 13(5): 1934578X1801300506.

[48]   Bose TK, Yadav LP. Commercial flowers. Calcutta Publication 1989; pp. 267-350.

[49]   Ghani A. Medicinal plants. Banglapedia: Natl. Encycl. Bangladesh 2004; 1-16.

[50]   Evans DA, Nelson JV, Vogel E, Taber TR. Stereoselective aldol condensations *via* boron enolates. J
        Am Chem Soc 1981; 103(11): 3099-111.
        [http://dx.doi.org/10.1021/ja00401a031]

[51]   Neuwinger HD. Fish poisoning plants in Africa. Bot Acta 1994; 107(4): 263-70.
        [http://dx.doi.org/10.1111/j.1438-8677.1994.tb00795.x]

[52] Samy RP, Thwin MM, Gopalakrishnakone P, Ignacimuthu S. Ethnobotanical survey of folk plants for the treatment of snakebites in Southern part of Tamilnadu, India. J Ethnopharmacol 2008; 115(2): 302-12.
[http://dx.doi.org/10.1016/j.jep.2007.10.006] [PMID: 18055146]

[53] Viswanathan N, Joshi BS. Toxic Constituents of some Indian plants. Curr Sci 1983; 52(1): 1-8.

[54] Khan M, Santhosh SR, Tiwari M, Lakshmana Rao PV, Parida M. Assessment of *in vitro* prophylactic and therapeutic efficacy of chloroquine against chikungunya virus in vero cells. J Med Virol 2010; 82(5): 817-24.
[http://dx.doi.org/10.1002/jmv.21663] [PMID: 20336760]

[55] Khan SA, Kumar P, Joshi R, Iqbal PF, Saleem K. Synthesis and *in vitro* antibacterial activity of new steroidal thiosemicarbazone derivatives. Eur J Med Chem 2008; 43(9): 2029-34.
[http://dx.doi.org/10.1016/j.ejmech.2007.12.004] [PMID: 18450330]

[56] Suri OP, Gupta BD, Suri KA, Sharma AK, Satti NK. A new glycoside, 3-O-demethylcolchicine-3-O-α-d-glucopyranoside, from *Gloriosa superba* seeds. Nat Prod Lett 2001; 15(4): 217-9.
[http://dx.doi.org/10.1080/10575630108041284] [PMID: 11833615]

[57] Kala CP, Farooquee NA, Dhar U. Prioritization of medicinal plants on the basis of available knowledge, existing practices and use value status in Uttaranchal, India. Biodivers Conserv 2004; 13(2): 453-69.
[http://dx.doi.org/10.1023/B:BIOC.0000006511.67354.7f]

[58] Custers JBM, Bergervoet JHW. Micropropagation of *Gloriosa*: Towards a practical protocol. Sci Hortic (Amsterdam) 1994; 57(4): 323-34.
[http://dx.doi.org/10.1016/0304-4238(94)90115-5]

[59] Hassan AK, Roy SK. Micropropagation of *Gloriosa superba* L. through high-frequency shoot proliferation. Plant Tissue Cult 2005; 15(1): 67-74.

[60] Somani VJ, John CK, Thengane RJ. *in vitro* propagation and corm formation in *Gloriosa superba*. Indian J Exp Biol 1989; 27: 578-9.

[61] Sivakumar G, Krishnamurthy KV. Micropropagation of *G. superba* L.—an overexploited medicinal plant species from India. Role of Plant Tissue Culture in India in Biodiversity Conservation and Economic Development. Nainital, India: Gyanodaya Prakashan Publications 2002; 345-50.

[62] Sivakumar G, Krishnamurthy KV. *In vitro* organogenetic responses of *Gloriosa superba*. Russ J Plant Physiol 2004; 51(5): 713-21.
[http://dx.doi.org/10.1023/B:RUPP.0000040761.45363.75]

[63] Jha S, Bandyopadhyay M, Chaudhuri KN, Ghosh S, Ghosh B. Biotechnological approaches for the production of forskolin, withanolides, colchicine and tylophorine. Plant Genet Resour 2005; 3(2): 101-15.
[http://dx.doi.org/10.1079/PGR200571]

CHAPTER 5

Iridaceae Family

Sibel Day[1,*]

[1] *Department of Field Crops, Faculty of Agriculture, Ankara University, Ankara, Türkiye*

Abstract: The *Iridaceae* family, with 92 genera, is distributed globally, and the family is more common in the southern hemisphere. The main genera are *gladiolus, iris, sisyrinchium, crocus, romulea, geissorhiza, babiana,* and *hesperantha*. These genera are important for phytochemical extracts and ornamental value. The *Crocus* and *Gladiolus* are mentioned in this chapter. *Crocus* is a genus of plants that grows naturally in a variety of environments. Türkiye has the largest diversity of *Crocus*, with more than 80 different species, but they can also be found in regions ranging from Western Europe and North Western Africa to Western China. *Gladiolus* is currently one of the most significant bulbous ornamental flowers in the world. There are 11 taxa of *Gladiolus* found in Türkiye. Most of the taxa prevailing in nature are in danger of extinction. Identification of these taxa and their cultivation and protection are important for the genetic pool. This chapter underlines the cultivation of *Crocus sativus* and *Gladiolus* cultivation.

Keywords: *Crocus*, Cultivation, Diseases, *Gladiolus*, Morphology, Pests, Saffron.

INTRODUCTION

Iridaceae is a family of plants that includes 92 genera and 1800 species [1]. It belongs to the monocot order Asparagales, and its plants are found in tropical and temperate regions worldwide. The greatest diversity of *Iridaceae* can be found in sub-Saharan Africa, followed by South America, Europe, and temperate regions of Asia [2]. Horticulturally, *Iridaceae* is considered one of the most important plant families. *Crocus* and *Iris* are common in the floral diversity of Eurasia and North America, while *Gladiolus* and *Morea* are major genera of the flora found in Sub-Saharan countries [3]. Though *Iridaceae* plants are distributed globally, the family is more common in the southern hemisphere [4].

The main genera are *gladiolus, iris, sisyrinchium, crocus, romulea, geissorhiza, babiana,* and *hesperantha* [5].

* **Corresponding author Sibel Day:** Department of Field Crops, Faculty of Agriculture, Ankara University, Ankara, Türkiye; E-mail:day@ankara.edu.tr

Leaves are usually narrow and sword-shaped, arranged in a two-ranked manner. They can be cylindrical or parallel to the stem. The inflorescences are diverse and range from terminal spikes to groups of flowers arranged in panicles or spikes. Usually, two bracts that resemble spathes subtend these inflorescences [6].

Leaves are typically narrow, ensiform (sword-shaped), and often arranged in a distichous (two-ranked) fashion. They may be unifacial (with the leaf plane parallel to the stem) or terete (cylindrical). Inflorescences are diverse, ranging from terminal spikes to solitary flowers or clusters of flowers arranged in spikes or panicles. These inflorescences are often subtended by two spathe-like bracts [6].

The *Iridaceae* family consists of four subfamilies: Isophysidoideae, Iridoideae, Aristeoideae (also known as Nivenioideae), and Crocoideae (also referred to as Ixioideae). Subfamilies are differentiated based on floral morphology, such as flower arrangement, presence or absence of spathe-like bracts, and ovary position [7].

Members of the Iridaceae family have a worldwide distribution, with a particular concentration of diversity in southern Africa.

Many species in the family, including irises, gladioli, freesias, and crocuses, are important as ornamental plants. This chapter includes two genera: *Crocus* and *Gladiolus*.

CROCUS

Crocus is a genus of plants that grows naturally in a variety of environments, such as scrub, meadows, and woodland. Türkiye is rich in crocus, with over 80 species. However, they can also be found in regions ranging from western Europe and northwest Africa to western China. The diversity found in Türkiye is given in Table 1 with 154 taxa (53 taxa given in Table 1 are endemic). Apart from the triploid *Crocus sativus*, all members of *Crocus* are diploid. *Crocus sativus* is only vegetatively reproduced by corms. Cultivated all over the world, it is the best-known species of the genus. *Crocus sativus* is best known for producing the spice saffron, but other species in the genus have medicinal, food, and ornamental uses [8].

A comprehensive literature review identified 16 *Crocus* species with ethnobotanical and ethnomedicinal uses, largely from Asia and Europe.

Table 1. Crocus taxa prevailing in Türkiye.

-	Taxa	Endemism
1	*C. abantensis* T.Baytop & B.Mathew	endemic
2	*C. abracteolus*	-
3	*C. adamioides*	-
4	*C. adanensis* T.Baytop & B.Mathew	endemic
5	*C. aerius* Herb.	endemic
6	*C. akdagensis*	-
7	*C. akkayaensis*	-
8	*C. ancyrensis* (Herb.) Maw	endemic
9	*C. ancyrensis* subsp. *guneri*	-
10	*C. antalyensioides*	-
11	*C. antalyensis* B.Mathew	-
12	*C. antalyensis* subsp. *antalyensis* B.Mathew	endemic
13	*C. antalyensis* subsp. *gemicii* Şık & Erol	endemic
14	*C. antalyensis* subsp. *striatus* Erol & Koçyiğit	endemic
15	*C. antherotes*	-
16	*C. arizelus*	-
17	*C. asumaniae* B.Mathew & T.Baytop	endemic
18	*C. babadagensis*	-
19	*C. baytopiorum* B.Mathew	endemic
20	*C. berytius*	-
21	*C. bifloriformis*	-
22	*C. biflorus* Mill.	-
23	*C. biflorus* subsp. *adamii* (Gay) B.Mathew	-
24	*C. biflorus* subsp. *albocoronatus* Kernd.	endemic
25	*C. biflorus* subsp. *artvinensis* (Philippov) B.Mathew	endemic
26	*C. biflorus* subsp. *atrospermus* Kernd. & Pasche	endemic
27	*C. biflorus* subsp. *biflorus* Mill.	-
28	*C. biflorus* subsp. *caelestis* Kernd. & Pasche	endemic
29	*C. biflorus* subsp. *caricus* Kernd. & Pasche	endemic
30	*C. biflorus* subsp. *crewei* (Hook.f.) B.Mathew	-
31	*C. biflorus* subsp. *fibroannulatus* Kernd. & Pasche	endemic
32	*C. biflorus* subsp. *ionopharynx* Kernd. & Pasche	endemic
33	*C. biflorus* subsp. *isauricus* (Siehe ex Bowles) B.Mathew	endemic

(Table 1) cont.....

-	Taxa	Endemism
34	*C. biflorus* subsp. *leucostylosus* Kernd. & Pasche	endemic
35	*C. biflorus* subsp. *nubigena* (Herb.) B.Mathew	-
36	*C. biflorus* subsp. *pseudonubigena* B.Mathew	endemic
37	*C. biflorus* subsp. *pulchricolor* (Herb.) B.Mathew	endemic
38	*C. biflorus* subsp. *punctatus* B.Mathew	endemic
39	*C. biflorus* subsp. *tauri* (Maw) B.Mathew	-
40	*C. biflorus* subsp. *yataganensis* Kernd. & Pasche	endemic
41	*C. beydaglarensis* Kernd. & Pasche	endemic
42	*C. boissieri* Maw	endemic
43	*C. bowlesianus*	-
44	*C. brachyfilus*	-
45	*C. brickellii*	-
46	*C. calanthus*	-
47	*C. cancellatus* Herb.	-
48	*C. cancellatus* subsp. *cancellatus* Herb.	endemic
49	*C. cancellatus* subsp. *damascenus* (Herb.) B.Mathew	-
50	*C. cancellatus* subsp. *lycius* B.Mathew	endemic
51	*C. cancellatus* subsp. *mazziaricus* (Herb.) B.Mathew	-
52	*C. cancellatus* subsp. *pamphylicus* B.Mathew	endemic
53	*C. candidus* E.D.Clarke	endemic
54	*C. chrysanthus* (Herb.) Herb.	-
55	*C. danfordiae* Maw	-
56	*C. danfordiae* subsp. *danfordiae* Maw	endemic
57	*C. fauseri* Kernd. & Pasche	endemic
58	*C. flavus* Weston	-
59	*C. flavus* subsp. *dissectus* T.Baytop & B.Mathew	endemic
60	*C. flavus* subsp. *flavus* Weston	-
61	*C. fleischeri* J.Gay	-
62	*C. gargaricus* Herb.	-
63	*C. gargaricus* subsp. *herbertii* B.Mathew	endemic
64	*C. graveolens* Boiss. & Reut.	-
65	*C. karduchorum* Kotschy ex Maw	endemic
66	*C. kerndorffiorum* Pasche	endemic
67	*C. kotschyanus* K.Koch	-

(Table 1) cont.....

-	Taxa	Endemism
68	*C. kotschyanus* subsp. *cappadocicus* B.Mathew	endemic
69	*C. kotschyanus* subsp. *hakkariensis* B.Mathew	endemic
70	*C. kotschyanus* subsp. *kotschyanus* K.Koch	-
71	*C. kotschyanus* subsp. *suworowianus* (K.Koch) B.Mathew	-
72	*C. leichtlinii* (Dewar) Bowles	endemic
73	*C. lydius* Kernd. & Pasche	endemic
74	*C. mathewii* Kernd. & Pasche	endemic
75	*C. minutus* Kernd. & Pasche	endemic
76	*C. nerimaniae* Yüzb.	endemic
77	*C. olivieri* J.Gay	-
78	*C. olivieri* subsp. *balansae* (J.Gay ex Maw) B.Mathew	-
79	*C. olivieri* subsp. *istanbulensis* B.Mathew	endemic
80	*C. olivieri* subsp. *olivieri* J.Gay	-
81	*C. pallasii* Goldb.	-
82	*C. pallasii* subsp. *dispathaceus* (Bowles) B.Mathew	-
83	*C. pallasii* subsp. *pallasii* Goldb.	-
84	*C. pallasii* subsp. *turcicus* B.Mathew	-
85	*C. paschei* Kernd.	endemic
86	*Crocus* x *paulineae* Pasche & Kernd.	endemic
87	*C. pestalozzae* Boiss.	endemic
88	*C. pulchellus* Herb.	-
89	*C. reticulatus* Steven ex Adams	-
90	*C. reticulatus* subsp. *hittiticus* (T.Baytop & B.Mathew) B.Mathew	endemic
91	*C. reticulatus* subsp. *reticulatus* Steven ex Adams	-
92	*C. roseoviolaceus* Kernd. & Pasche	endemic
93	*C. sativus* L.	-
94	*C. scharojanii* Rupr.	-
95	*C. scharojanii* subsp. *lazicus* (Boiss.) B.Mathew	endemic
96	*C. scharojanii* subsp. *scharojanii* Rupr.	-
97	*C. sieheanus* Barr ex B.L.Burtt	endemic
98	*C. speciosus* M.Bieb.	-
99	*C. speciosus* subsp. *ibrahimii* Rukšāns	endemic
100	*C. speciosus* subsp. *ilgazensis* B.Mathew	endemic
101	*C. speciosus* subsp. *speciosus* M.Bieb.	-

(Table 1) cont.....

-	Taxa	Endemism
102	*C. speciosus* subsp. *xantholaimos* B.Mathew	endemic
103	*C. vallicola* Herb.	-
104	*C. wattiorum* (B.Mathew) B.Mathew	endemic
105	*C. chrysanthus* subsp. *chrysanthus var. atroviolaceus*	-
106	*C. chrysanthus* subsp. *chrysanthus var. bicoloraceus*	-
107	*C. chrysanthus* subsp. *kesercioglui*	-
108	*C. chrysanthus* subsp. *punctatus*	-
109	*C. chrysanthus* subsp. *sipyleus*	-
110	*C. coloreus*	-
111	*C. concinnus*	-
112	*C. demirizianus*	-
113	*C. dilekyarensis*	-
114	*C. heilbronniorum*	-
115	*C. henrikii*	-
116	*C. incognitus*	-
117	*C. kangalensis*	-
118	*C. karamanensis*	-
119	*C. kartaldagensis*	-
120	*C. katrancensis*	-
121	*C. kofudagensis*	-
122	*C. lyciotauricus*	-
123	*C. malatyensis*	-
124	*C. marasensis*	-
125	*C. mawii*	-
126	*C. mediotauricus*	-
127	*C. mersinensis*	-
128	*C. muglaensis*	-
129	*C. multicostatus*	-
130	*C. munzurense*	-
131	*C. musagecitii*	-
132	*C. mysius*	-
133	*C. oreogenus*	-
134	*C. pelitensis*	-
135	*C. pestalozzae* subsp. *violaceus*	-

(Table 1) cont.....

-	Taxa	Endemism
136	*C. ponticus*	-
137	*C. rechingeri*	-
138	*C. romuleoides*	-
139	*C. salurdagensis*	-
140	*C. schneideri*	-
141	*C. simavensis*	-
142	*C. sivasensis*	-
143	*C. sozenii*	-
144	*C. striatulus*	-
145	*C. tahtaliensis*	-
146	*C. taseliensis*	-
147	*C. thracicus*	-
148	*C. tuna-ekimii*	-
149	*C. uschakensis*	-
150	*C. xanthosus*	-
151	*C. yakarianus*	-
152	*C. yaseminiae*	-
153	*C. zetterlundii*	-
154	*C. ziyaretensis*	-

[17] Bizimbitkiler <http://www.bizimbitkiler.org.tr>.

The dried stigma (Saffron) of the plant has been utilized as a colorant, drug, flavoring, and perfume in ancient Egypt, Greece, India, Persia, and Rome [8, 9]. Today, saffron is mostly used as a culinary ingredient.

In various traditional medicines, saffron has been used for a variety of purposes, including as a nerve tonic, laxative, and aphrodisiac, and for the treatment of diarrhea, stomach ulcers, and premature ejaculation [10]. In Iran, the saffron stigma is used to strengthen the heart [11]. In traditional Hindu medicine, stigmas are used as a general tonic to boost immunity, as well as a nerve sedative, appetizer, stimulant, and aphrodisiac [12]. Chinese medicine recommends the topical application of stigmas for neurological diseases, asthma, whooping cough, and inflammatory conditions [13]. The stigma and style have been used in Iraq and Spain for the treatment of insomnia and migraine, as a metabolism stimulant, and for toothache [14, 15]. In Italy, saffron infusion is used as a digestion and calming agent [16]. Besides *Crocus sativus*, other species belonging to the *Crocus* genus are also highly valued as sources of nutritional, medicinal, and ornamental value [17]. Some species have cultural significance and are used as food sources by indigenous peoples. *Crocus sativus* is notable for producing saffron, a highly prized spice derived from the styles and stigmas of its flowers.

Taxonomy and Properties

The taxonomical hierarchy of *Crocus* is as follows [18].

Regnum: Plantae

Division: Magnoliophyta

Familia: Iridaceae

Genus: *Crocus*

CROCUS SATIVUS (SAFFRON)

Saffron, also known as red gold, is a pricey and valuable spice crop that belongs to the family Iridaceae [19]. It is propagated through corms and is a triploid plant [20]. Saffron is mainly cultivated in Iran, Afghanistan, Morocco, India, Spain, Greece, and Italy [8]. Studies have shown that saffron is a valuable crop with many benefits [21].

The dried stigmas of the crop are highly valued all over the world [22]. Saffron stigmas contain 14-16% water, 11-13% nitrogenous matter, 12-15% sugars, 41-44% soluble extracts, 0.6-0.9% essential oil, 4-5% fiber, and 4-6% ashes. It is rich in vitamins and secondary metabolites like terpenes, flavonoids, anthocyanins, and carotenoids such as lycopene, α- and β-carotene, zeaxanthin, and crocetin. These compounds are essential for human nutrition and may help prevent cancer and heart disease [23]. A substantial body of literature exists attesting to the beneficial properties and applications of saffron in a range of sectors [24, 25].

The traditional method of cultivating saffron involves planting saffron corms [26]. The saffron plant height is typically between 10 to 25 cm and has a spherical corm with a diameter of 2.5 to 3.0 cm. A single corm can produce one to five flowers, each having six violet petals and three pantone red stigmas. The saffron has a distinctive and powerful aroma. The major compounds that determine its color, bitterness, and fragrance are crocins, picrocrocin, and safranal, respectively. Several studies have reported on the properties of these compounds [27 - 30].

The saffron crop goes through four distinct periods [31]:

- **Vegetative Period:** The corm develops throughout autumn and winter, determining the final size, quality, and number of flowers per plant.
- **Reproductive Period:** It occurs in the first month of spring and is critical for saffron plant development.
- **Dormant Period:** It usually begins in the second month of spring when temperatures are high.
- **Flowering Period:** It begins in September and concludes with the blooming of the saffron flower. The saffron flower requires a short photoperiod of less than 11.5 hours and a low temperature, usually between 10 °C and 15 °C, to blossom.

Corm planting is usually done in the second half of the spring season. The saffron production follows a four-year cycle, after which new corms are planted and soil fertility is restored [32, 33]. The corms multiply each year and produce around five new corms from each planted corm [34]. Lifting and separating the corms allows for replanting.

The management of corms is highly automated and can be partly carried out by farm vehicles such as tractors, mechanization methods, and specialized tools [35]. However, harvesting and separating the stigma from the rest of the flower is still done manually. This is the most sensitive stage of the operation, as it requires cutting the blossom in the right position to achieve the desired quality [36]. To obtain the best quality saffron, the lower part of the stigmas should not be involved.

Plant Morphology

Saffron, which comes from the Arabic word "Zafaran", which means yellow, has an unclear place of origin. Some authors suggest that the origin of this cultural phenomenon can be traced back to the Middle East (Iran) or Greece (southern Aegean islands Crete and Santorini), and it later spread to India, China, the Mediterranean basin, and Eastern Europe. The triploid genome of saffron ($x = 8$; $2n = 3x = 24$) causes an abnormal pairing of the chromosomes during the prophase of meiosis and an irregular distribution of chromosomes during metaphase, which leads to the production of infertile gametes [8, 37]. Saffron is reproduced only *via* corms due to self-sterility, as it has a higher percentage of abnormal pollen grains and a lower percentage of viable and germinating ones. However, its progenitors and methods of polyploidy remain unclear. Possible parents include *C. almehensis, C. cartwrightianus, C. haussknechtii, C. hadriaticus, C. mathewii, C. michelsonii, C. pallasii, C. serotinus,* and *C. thomasii* [8]. Recent analyses show that the crop is an autotriploid that evolved in Attica, Greece, by combining two different genotypes of *C. cartwrightianus* [8, 37, 38].

The corm is mainly composed of parenchyma cells that are rich in starch. It has a circular basal node from which roots grow. The shape of the corm can vary. It can be flattened to ovoid or sub-globose depressed. The horizontal diameter can range from 0.5 to 6.5 cm, and its weight can be from 0.5 to 70 g. The minimum size required for a corm to flower is 2.5 cm [39, 40]. A medium-sized corm, about 3-3.5 cm, has 2-3 apical buds that produce leaves, a floral axis, and daughter corms. It has 4-7 secondary buds that are irregularly placed in a spiral form in the lower section. These secondary buds produce a cauline axis and a tuft of leaves that draw nutrients and grow through photosynthesis.

Corm contains various compounds, including glucose, aspartic acid, glutamic acid, cysteine, serine, glycine, threonine, tyrosine, alanine, arginine, histidine, lysine, proline, phenylalanine, leucine, valine, methionine, two saponins (one triterpene and another steroid), and a high molecular weight protein [41].

Saffron has the ability to produce flowers before or after the leaves as an adaptation to drought conditions [42]. This feature also makes it easier to mechanically harvest flowers. In addition, hysteresis can be activated by storing the corm at 15 °C for 35 days. This makes it easier to control the timing of flowering and leafing [43].

The flower has six violet tepals, each 20-47 mm long and 11-23 mm wide. It also has a pistil and three stamens. The flower consists of short filaments and yellow anthers, which contain pollen. The flower is approximately 15 mm long [39].

The pistil is formed by three loggias and has an inferior ovary that is both tricarpellate and trilocular. It has an axial oviposition with 18-20 eggs per loggia, arranged in two rows. The pistil extends into a yellow-green filiform stylus, which is about 9 cm long. The stylus passes through the perigonium tube and culminates in a divided red stigma.

Stigmas have red-colored filaments (Fig. **1**), which are 30-40 mm long and have a trumpet-shaped enlarged tip. During flowering, the stigmas are typically upright, longer than the anthers, and often surpass the length of the petals. They bend over when the flower opens. Occasionally, a physiological and non-genetic abnormality during flower formation can result in a higher number of stigmas, stamens, and tepals [44]. The fresh weight of each flower varies between 300 and 500 mg, with fresh stigmas weighing between 25 and 47 mg and dry stigmas between 6 and 9 mg. This means that it takes around 160,000-110,000 flowers to obtain 1 kg of spice [21].

Fig. (1). Saffron in the field.

Various observations demonstrated that when *C. sativus* is hand-pollinated with *C. cartwrightianus* pollen, a large capsule develops and matures in May, dispersing its seeds onto the soil [45].

Saffron plants have two different kinds of roots: fibrous and contractile. As the shoots begin to grow, fibrous roots come up from the bottom of the corm. The fibrous roots are thin, straight, and about 15-20 cm long. They absorb water and nutrients. Contractile roots are a type of root that helps plants to anchor themselves in the soil. They are generally large, whitish, and have thick layers that form as the daughter corms grow. The purpose of these roots is to pull the corm deeper into the soil, which helps to protect the plant from harsh weather conditions and other external factors. Contractile roots are produced in response to changes in soil temperature and light conditions [39].

The leaves of the plant are elongated, measuring about 40-70 cm in length and 2-3 cm in width. They are dark green in color, with a white stripe running down the center that corresponds to the water-storing tissue and two lateral stripes of a darker shade. The number of leaves is determined by the corm weight and horizontal diameter, ranging from 29 to 52 in corms weighing between 6-12 g and 36-42 g, respectively [46]. When the leaves first emerge, they are in a vertical position. However, during the development phase, they change to a horizontal position [47]. The leaves' photosynthesis activity is crucial for the multiplication of daughter corms. They grow from September to May (Fig. **2**), after which they dry up, marking the beginning of the plant's senescence phase [46].

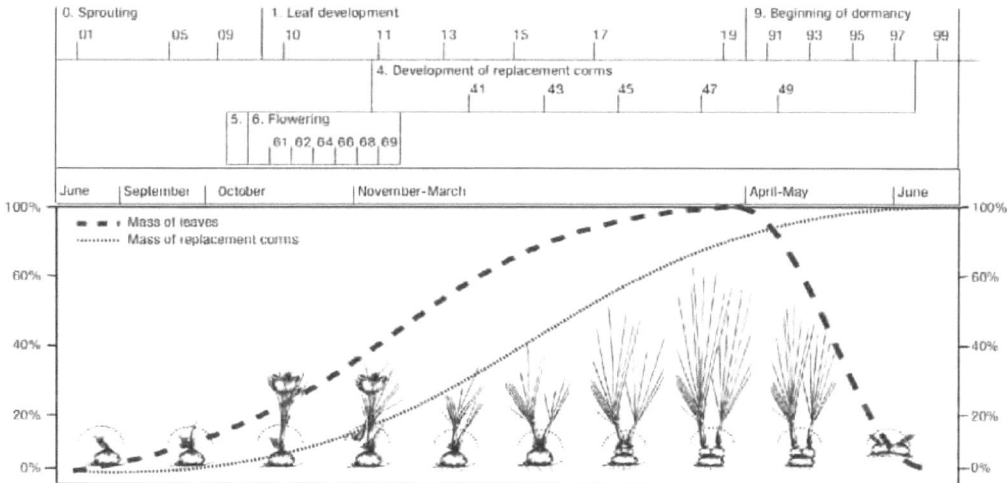

Fig. (2). The growth stages of saffron [54].

The Soil and Climate Requirement

Environmental factors (soil, altitude, temperature, and photoperiod) play a critical role in saffron production [27, 48, 49]. It grows best in loose, low-density, well-drained clay calcareous soils with optimum pH between 6.8-7.8 and E.C. below 2 dS m^{-1} and with proper irrigation. Studies indicate that rainfall of 600 mm is adequate for saffron cultivation under rain-fed conditions, although this may vary based on soil characteristics and fertilization practices [50 - 53]. It was reported that the highest number of flowers and dry stigma yield was observed when corms were planted at high density in sandy soil. On the other hand, the highest stigma weight was obtained when corms were sown in clay soil. The optimal temperature for flowering is between 23 and 27 °C [42].

Cultivation Practises

Planting saffron can be done by hand or using machines for potatoes or onions. Based on the length of the growing cycle, saffron can be grown annually or for multiple years. In the town of Navelli, Italy, the soil is medium humus-clay or sandy soil, with good active limestone content, high organic matter, low phosphates, and optimal potassium. Before planting in August, the soil is plowed at a depth of 25-30 cm in winter. The planting is done in four rows per patch, with a depth of 10-15 cm and a spacing of 10-15 cm between corms and 20-25 cm between rows. On the other hand, in Sardinia, where the soil is rich in alluvial deposits, has uniform sandy clay texture, and is well-drained, planting is done at a depth of 15-20 cm from 15 August to 15 September [55]. In Spain, where the soil is deep, slightly calcareous, and crumbly, planting is carried out between the latter part of June and the early part of September. The density of the plantations varies from 60 plants per m^2 for Spain to between 10 to 50 plants per m^2 for Sardinia [56 - 58].

The depth at which the corms of saffron are planted significantly affects the yield of the plant. If corms are planted less than 8-10 cm deep, contractile roots become large. This can prevent the growth of the daughter corm because the reserve materials are stored in these roots, which consume the entire mother corm [59]. Saffron cultivation has been studied in different types of soil, including sandy soils in Israel and Soan Valley, Khushab, Iran. In Israel, saffron has been found to emerge from depths of up to 30 cm when planted, according to research by Hagiladi *et al.* [60]. However, Nazir *et al.* [61] found that planting saffron at a depth between 7.5 and 17.5 cm in Soan Valley, Khushab, Iran, resulted in longer leaves (48.70 cm), more tillers per plant (29.24), and more flowers per plant (22.33). Meanwhile, Dhar [62] advised against shallow planting as it exposes the corms to cold in winter and high temperatures in summer, which can adversely affect growth. The recommended planting depths for corms can vary from 7.5-10 to 15-22 cm depending on the soil texture in different regions. In Italy, it was found that planting the corms at a depth of 15 cm resulted in better yield compared to shallower or deeper planting. It is worth noting that planting depth has a significant impact on corm production. Corms planted closer to the surface tend to produce more buds than those planted deeper, which ultimately leads to more daughter corms [57].

Several studies have examined the use of soilless farming. However, their findings are inconsistent. Controlled planting can be an alternative to open field cultivation, particularly in inadequate climates, to cope with environmental restrictions and to avoid the negative effects of climate change. This cultivation method offers many benefits, including higher crop density, improved spice quality and yield, improved hygiene and sanitation, faster sprouting than soil cultivation, and better pest and pathogen control [42, 63].

Adding manure alone is insufficient to meet the nutritional requirements of saffron. However, a combination of nitrogen (N), phosphorus (P), and potassium

(K) with organic manure can enhance flower production and yield, as well as improve quality. Organic manure is particularly important in soils that have low levels of organic carbon, as it promotes saffron production. Therefore, it is necessary to supplement manure with chemical fertilizers to achieve higher yields. One 8-year study conducted in Iran found that adding 30 tons of cow manure with 50 kg of ammonium phosphate per hectare significantly increased saffron yield due to the low organic compound of the soil in one site, while another site yielded the highest flower yield with 100 kg of urea per hectare alone. Fertilizer application should be done after flower-picking and just before the second irrigation. In a separate 8-year study, Behzad *et al.* [64, 65] compared the effects of different combinations of N, P, K, and cow manure on saffron production and found that N had the greatest impact on increasing flower yield. In sandy soils, adding 20 tons of organic matter along with 100 kg of (N+P+K) per hectare resulted in the highest saffron yield [66].

Saffron soil fertility management practices in different countries are as follows. In Italy, cow or sheep manure (20-30 t ha^{-1}) is used [43], and to avoid harming the soil and excessive use of mineral fertilizers, crop rotation is recommended with fava beans to increase stigma yield, weight, and the number of replacement corms [67]. In Greece, 40, 30, and 40 kg ha^{-1} of N, P_2O_5, and K_2O, respectively, are incorporated in September, and 30 units of NO_3^- form in March [68]. In Morocco, farm manure (10-20 t ha^{-1}) is used in the first, third, or fourth cultivation years [69]. In Iran, the application of vermicompost (10.2 t ha^{-1}) resulted in a significant increase in the number, weight, and N and P contents of medium and large daughter corms per plant compared to mineral fertilizer [70]. An experiment conducted in Türkiye revealed that the application of urea fertilizers resulted in an increase in the number of flowers with the highest fresh and dry saffron weight, whereas calcium ammonium nitrate led to maximum plant height [71].

Compared to other crops, saffron requires less water due to its drought resistance and dormant phase from May to August, which eliminates the need for irrigation [47, 72]. In some cultivated areas like Abruzzo, Sardinia, and Greece, farmers do not use irrigation. Instead, they rely on the rain, which usually comes at the end of summer, which is the most important time for irrigation [57]. However, more than 70% of the cultivated area in Castilla-La Mancha, a semi-arid region of Spain, is irrigated. Irrigation plays a crucial role in Morocco. Farmers in the region typically use volumes ranging from 350 to 500 m^3 ha^{-1}, which are distributed on a weekly basis during the period between September and November. As winter sets in, the intervals between irrigation sessions increase to 15 days, ensuring that crops receive ample moisture without being over-watered. This approach helps to optimize crop yields and promotes sustainable practices in the region's farming communities [68].

Depending on the climate and soil type, the watering methods are surface, sprinkler, and drip/micro [43]. The management of irrigation for saffron involves six specific applications that are critical for the successful growth of the flowers. The first application takes place in July to promote blooming. The second application takes place in early October to make it easier to harvest the flowers. The third application is in November after the flowers have been collected and new leaves have appeared. The fourth application takes place in late December to early January after weeding and fertilizer spreading. The fifth application is in early March, and the sixth is in early April to ensure the complete growth of daughter corms. The crop coefficient (Kc) values are influenced by the age of the field and the prevailing climatic conditions. The Kc values differ for the different growth stages, ranging from 0.41 to 0.45, 0.93 to 1.05, and 0.29 to 0.31. Generally, the highest Kc value is recorded in January [73].

Flower and Corm Harvesting

The process of saffron harvesting involves handpicking closed flowers at dawn to yield high-quality pistils [74]. Alternatively, a machine or mechanical system can detach the corolla from the stem and collect the flower with a vacuum [75]. Producing 1 kg of dried saffron requires 370-470 hours of labor. The harvesting of 1000 flowers with workers takes approximately 45-55 minutes, with a further 100-130 minutes for the separation of the stigmas, which are to be dried [76].

Depending on various factors, the yield of stigma can range from 2 to 28 kilograms per hectare [21]. Several studies have shown that the duration of the crop cycle has an impact on crop yields and productivity [56]. Different factors such as climate, corms' size and origin [21, 77], planting time, density, and depth [43], as well as fertilization and irrigation methods [78, 79], have a significant impact on the yield of saffron. Cardone *et al.* [21] found that the best saffron yield was achieved at a temperature of 15-16 °C and moderate rainfall during the biennial flowering period. According to Douglas *et al.* [77], planting corms weighing between 38-52 g for three consecutive years leads to a high stigma yield. In a study conducted by Gresta *et al.* [43], it was found that planting at the end of July (an earlier planting time) also contributes to a high stigma yield. Temperini *et al.* [80] conducted a multi-year study and recommended a two to three-year crop cycle to maintain flower number and spice yield over time, as there was a decrease observed in both during a four-year crop cycle.

The saffron plant is harvested for both its flowers and corms. The timing of corm harvesting depends on the country. In Iran and India, it takes 6-8 years; in Morocco, it takes 5-6 years; in Greece, it takes 10-12 years; in Spain and Sardinia, it takes 3-4 years; and in Abruzzo and Toscany, it takes 1 year. The process of harvesting corms involves lifting, cleaning, and sorting them by size. After that, they are disinfected with copper oxychloride or prochloraz solution before being planted in June and July. Additionally, the temperature during corm storage plays a crucial role in determining the growth and flowering of the plant. To increase flowering, it is recommended to store the corms for 90-150 days at a temperature ranging from 23-27 °C [42].

Pest and Diseases

Corm Rot

Several soil-borne fungi, such as *Rhizoctonia* sp., *Phytium* sp., *Macrophomina phaseolina, Fusarium solani, Basidomycota* sp., and *Phoma crocophila,* can cause this issue [81, 82]. Symptoms of rot appear during the flowering stage, causing yellowing and wilting of shoots due to basal stem rot and the development of white rounded spots on the corm [83]. Breeding resistant cultivars, improved cultural practices, crop rotation, and chemical management are some of the practices against corm rot.

Mice and Moles

Mice and moles cause damage to corms and affect sprouting flowers [81].

Weed Management

Saffron's slow-growing morphology leads to crops infested with weeds. Weed control is done mechanically. The mechanical weeding is done in August [39].

GLADIOLUS

The name of the genus, *Gladiolus*, is derived from the Latin "gladius", meaning sword. All members of the genus have this name because of the shape of the leaves. The Romans were aware of this genus and used to refer to it by this name. The ancient Greek name for the wild *Gladiolus* was "xiphium", which is derived from the Greek word "xiphos". Xiphos also means sword [84].

It is said that *gladioli* have been cultivated since the days of ancient Greece. Lyte's Nievve Herball, a record from 1578, provides evidence of its existence. *Gladioli* were initially introduced in France and then spread to other countries, including England, Germany, Holland, and North America. In 1596, John Gerard, a gardener to Lord Burleigh, owned his own "Physic Garden" in Holborn and had two European species of *gladioli: G. communis* from the Mediterranean region and *G. segetum* from South Europe, the canaries, and the Mediterranean region. Gerard grew around 1,030 plantlets during that period, as evidenced by the catalog. In 1597, Gerard published his famous book, Herball, General History of Planets, which described these two species [84].

Before 1730, the primary garden species in England were *G. communis*, *G. segetum*, and *G. byzantius*. The latter was introduced in 1629 from Istanbul. In 1737, several South African species were sent to England following the establishment of trade routes from England to India *via* the Cape of Good Hope [84].

According to Goldblatt and Manning [3], the genus *Gladiolus* has over 255 species, which are primarily found in southern Africa but also extend to tropical Africa, Madagascar, the Arabian Peninsula, the Mediterranean region, Europe, and as far east as Iran and Afghanistan.

Gladiolus can be propagated through cormels. These small corms grow in clusters on outgrowths called stolons, which are found between the mother and daughter corms.

Gladiolus is currently one of the most significant ornamental flowers in the world. It is highly prized both as a garden plant and as a cut flower, often used in bouquets and floral decorations. New *Gladiolus* varieties provide a wide range of colors, shapes, and sizes that are rarely found in other flowering plants. It is grown in almost every part of the world where climatic conditions are favorable [84].

Taxonomy

The taxonomical hierarchy of *Gladiolus* is as follows [85].

Kingdom: Plantae

Subkingdom: Viridaeplantae

Phylum: Tracheophyta

Class: Liliopsida

Order: Iridales

Family: Iridaceae

Subfamily: Ixioideae

Genus: *Gladiolus* L.

There are 11 taxa of *Gladiolus* found in Türkiye, with 4 of them being endemic (Table **2**).

Table 2. *Gladiolus* taxa in Türkiye.

1	G. anatolicus (Boiss.) Stapf	-
2	G. antakiensis A.P.Ham.	-
3	G. atroviolaceus Boiss.	-
4	G. attilae Kit Tan, B.Mathew & A.Baytop	Endemic
5	G. halophilus Boiss. & Heldr.	Endemic
6	G. humilis Stapf	Endemic
7	G. illyricus W.D.J.Koch	-
8	G. italicus Mill.	-
9	G. kotschyanus Boiss.	-
10	G. micranthus Stapf	Endemic
11	G. osmaniyensis	-

[17] Bizimbitkiler http://www.bizimbitkiler.org.tr

Morphology

The *Gladiolus* corm is formed from the shortening of 5-8 basal internodes of the flower stalk. Alternating nodes of the corm contain buds, and usually, one or two apical buds develop into a shoot. The leaves of the corm overlap at the base and may range from 1 to 12. The corm is surrounded by husks, which are the dry bases of foliage leaves. Every new growing season, a new corm is produced over the mother corm. Meanwhile, cormels are formed at the tip of branched stolons that sprout from buds located at the base of the new corm. Wild species generally produce only one corm, sometimes two, and a few cormels, while modern cultivars can produce between 2-4 corms and 30 to over 400 cormels [84, 85].

Gladiolus is a type of herbaceous plant that has deciduous leaves. The leaves have overlapping bases and the stem bears a spike of flowers at the top. Usually, the leaves can be found along with the flowers on the same stem, but sometimes, they may appear earlier or later than the flowers on separate stems. They come in pairs of two to several and can be located at the base of the plant or above ground level. The base of the leaf is sheathed and the blade is unifacial with an isobilateral shape. Sometimes, the blade is reduced or absent, resulting in a partially or fully sheathed leaf. The shape of the blade can vary from linear to lanceolate, and the margins, midrib, and other veins may or may not be thickened and hyaline. Occasionally, the midrib and margins can be significantly raised, and the blade may even be winged in a shape resembling an H or X. In some cases, the midrib and margins can be heavily thickened, and the blade is terete with four narrow longitudinal grooves [84].

The flowering stems are aerial, cylindrical, and can be either simple or branched. They are usually erect or flexed downward above the sheath of the uppermost leaf. The flowers are arranged in a second or distichous order in a spike inflorescence, though it may be reduced to a single flower in some species. Two floral bracts are present, usually green and sometimes dry above or entirely. These bracts are usually relatively large, with the inner one being slightly smaller than the outer one. In some cases, the inner bract may be much smaller or slightly longer than the outer one. The bracts are usually notched apically for 1-2 mm, although they may occasionally be entirely smooth [84].

The flowers of the *Gladiolus* plant are usually bilaterally zygomorphic, but a few species in tropical Africa, Madagascar, and South Africa have actinomorphic flowers. The tepals of the flower are joined together at the bottom to form a tube. The lower tepals usually contain markings that act as a guide for collecting nectar. The stamens of the flower are curved and positioned on one side, facing upwards or horizontally. The style of the flower is arched over the stamens and often closes at night. The perianth tube is typically an oblique funnel shape, often shorter than the bracts but occasionally longer. The tepals in a *Gladiolus* flower are typically asymmetrical. The top tepal is broad and curved, forming a hood over the stamens. The bottom three tepals are narrow, and in some species, they are clawed at the base and partially united. In subgenus *Gladiolus*, the lower tepals may be shorter, longer, or the same length as the upper tepals. The flowers of this plant can have up to 30 or more florets, which can be either bilateral or radially symmetric. The size of the flowers can range from 2 to 20 cm in diameter. The filaments are slender and are inserted at the base of the upper part of the perianth tube, which may be visible or extend only up to the mouth of the tube. In species with actinomorphic flowers, the anthers are symmetrically arranged around the style. The anthers typically lie below the dorsal tepal and are usually unilateral and either parallel-ascending or horizontal. They develop longitudinally and are sub-basifixed to centrifixed. Occasionally, they have sterile tails. In some tropical African species, the connective is obtusely mucronate above or prolonged into a prominent acute to apiculate appendage [84].

The flowers that are enveloped by two bracts have a more or less tubular shape with a perianth of six members, three stamens, an inferior ovary, and a capsule divided into three chambers. The ovary is either ovoid or oblong, while the style is filiform and divides opposite to or beyond the anthers. The branches of the style are simple and filiform below, expanding gradually or abruptly above and channeled to bilobed. The capsules are usually slightly inflated, large, and ovoid to ellipsoid or globose, with some being elongated and nearly cylindric.

The capsule holds anywhere between 50 to 100 ovules, which usually mature within 30 days after fertilization. The capsules are typically softly cartilaginous and have a slightly inflated oblong to ellipsoid or globose shape. The seeds can be either discoid with a broad membranous, circumferential wing and many per locule, or wingless and more or less globose to angle by pressure, and few per locule [84].

Soil and Climate Requirement

Gladiolus grows in all types of well-prepared soil. Good soil tillage is important. Soil pH should be 6-7, and development is slow in very calcareous soils.

Light and temperature are important factors for cultivation. Since *Gladiolus* grows best under plenty of sunlight, greenhouse conditions and planting distances should be adjusted accordingly. Temperatures between 10-25°C are the most suitable for the development of gladiolus. High temperatures and low lighting in the greenhouse during the winter months can cause poor-quality flowers [86].

Cultivation

Gladiolus cut flower cultivation can be done both in open and closed areas all year round. Commercial growers typically use medium-sized whole corms (2.5 to 3.8 cm) to produce standard-sized flower spikes, daughter corms, and cormels. However, if the goal is to obtain maximum production of corms and cormels, it is better to use large (3.8 to 5.1 cm) and jumbo (>5.1 cm) corms. Commercial producers can cut large corms into pieces to obtain maximum corm and cormel production. Gromov [87] suggested that small corms should be divided into 3 to 4 parts, large corms into 7 to 10 parts, and very large corms into 12 to 15 parts, depending on the number of buds. Each piece should contain a bud and a portion of the root zone. McKay *et al.* [88] found that larger corms (size 3 or larger) produce a greater yield of new corms compared to smaller corms. They also reported that larger corms produce higher-quality inflorescences with greater yields compared to smaller corms. Planting depth is 15-23 cm for large corms and 13-16 cm for medium-sized corms.

To grow *Gladiolus* successfully, it is important to cultivate the soil deeply, as the root part can extend up to 40-50 cm deep. Sandy soils require frequent fertilization, especially during rainy periods. The nutrient requirement of *Gladiolus* depends on the fertilization of the main corm in the previous period. Nitrogen, potassium, and phosphorus fertilizers should be added to the soil for

Gladiolus grown in sandy soils. Other nutrients such as calcium, magnesium, and iron should be added as traces during soil preparation based on the results of soil analysis. It is recommended to apply fertilizers in four periods for better growth.

- Before planting.
- Prior to the formation of the second and third leaves.
- The period when the outline of the flower begins to emerge among the leaves.
- Two weeks after flowering for the development of new corms and cormels.

The application of 150 kg ha^{-1} of nitrogen and 100 kg ha^{-1} phosphorous had a significant positive effect on plant height growth due to the fertilizer treatment [89]. Growth is much better if *Gladiolus* is planted in soil that has been thoroughly fertilized and cultivated a year in advance. When well-burned farm manure is mixed at the rate of 4-5 tons per decare, it positively affects the soil structure. In greenhouses, sterilization of the soil by steam or chemical methods is beneficial.

Regular watering is important after planting. Flood or sprinkler irrigation can be done. Sprinkler irrigation in extremely humid regions and seasons may cause botrytis damage. However, in dry summer months, sprinkler irrigation is a useful form of irrigation to prevent leaf tips and buds from burning. After planting gladiolus, superficial hoeing should be done against weeds. Water should not be given until the soil is thoroughly dried. The soil should be kept constantly moist to prevent ponding until the *Gladiolus* reaches 25-30 cm in height. In the following period, the amount of water should be reduced slightly. Starting from the period when the flower stem begins to form (which can be determined by checking the bottom leaves manually), the amount of water can be increased again. Considering that the plant will form roots at a depth of 40–50 cm, water should be ensured to reach this depth.

Tissue culture techniques have enabled the commercial mass propagation of cormels. Developed countries are utilizing highly sophisticated methods to produce desired varieties for international markets. This technology also allows for the production of disease-free and true-to-type planting material. *In vitro* techniques are especially useful for the propagation of corm-producing species since most hybrid cultivars of *Gladiolus* have a very low multiplication rate.

The primary objective of *in vitro* propagation of *Gladiolus* is to produce a large number of cormels [90]. Cormels grown in *in vitro* conditions are easy to store and sow. The appropriate growth medium is critical for successful micropropagation and cormel development in *Gladiolus* tissue culture. Murashige and Skoog's (1962) medium, supplemented with auxins and cytokinins, is ideal for initiating shoots, multiplying them, and promoting rooting [91].

Harvesting

Gladiolus grows into a spike after 6-7 leaves. When the spike reaches a certain length, flower color begins to appear from the lowest bulbs. When the lowest bulbs start to show color, it means it is time for flower cutting. It is cut 10-15 cm above the soil level with a sharp knife, leaving 1-2 leaves. The cut flowers are sized and stacked in flower boxes in the form of bunches of 10. The bundles in the boxes are cooled by sprinkling some water on them. If flower boxes are to be kept in storage, they are kept in an upright position. While waiting for 1-2 days, the flower length increases by 3-7 cm. In the horizontal position, the flowers curl at the ends due to geotropism [92].

Diseases

Corm Rot (Fusarium wilt)

This soil-borne disease is caused by fungal pathogens *Fusarium oxyporum f. sp. gladioli, Curvularia trifolii, Rhizopus arrhizus, Botrytis gladiolorum, Stromatinia gladioli*, and *Penicillium gladioli* [93]. When plants are infected, they produce smaller spikes and bloom later than healthy plants. A dark green color develops in spikes, and the petals become darker. Roots may show brown lesions. Planting healthy corms in disease-free soil, using calcium, potassium, and sodium nitrate in cool, moist soils, using ammonium nitrate in warm, dry soils, crop rotation, soil solarization, and sterilization are some of the effective cultural practices [94].

Botrytis blight

It is caused by *Botrytis gladiolorum*. It causes a destructive disease of *Gladiolus* flowers and corms in all regions where the plant is commercially grown worldwide [95]. The disease causes light brown spots at first then dark brown in leaves. If the corms are infected, soft and spongy areas are seen. Management of botrytis blight includes breeding resistant cultivars, sanitation, irradiation, using calcium nutrients, chemical control, ethylene management, relative humidity, and temperature control [96].

CONCLUSION

Iridaceae family, with 92 genera, is one of the important plant families. *Crocus* and *Iris* are common in the floral diversity of Eurasia and North America, while *Gladiolus* and *Morea* are major genera of the flora found in Sub-Saharan countries. Most of the species in the family are important as ornamental plants. Their propagation and cultivation practices should be improved. Saffron, in particular, holds special significance in the traditional medicine of many countries. *Gladiolus* is currently valued both as a garden plant and as a cut flower crop, often used for bouquets and floral arrangements. Particularly, cultivation practices and disease management should be improved, and the source of genetic variability should be searched for breeding activities.

REFERENCES

[1]   Goldblatt P. Phylogeny and classification of the Iridaceae and the relationships of Iris. Ann Bot 2000; 58.

[2]   Bahali DD. Habitat of iridaceae in India. Bulletin of the National Institute of Ecology 2006; 17: 1.

[3]   Goldblatt P, Manning J, Anderson F, Batten A. *Gladiolus* in Southern Africa. Fernwood Press (Pty) Ltd. 1998.

[4]   Goldblatt P. Phylogeny and classification of Iridaceae. Ann Mo Bot Gard 1990; 77(4): 607-27.

[5]   Rashed-Mohassel MH. Evolution and botany of saffron (*Crocus sativus* L.) and allied species. Saffron Woodhead Publishing 2020; 37-57.

[6]   Goldblatt P, Manning JC, Rudall P. Iridaceae In Kubitzki K, Ed, Flowering Plants Monocotyledons: Lilianae (except Orchidaceae). Berlin, Heidelberg: Springer Berlin Heidelberg 1998; pp. 295-333.

[7]   Rudall P. Anatomy and systematics of Iridaceae. Bot J Linn Soc 1994; 114(1): 1-21.

[8]   Cardone L, Castronuovo D, Perniola M, Cicco N, Candido V. Saffron (*Crocus sativus* L.), the king of spices: An overview. Sci Hortic (Amsterdam) 2020; 272: 109560.

[9]   Mati E, de Boer H. Ethnobotany and trade of medicinal plants in the Qaysari Market, Kurdish Autonomous Region, Iraq. J Ethnopharmacol 2011; 133(2): 490-510.
        [PMID: 20965241]

[10]   Emami SA, Nadjafi F, Amine GH, Amiri MS, Khosravi Mt NM. Les espèces de plantes médicinales utilisées par les guérisseurs traditionnels dans la province de Khorasan, nord-est de l'Iran. J Ethnopharmacol 2012; 48: 48-59.

[11]   Ghasemi Pirbalouti A, Momeni M, Bahmani M. Ethnobotanical study of medicinal plants used by Kurd tribe in Dehloran and Abdanan Districts, Ilam Province, Iran. Afr J Tradit Complement Altern Med 2012; 10(2): 368-85.
        [PMID: 24146463]

[12]   González JA, García-Barriuso M, Amich F. Ethnobotanical study of medicinal plants traditionally used in the Arribes del Duero, western Spain. J Ethnopharmacol 2010; 131(2): 343-55.
        [PMID: 20643201]

[13]   Idolo M, Motti R, Mazzoleni S. Ethnobotanical and phytomedicinal knowledge in a long-history protected area, the Abruzzo, Lazio and Molise National Park (Italian Apennines). J Ethnopharmacol 2010; 127(2): 379-95.
        [PMID: 19874882]

[14]   Günbatan TU, Gürbüz IL, Özkan AM. The current status of ethnopharmacobotanical knowledge in Çamlıdere (Ankara, Turkey). Turk J Bot 2016; 40(3): 241-9.

[15]   Egamberdieva D, Mamadalieva N, Khodjimatov O, Tiezzi A. Medicinal plants from Chatkal Biosphere Reserve used for folk medicine in Uzbekistan. Med Aromat Plant Sci Biotechnol 2013; 7(1): 56-64.

[16]   Arnold N, Baydoun S, Chalak L, Raus T. A contribution to the flora and ethnobotanical knowledge of Mount Hermon. Lebanon Fl Medit 2015; 25: 13-55.

[17]   Mohtashami L, Amiri MS, Ramezani M, Emami SA, Simal-Gandara J. The genus *Crocus* L.: A review of ethnobotanical uses, phytochemistry and pharmacology. Ind Crops Prod 2021; 171: 113923.

[18]   Bizimbitkiler. Available from: http://www.bizimbitkiler.org.tr [access date: 02 03 2024]

[19]   Gómez-Gómez L, Parra-Vega V, Rivas-Sendra A, *et al.* Unraveling massive crocins transport and accumulation through proteome and microscopy tools during the development of saffron stigma. Int J Mol Sci 2017; 18(1): 76.
[PMID: 28045431]

[20]   Bayat M, Rahimi M, Ramezani M. Determining the most effective traits to improve saffron (*Crocus sativus* L.) yield. Physiol Mol Biol Plants 2016; 22(1): 153-61.
[PMID: 27186029]

[21]   Cardone L, Castronuovo D, Perniola M, Cicco N, Candido V. Evaluation of corm origin and climatic conditions on saffron (*Crocus sativus* L.) yield and quality. J Sci Food Agric 2019; 99(13): 5858-69.
[PMID: 31206680]

[22]   Skinner M, Parker BL, Ghalehgolabbehbahani A. Saffron production: life cycle of saffron (*Crocus sativus*). North Am Cent Saffron Res Dev. University of Vermont 2017.

[23]   José Bagur M, Alonso Salinas GL, Jiménez-Monreal AM, *et al.* Saffron: An old medicinal plant and a potential novel functional food. Molecules 2017; 23(1): 30.
[PMID: 29295497]

[24]   Leone S, Recinella L, Chiavaroli A, *et al.* Phytotherapic use of the *Crocus sativus* L. (Saffron) and its potential applications: A brief overview. Phytother Res 2018; 32(12): 2364-75.
[PMID: 30136324]

[25]   Muzaffar S, Sofi TA, Khan KZ. Chemical composition of saffron: A review. Int J Biol Med Res 2019; 10(4): 6910-9.

[26]   Sampathu SR, Shivashankar S, Lewis YS, Wood AB. Saffron (*Crocus sativus* Linn.)—Cultivation, processing, chemistry and standardization. Crit Rev Food Sci Nutr 1984; 20(2): 123-57.

[27]   Siracusa L, Gresta F, Avola G, Lombardo GM, Ruberto G. Influence of corm provenance and environmental condition on yield and apocarotenoid profiles in saffron (*Crocus sativus* L.). J Food Compos Anal 2010; 23(5): 394-400.
[http://dx.doi.org/10.1016/j.jfca.2010.02.007]

[28]   García-Rodríguez MV, López-Córcoles H, Alonso GL, Pappas CS, Polissiou MG, Tarantilis PA. Comparative evaluation of an ISO 3632 method and an HPLC-DAD method for safranal quantity determination in saffron. Food Chem 2017; 221: 838-43.
[PMID: 27979282]

[29]   Giorgi A, Pentimalli D, Giupponi L, Panseri S. Quality traits of saffron (*Crocus sativus* L.) produced in the Italian Alps. Open Agric 2017; 2(1): 52-7.
[http://dx.doi.org/10.1515/opag-2017-0005]

[30]   Mykhailenko O, Desenko V, Ivanauskas L, Georgiyants V. Standard operating procedure of Ukrainian saffron cultivation according with good agricultural and collection practices to assure quality and traceability. Ind Crops Prod 2020; 151: 112376.

[31]   Perez-Vidal C, Gracia L. Computer based production of Saffron (*Crocus sativus* L.): From mechanical design to electronic control. Comput Electron Agric 2020; 169: 105198.

[32]   Rubio Terrado P. El azafrán. Aspectos socioeconómicos y culturales. STVDIVM. Revista de Humanidades 2007; 13: 199-228.

[33]   Lal R. Restoring soil quality to mitigate soil degradation. Sustainability 2015; 7(5): 5875-95.

[34]   Mollafilabi A, Koocheki A, Moeinerad H, Kooshki L. Effect of plant density and weight of corm on yield and yield components of saffron (*Crocus sativus* L.) under soil, hydroponic and plastic tunnel cultivation. International symposium on Medicinal and Aromatic Plants-SIPAM Acta Horticulturae 2013; 997(997): 51-8.

[35]   Mohammad-Abadi AA, Rezvani-Moghaddam P, Sabori A. Effect of plant distance on flower yield and qualitative and quantitative characteristics of forage production of saffron (*Crocus sativus*) in Mashhad conditions. II Int Symp Saffron Biol Technol 2006; 739: 151-3.

[36]   Souret FF, Weathers PJ. The growth of saffron (*Crocus sativus* L.) in aeroponics and hydroponics. J Herbs Spices Med Plants 2000; 7(3): 25-35.

[37]   Shokrpour M. Saffron (*Crocus sativus* L.) breeding: opportunities and challenges. In: Al-Khayri JM, Jain SM, Johnson DV, Eds., Advances in Plant Breeding Strategies: Industrial and Food Crops 2019; 6: 675-706.

[38]   Nemati Z, Harpke D, Gemicioglu A, Kerndorff H, Blattner FR. Saffron (*Crocus sativus*) is an autotriploid that evolved in Attica (Greece) from wild *Crocus cartwrightianus*.. Mol Phylogenet Evol 2019; 136: 14-20.
[PMID: 30946897]

[39]   Kumar R, Singh V, Devi K, Sharma M, Singh MK, Ahuja PS. State of art of saffron (*Crocus sativus* L.) agronomy: A comprehensive review. Food Rev Int 2008; 25(1): 44-85.

[40]   Mathew BR. Botany, taxonomy and cytology of *C. sativus* L. and its allies. In: Negbi M, Ed., Saffron: *Crocus sativus* L. 1999; 17-30.

[41]   Rubio-Moraga Á, Gómez-Gómez L, Trapero A, Castro-Díaz N, Ahrazem O. Saffron corm as a natural source of fungicides: The role of saponins in the underground. Ind Crops Prod 2013; 49: 915-21.

[42]   Molina RV, Valero M, Navarro Y, Guardiola JL, Garcia-Luis AJ. Temperature effects on flower formation in saffron (*Crocus sativus* L.). Sci Hortic (Amsterdam) 2005; 103(3): 361-79.

[43]   Gresta F, Lombardo GM, Siracusa L, Ruberto G. Effect of mother corm dimension and sowing time on stigma yield, daughter corms and qualitative aspects of saffron (*Crocus sativus* L.) in a Mediterranean environment. J Sci Food Agric 2008; 88(7): 1144-50.

[44]   Gresta F, Lombardo GM, Avola G. Saffron stigmas production as affected by soil texture. In III International Symposium on Saffron: Forthcoming Challenges in Cultivation. Res Econ 2009; 850: 149-52.

[45]   Caiola MG, Canini A. Looking for saffron's (*Crocus sativus* L.) parents. Funct Plant Sci Biotechnol 2010; 4(2): 1-4.

[46]   Renau-Morata B, Nebauer SG, Sánchez M, Molina RV. Effect of corm size, water stress and cultivation conditions on photosynthesis and biomass partitioning during the vegetative growth of saffron (*Crocus sativus* L.). Ind Crops Prod 2012; 39: 40-6.

[47]   Kafi M, Koocheki A, Rashed Mohassel MH, Nassiri M. Saffron, production and processing. Language and Literature Publications 2002; p. 252.

[48]   Rahimi H, Shokrpour M, Tabrizi Raeini L, Esfandiari E. A study on the effects of environmental factors on vegetative characteristics and corm yield of saffron (*Crocus sativus*). Iran J Hortic Sci 2017; 48: 45-52.

[49]   Cardone L, Castronuovo D, Perniola M, Scrano L, Cicco N, Candido V. The influence of soil physical and chemical properties on saffron (*Crocus sativus* L.) growth, yield and quality. Agronomy (Basel) 2020; 10(8): 1154.

[50]   Fallahi HR, Mahmoodi S. Influence of organic and chemical fertilisation on growth and flowering of saffron under two irrigation regimes. Saffron Agron Technol 2018; 6: 147-66.
[http://dx.doi.org/10.22048/jsat.2017.71511.1207]

[51]   Fallahi HR, Mahmoodi S. Impact of water availability and fertilization management on saffron (*Crocus sativus* L.) biomass allocation. J Hortic Postharvest Res 2018; 1(2): 131-46.

[52]   Zarghani F, Karimi A, Khorasani R, Lakzian A. To evaluate the effect of soil physical and chemical characteristics on the growth characteristics of saffron (*Crocus sativus* L.) corms in Tornbat-e

Heydariyeh area. J Agroecol 2016; 8: 120-33.
[http://dx.doi.org/10.22067/jag.v8i1.48511]

[53]   Gresta F, Lombardo GM, Siracusa L, Ruberto G. Saffron, an alternative crop for sustainable agricultural systems: a review. Sustain Agric 2009; 355-76.

[54]   Lopez-Corcoles H, Brasa-Ramos A, Montero-Garcia F, Romero-Valverde M, Montero-Riquelme F. Phenological growth stages of saffron plant (*Crocus sativus* L.) according to the BBCH Scale. Span J Agric Res 2015; 13(3): e09SC01.

[55]   Colla G, Rouphael Y. Evaluation of saffron (*Crocus sativus* L.) production in Italy: Effects of the age of saffron fields and plant density. J Food Agric Environ 2009; 7(1): 19-23.

[56]   Branca F, Argento S. Evaluation of saffron pluri annual growing cycle in central Sicily. In III International Symposium on Saffron: Forthcoming Challenges in Cultivation. Res Econ 2009; 850: 153-8.

[57]   Tammaro F. Saffron (*Crocus sativus* L.) in Italy. Saffron CRC Press 1999; 48-55.

[58]   Fernández JA. Biology, biotechnology and biomedicine of saffron. Recent Research Developments in Plant Science 2004; 2: 127-59.

[59]   Negbi M, Dagan B, Dror A, Basker D. Growth, flowering, vegetative reproduction, and dormancy in the saffron *Crocus* (*Crocus sativus* L.). Isr J Plant Sci 1989; 38(2-3): 95-113.

[60]   Hagiladi A, Umiel N, Ozeri Y, *et al.* The effect of planting depth on emergence and development of some geophytic plants. VI Int Symp Flower Bulbs. 325: 131-8.

[61]   Nazir MM, Nasir MA, Allah B, Khan MN, Summrah MA, Nawaz MZ. Effect of different planting depth of corms on the yield of saffron under Soan Valley climatic conditions. Sarhad J Agric 2000; 16(5): 485-7.

[62]   Dhar AK. Saffron: biology, utilization, agriculture, production and quality. Curr Res Med Aromat Plants 2000; 22: 355-60.

[63]   Askari-Khorasgani O, Pessarakli M. Shifting saffron (*Crocus sativus* L.) culture from traditional farmland to controlled environment (greenhouse) condition to avoid the negative impact of climate changes and increase its productivity. J Plant Nutr 2019; 42(19): 2642-65.

[64]   Behzad S, Razavi M, Mahajeri M. The effect of various amount of ammonium phosphate and urea on saffron production. Int Symp Medicinal Arom Plants, XXIII IHC. 306: 337-9.

[65]   Behzad S, Razavi M, Mahajeri M. The effect of mineral nutrients (NPK) on saffron production. Acta Hortic 1992; (306): 426-30.

[66]   Bullitta P, Milia M, Pinna ME, Satta M, Scarpa GM. Initial results of the effects of different agronomic treatments on *Crocus* sativus L. in Sardinia. Riv Ital EPPOS 1996; 19: 131-7.

[67]   Gresta F, Santonoceto C, Avola G. Crop rotation as an effective strategy for saffron (*Crocus sativus* L.) cultivation. Sci Hortic (Amsterdam) 2016; 211: 34-9.

[68]   Goliaris AH. Saffron cultivation in Greece. Saffron: Crocus sativus. CRC Press 1999; pp. 65-76.

[69]   Ait-Oubahou AH, El-Otmani MO. Saffron cultivation in Morocco Saffron: Crocus sativus L. Amsterdam, The Netherlands: Harwood Academic Publications 1999; pp. 87-94.

[70]   Husaini AM. Challenges of climate change: omics-based biology of saffron plants and organic agricultural biotechnology for sustainable saffron production. GM Crops Food 2014; 5(2): 97-105. [PMID: 25072266]

[71]   Unal M, Cavusoglu A. The effect of various nitrogen fertilizers on saffron (*Crocus sativus* L.) yield. Akdeniz Üniv Ziraat Fak Derg 2005; 18(2): 257-60.

[72]   Dastranj M, Sepaskhah AR. Response of saffron (*Crocus sativus* L.) to irrigation water salinity, irrigation regime and planting method: Physiological growth and gas exchange. Sci Hortic

(Amsterdam) 2019; 257: 108714.

[73]   Yarami N, Kamgar-Haghighi AA, Sepaskhah AR, Zand-Parsa S. Determination of the potential evapotranspiration and crop coefficient for saffron using a water-balance lysimeter. Arch Agron Soil Sci 2011; 57(7): 727-40.

[74]   Erden K, Özel A. Influence of delayed harvest on yield and some quality parameters of saffron (*Crocus sativus* L.). J Agric Biol Sci 2016; 11: 313-6.

[75]   Ruggiu M, Bertetto AM. A mechanical device for harvesting *Crocus sativus* (saffron) flowers. Appl Eng Agric 2006; 22(4): 491-8.

[76]   Golmohammadi F. Saffron and its farming, economic importance, export, medicinal characteristics and various uses in South Khorasan Province-East of Iran. International Journal of Farming and Allied Sciences 2014; 3(5): 566-96.

[77]   Douglas MH, Smallfield BM, Wallace AR, McGimpsey JA. Saffron (*Crocus sativus* L.): The effect of mother corm size on progeny multiplication, flower and stigma production. Sci Hortic (Amsterdam) 2014; 166: 50-8.

[78]   Ghanbari J, Khajoei-Nejad G, Van Ruth SM, Aghighi S. The possibility for improvement of flowering, corm properties, bioactive compounds, and antioxidant activity in saffron (*Crocus sativus* L.) by different nutritional regimes. Ind Crops Prod 2019; 135: 301-10.

[79]   Koocheki A, Seyyedi SM. Effects of different water supply and corm planting density on crocin, picrocrocin and safranal, nitrogen uptake and water use efficiency of saffron grown in semi-arid region. Not Sci Biol 2016; 8(3): 334-41.

[80]   Colla G, Rouphael Y. Evaluation of saffron (*Crocus sativus* L.) production in Italy: Effects of the age of saffron fields and plant density. J Food Agric Environ 2009; 7(1): 19-23.

[81]   Dhar AK. Saffron breeding and agrotechnology-A status report. PAFAI J 1990; 12: 18-22.

[82]   Thakur RN. Corm rot in saffron and its control Supplement to cultivation and utilization of aromatic plants. Jammu, India: Regional Research Laboratory 1997; pp. 447-58.

[83]   Hassan MG, Devi LS. Corm rot diseases of saffron in Kashmir valley. Indian Phytopathol 2003; 56(1): 122.

[84]   Cantor M, Tolety J. Gladioulus In Kole C, Ed., wild crop relatives: genomic and breeding resources: plantation and ornamental crops. Berlin, Heidelberg: Springer Berlin Heidelberg. 2011; pp. 133-59.

[85]   Dhiman MR, Thakur N, Gupta YC, Sharma N. *Gladiolus*. In: Datta SK, Gupta YC, Eds., Floriculture and Ornamental Plants. Singapore: Springer Nature Singapore 2022; pp. 47-79.

[86]   Mazzini-Guedes RB, Guedes Filho O, Bonfim-Silva EM, Couto JC, Pereira MT, da Silva TJ. Management of corm size and soil water content for *Gladiolus* flower production. Ornam Hortic (Campinas) 2017; 23(2): 152-9.

[87]   Gromov AN. The world of the *Gladiolus*. USA: NAGC 1972; pp. 98-102.

[88]   McKay ME, Byth DE, Tommerup J. The effect of corm size and division of the mother corm in gladioli. Aust J Exp Agric 1981; 21(110): 343-8.

[89]   Dhakal K, Khanal D, Ayer DK, *et al.* Effect of nitrogen and phosphorous on growth, development and vase life of gladiolus. RRJoAST 2017; 6: 1-7.

[90]   Nagaraju V, Bhowmik G, Parthasarathy VA. Effect of paclobutrazol and sucrose on *in vitro* cormel formation in *Gladiolus*. Acta Bot Croat 2002; 61(1): 27-33.

[91]   Wahocho NA, Miano TF, Leghari MH. Propagation of *Gladiolus* corms and cormels: A review. Afr J Biotechnol 2016; 15(32): 1699-710.

[92]   Kushal Singh KS, Ranjit Singh RS. Optimizing harvesting stage of *Gladiolus* spikes for wet refrigerated storage. Asian J Hortic 2013; 8(2): 561-4.

[93]   Mishra PK, Mukhopadhyay AN, Fox RT. Integrated and biological control of *Gladiolus* corm rot and wilt caused by *Fusarium oxysporum* f. sp. *gladioli.*. Ann Appl Biol 2000; 137(3): 361-4.

[94]   Baiswar P, Chandra S, Kumar R. Status of *Gladiolus* diseases and their management in India-A review. J Ornam Hortic 2007; 10(4): 209-14.

[95]   Singh PJ, Kumar A, Kaul VK. Morphological and anatomical basis of resistance to blight caused by *Botrytis gladiolorum* in *Gladiolus*. Plant Dis Res 2009; 24(2): 156-62.

[96]   Bika R, Baysal-Gurel F, Jennings C. *Botrytis cinerea* management in ornamental production: a continuous battle. Can J Plant Pathol 2021; 43(3): 345-65.

CHAPTER 6

Liliaceae Family

Sibel Day[1,*]

[1] *Department of Field Crops, Faculty of Agriculture, Ankara University, Ankara, Türkiye*

Abstract: Liliacea family consists of 15 genera, which are distributed in the Northern Hemisphere and Eurasia. *Fritillaria* and Tulip are the most famous genera known all over the world. *Fritillaria* and *Tulipa* are the most common ornamental plants. *Fritillaria* is also valued for its chemical components and is used in conventional medicine. Protection of the wild genus of Fritillaria and Tulip is important for new germplasm against some of the important pests and diseases of these plants. *Fritillaria* and Tulip cultivation, especially *fritillaria* cultivation and its development, is important to prevent collection from nature. In this chapter, their taxa in Türkiye, as well as their importance and cultivation, are discussed.

Keywords: Cultivation, *Fritillaria*, *Fritillaria imperialis*, Morphology, Tulip.

INTRODUCTION

Liliaceae was initially presented to the scientific community by Antoine Laurent de Jussieu in 1789. The families known as Liriaceae, Tulipaceae, Erythroniaceae, and Fritillariaceae are considered synonyms of Liliaceae [1, 2].

The Liliaceae family consists of 15 genera and 635 species in the Northern Hemisphere and temperate Eurasia. The genera of the family include *Amana, Calochortus, Cardiocrinum, Clintonia, Erytronium, Fritillaria, Gagea, Lilium, Medeola, Notholirion, Prosartes, Scoliopus, Streptopus, Tricyrtis*, and *Tulipa* [3].

In Türkiye, the Liliaceae family is used in ethnomedicine for treating abdominal pain, including in infants, as well as abscesses, edema, halitosis, headaches, menstrual pain, rheumatism, skin firming, toothaches, and wounds [4 - 12]. This chapter includes the properties and cultivation of *Fritillaria* and *Tulipa*.

---

[*] **Corresponding author Sibel Day:** Department of Field Crops, Faculty of Agriculture, Ankara University, Ankara, Türkiye; E-mail: day@ankara.edu.tr

FRITILLARIA

There are 148 accepted species of *Fritillaria* that have been reported. According to reports, the genetic diversity center of the *Fritillaria* genus is located in Iran, where subgenera from central Asia, the Mediterranean, and the Caucasus meet [13]. The genus consists of species that are native to Cyprus, Iran, and Southern Türkiye [14]. The highest number of *Fritillaria* taxa have been reported in Türkiye, with 19 of them being endemic and a total of 46 taxa (Table 1). Iran has 18 endemic taxa. China, Greece, California, and India have reported 30, 24, 18, and 6 taxa, respectively [15].

Table 1. *Fritillaria* species in Türkiye [22] (www.bizimbitkiler.org.tr.).

1	*Fritillaria ozdemir-elmasii* Yıldırım & Tekşen	Endemic
2	*Fritillaria acmopetala* Boiss.	-
3	*Fritillaria alburyana* Rix	Endemic
4	*Fritillaria alfredae* Post	-
5	*Fritillaria alfredae* subsp. *glaucoviridis* (Turrill) Rix	Endemic
6	*Fritillaria alfredae* subsp. *platyptera* (Sam. ex Rech.f.) Rix	-
7	*Fritillaria assyriaca* Baker	-
8	*Fritillaria assyriaca* subsp. *assyriaca* Baker	-
9	*Fritillaria assyriaca* subsp. *melananthera* Rix	Endemic
10	*Fritillaria aurea* Schott	Endemic
11	*Fritillaria baskilensis* Behcet	Endemic
12	*Fritillaria bithynica* Baker	-
13	*Fritillaria byfieldii* N.Özhatay & Rix	Endemic
14	*Fritillaria carica* Rix	-
15	*Fritillaria caucasica* Adam	-
16	*Fritillaria crassifolia* Boiss. & A. Huet	-
17	*Fritillaria crassifolia* subsp. *crassifolia* Boiss. & A. Huet	Endemic
18	*Fritillaria hakkarensis* (Rix) Tekşen	-
19	*Fritillaria crassifolia* subsp. *kurdica* (Boiss. & Noë) Rix	-
20	*Fritillaria elwesii* Boiss.	-
21	*Fritillaria fleischeriana* Steud. & Hochst. ex Schult. & Schult.f.	Endemic
22	*Fritillaria forbesii* Baker	-
23	*Fritillaria frankiorum* R.Wallis & R.B.Wallis	-
24	*Fritillaria amana* (Rix) Tekşen	-
25	*Fritillaria imperialis* L.	-

(Table 1) cont.....

26	*Fritillaria kittaniae* Sorger	Endemic
27	*Fritillaria latakiensis* Rix	-
28	*Fritillaria latifolia* Willd.	-
29	*Fritillaria michailovskyi* Fomin	Endemic
30	*Fritillaria milasense* Tekşen & Aytaç	Endemic
31	*Fritillaria minima* Rix	Endemic
32	*Fritillaria minuta* Boiss. & Noë	-
33	*Fritillaria mughlae* Tekşen & Aytaç	Endemic
34	*Fritillaria persica* L.	-
35	*Fritillaria pinardii* Boiss.	-
36	*Fritillaria pontica* Wahlenb.	-
37	*Fritillaria serpenticola* (Rix) Tekşen & Aytaç	Endemic
38	*Fritillaria enginiana* (Byfield & Özhatay) Tekşen	Endemic
39	*Fritillaria sibthorpiana* (Sm.) Baker	-
40	*Fritillaria straussii* Bornm.	-
41	*Fritillaria stribrnyi* Velen.	-
42	*Fritillaria uva-vulpis* Rix	-
43	*Fritillaria viridiflora* Post	-
44	*Fritillaria whittallii* Baker	Endemic
45	*Fritillaria wendelboi* (Rix) Tekşen	Endemic
46	*Fritillaria asumaniae* R.Wallis, R.B.Wallis & Özhatay	Endemic

Fritillaria is a significant genus in the Liliaceae family and is valued for its chemical components employed in conventional medicine by various societies, including Türkiye [16], Southeast Asia [17], China, Pakistan, and Japan [18]. The genus is also commonly used in therapeutic plants [19] and floriculture [20]. Moreover, *Fritillaria* is widely consumed globally as both a food source and medication; Native Americans use roasted bulbs of certain species as food. The dried bulbs of certain *Fritillaria* species are used in traditional Turkish, Chinese, and Japanese medicine to treat various ailments, including asthma. Additionally, the bulbs of the plant are employed in traditional medicine to mitigate pain, reduce phlegm, lower fever, relieve coughs, and facilitate detoxification. However, the slow-growing nature of *Fritillaria* plants results in minimal annual growth and medicinal yield, with seed germination to flowering taking as long as 4-5 years. In Türkiye, the combination of *Fritillaria* germplasm resources, habitat degradation, and animal and human intervention has resulted in the overexploitation and severe endangerment of wild *Fritillaria* resources. The collection and destruction of this species are prohibited and are updated annually in Türkiye's national key protected wild plants [21].

Taxonomy and Properties

Kingdom: Plantae

Subkingdom: Tracheobionta

Divison: Magnoliophyta

Class: Liliopsida

Subclass: Liliidae

Order: Liliales

Family: Liliaceae

Genus: *Fritillaria*

Fritillaria imperialis

Morphology

The plant has oval bulbs that are 4-4.5 cm in diameter. Its trunk is thick, brown to vibrant green, and smooth, with a height of 30-100 cm and a straight appearance. The vibrant green leaves are stemless, and there are 20-29 of them. The lowest leaf is oval-lance-shaped, pointed, and 7-18 × 5-10 cm in size. There are also 10-23 bracket leaves that are spear-shaped, vibrant green, and 6-12 × 0.5-1.5 cm in size, arranged vertically upwards from the bottom of the flower cluster [13, 23, 24].

The inflorescence is in the form of an umbrella, with 1-15 flowers in each cluster. The perianth is wide and bell-shaped, and the color of the flowers ranges from red to orange. The outer tops of the flowers may turn slightly pink as they dry, and the curl of the outer tops and nectar area are visible. The inner tops of the flowers are black. The tepals are lanceolate, 4-5.5 cm long, with a pointed apex and base. The nectaries, which are white and circular in shape, are located at the base of the perianth and measure up to 5 mm in diameter [13, 23, 24].

The filaments are 25-45 mm long and white to green. The anthers are 13-18 mm long and light yellow. The style is 40-43 mm long, 3-part, and light yellow to green towards the ovary. The capsule is 19-24 mm, brownish, and 6-winged [13, 23, 24].

Fritillaria persica

<u>Morphology</u>

The bulb is 5 cm in diameter and 6 cm in height, swollen in the middle. The plant is 55-82 cm tall, with a thick and dull bluish-green stem. The leaves are sessile, dull bluish-green, and there are around 50-60 pieces. At the bottom of the leaf, the size is 8-9.5 × 1.5-2.5 cm, and it is ovate-lanceolate. The leaf apex is acute acuminate, integer, and alternate. Bract leaves may or may not be present.

The inflorescence is a raceme with 12-28 flowers (Fig. **1**). The perianth is narrowly campanulate, dark purple, and the tepals are 14-17 × 7-10 mm (Fig. **2**). The tepals are elliptic-oblanceolate, and the tepal apex and base are obtuse. The nectaries are purple, 1-1.5 mm in diameter, and triangular at the filament base. The filaments are 8-11 mm long, yellow-green, and the anthers are 2 mm long, dark yellow or purple. The style is 7-7.5 mm long and smooth, while the stigma is flat [13]. The flowering period is between March and May.

Propagation

There are two species of *Fritillaria*, namely *F. persica* and *F. imperialis,* which are produced and exported from Türkiye. It is important to note that collecting and exporting these species, as well as other *Fritillaria* species, from nature is strictly prohibited. In 2006, the export of 150,000 *F. persica* bulbs and 100,000 *F. imperialis* bulbs was allowed, but only from cultivated sources. Bulbous and tuberous plants can be propagated through generative or vegetative methods. Vegetative propagation techniques are more commonly used nowadays. Some of these techniques include separating bulbs that naturally produce tillers, ensuring bulblet formation on the stem, dividing the bulb into pieces, cutting the bulb from the base, dividing the bulb into 3-4 parts while leaving a portion of the base on the cut piece, injuring the bulb, using bulb scales, and tissue culture [25, 26].

The process of vegetative propagation in *Fritillaria* is slow, as one mother bulb can only produce two to three daughter bulbs, depending on the ecological niche conditions and cultivation procedures [27]. The rate of propagation through seeds is even lower than that of vegetative propagation, with seedlings taking about 4-6 years to mature into plants [28]. To overcome these challenges, various attempts have been made since the early 1980s to regenerate or morphogenetically create medicinal *Fritillaria* species using *in vitro* regeneration techniques. In plant tissue culture technology, initial explants such as bulb scales, bulb segments (transverse or vertical cuts), or whole bulbs are used for the micropropagation of *Fritillaria*. Calli, somatic embryos, and bulblets are induced and regenerated using different concentrations and combinations of plant regulators under culture conditions optimized for the effective morphogenetic response of *Fritillaria* species, such as photoperiod, light flux, humidity, and temperature [29].

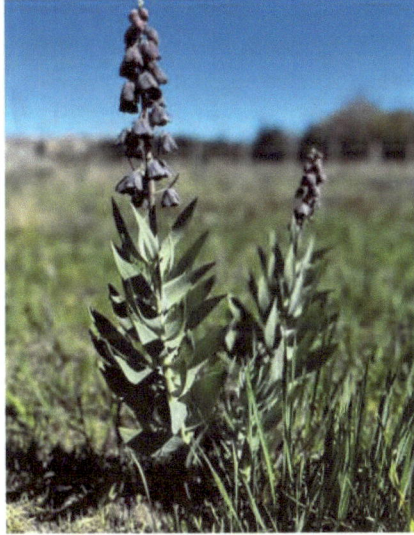

Fig. (1). *Fritillaria persica* morphology.

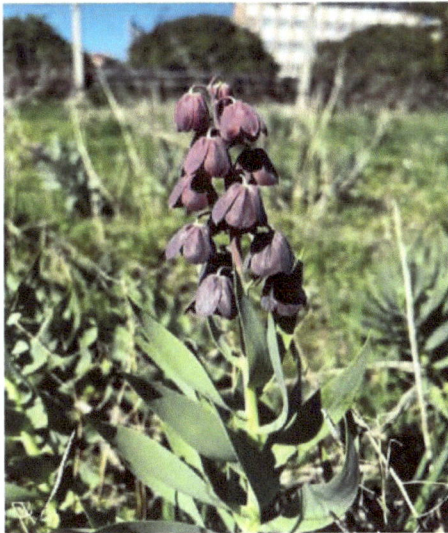

Fig. (2). The plant morphology of *Fritillaria persica.*

Inverted tulips are best planted in the autumn. Peat and fertilizer should be added to the soil 10 days before planting to ensure good aeration. This plant is usually planted as a bulb and blooms in late February or early March. Fertilizer should be applied immediately after flowering to keep the flowers vibrant [30].

Pests and Diseases

Lilioceris chodjaii

During winters, the adult *Lilioceris chodjaii* pests were found to be overwintering and entering a dormant phase in the soil below the *Fritillaria* plant. In May, the adults emerge and start feeding on young leaves of *Fritillaria imperialis*. The eggs were then observed as reddish-orange in color, numbering around 6, and arranged in irregular lines on and under the leaves of the host plant. Pest monitoring and management programs should be implemented to prevent future pest damage [31].

Lilioceris merdigera

Newly hatched *L. merdigera* larvae in their first instar cause damage to the plant by gnawing through the entire beginning of the instar, creating openings in the middle of the plant's growth. These larvae initially have a web-like structure on the upper leaves, and as they grow, they can cause further damage to the leaves by feeding on them. The feeding of the larvae starts from the tip of the body and continues towards the base [32].

Eumerus amoenus

E. amoenus larvae have been found to cause decay by feeding on the bulbs of the *F. imperialis* plant [32]. Speight *et al.* [33] found in their study that the larvae infect *F. imperialis* bulbs and feed on the internal tissues of the plant's bulbs, causing the bulbs to rot rapidly.

TULIPA

The tulip has been cultivated by the Turks since 1000 AD. During the Seljuk Empire, it was stylized and used in decorative art. In the first period of the Ottoman Empire, the people had a fondness for tulips, and Mehmed II, the conqueror of Istanbul, was particularly interested in literature, art, gardening, and tulip growing. After conquering Istanbul, Mehmed II initiated the construction of the Topkapı Palace, an extensive garden with a magnificent view over the Bosporus, where plants, especially tulips, were planted.

Süleyman the Magnificent, the great-grandson of Mehmed II, ascended to the throne in 1520 at the height of the Ottoman Empire's power and size. It was at this time that the Turks began to breed tulips rather than simply collect them from the wild. The passion for tulips nurtured by Süleyman and later his son Selim II declined towards the end of the 16th century with the accession of Mehmed III in

1595.

It was not until 1647 when Mehmed IV became Sultan that the tulip regained royal favor. He restored the imperial gardens and decreed that all new flower species should be registered and classified, and he established a council of florists to judge all new tulip cultivars [34].

In the seventeenth century, the tulip appeared as the most dominant flower in the decoration of wall tiles. The tulip held an important place in the works of the poets, and it appeared in frescoes, fabrics, and book illuminations. By 1630, there were eight flower shops and 300 professional florists [34].

Despite the existence of much literature about tulips, their taxonomy is generally considered difficult.

Taxonomy and Properties

Kingdom: Plantae

Subkingdom: Tracheobionta

Division: Magnoliophyta Cronquist, Takht & Zimmerm. ex Reveal

Class: Lilliopsida Batsch

Subclass: Liliidae J. H. Schaffn.

Order: Liliales Perleb

Family: Liliaceae Juss.

Genus: *Tulipa* L.

Tulips are mainly popular in landscaping, cut flowers, and potted plants. Mainly world tulip bulb production is in the Netherlands. Most tulip species are diploid, 2n=24, and polyploidy is common, *e.g.*, triploidy (2n=3x=36) in *T. aleppensis, T. radii,* and *T. orphanidea*, tetraploidy (2n=4x=48) in *T. sylvestris* subsp. *Sylvestris,* pentaploidy (2n=5x=60) in *T. clusiana* have been reported [35]. The total number of species in the world is given in Table **2**.

Table **2**. Distribution and number of species of tulips in the world [35].

Country	Number of species
Türkiye	18 species (19 taxa)
Russia, Central Asia, and Caucasus	65 species

(Table 2) cont.....

Kazakhstan	32 species
Tajikistan	25 species
Uzbekistan	21 species
Russia	6 species
Armenia	7 species
Iran, Afghanistan, western Pakistan, northern Iraq, Azerbaijan, Turkmenistan	36 species (38 taxa)
Iraq	3 species (4 taxa)
Syria, Palestine, and Sinai	10 species
Palestine	3 species (4 taxa)
Israel	4 species
Jordan	3 species
Saudi Arabia	1 species
Pakistan	6 species
Afghanistan	8 species
India	2 species (6 taxa)
Balkans	8 species
Greece	6 species
Bulgaria	4 species (7 taxa)
Croatia	2 species
Romania	6 species (7 taxa)
Serbia	5 species
Switzerland	2 species
Malta	2 species
Flora Europa	11 species (12 taxa)
Italy	9 species
Iberian Peninsula	5 species (6 taxa)
Cyprus	2 species
Crete	4 species
Chios	4 species
Corsica	2 species
Morocco	1 species (2 taxa)
Egypt	2 species
Algeria	1 species
North Africa	4 species (9 taxa)
China	13 species

(Table 2) cont.....

Hungary	1 species
Mongolia	1 species

The total number of taxa in Türkiye increased from 19 taxa [35] to 23 taxa with 7 endemic taxa (Table **3**).

Table 3. Tulip taxa in Türkiye [22] www.bizimbitkiler.org.tr.

1	*Tulipa raddii* Reboul	endemic
2	*Tulipa agenensis* DC.	-
3	*Tulipa aleppensis* Boiss. ex Regel	-
4	*Tulipa armena* Boiss.	-
5	*Tulipa armena* var. *armena* Boiss. (Fig. **3**)	-
6	*Tulipa armena* var. *galatica* (Freyn) Eker	-
7	*Tulipa biflora* Pall.	-
8	*Tulipa cinnabarina* K.Perss.	endemic
9	*Tulipa clusiana* DC.	-
10	*Tulipa humilis* Herb.	-
11	*Tulipa julia* K.Koch	-
12	*Tulipa koyuncui* Eker & Babaç	endemic
13	*Tulipa orphanidea* Boiss. ex Heldr.	-
14	*Tulipa pulchella* (Fenzl ex Regel) Baker	endemic
15	*Tulipa saxatilis* Sieber ex Spreng.	-
16	*Tulipa sintenisii* Baker	endemic
17	*Tulipa sprengeri* Baker	endemic
18	*Tulipa sylvestris* L.	-
19	*Tulipa sylvestris* var. *australis* (Link) Pamp.	-
20	*Tulipa sylvestris* var. *sylvestris* L.	-
21	*Tulipa systola* Stapf	-
22	*Tulipa undulatifolia* Boiss.	-
23	*Tulipa cinnabarina* subsp. *toprakii* Yıldırım & Eker	endemic

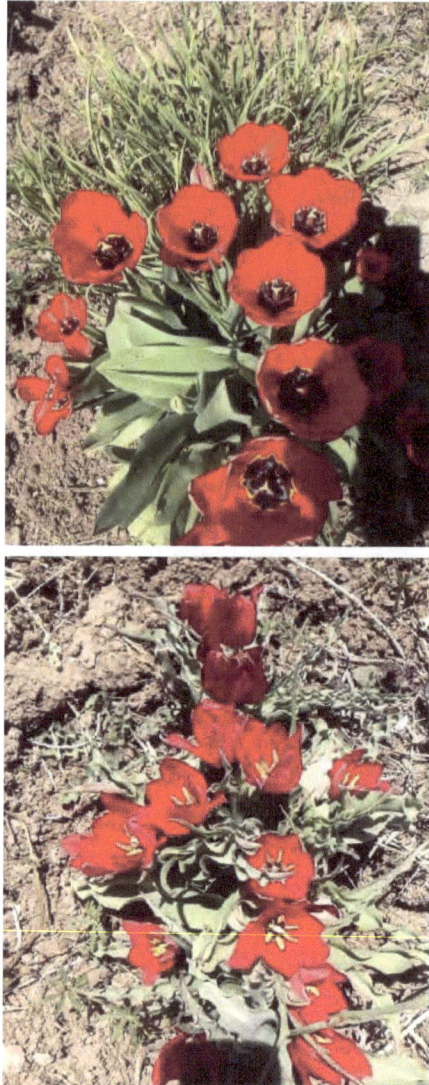

Fig. (3). View of *Tulipa armena var. armena* Boiss.

General Morphology of Tulip Genus

The bulb is a specialized organ that serves not only for vegetative reproduction but also for storing nutrients. Typically, a mature bulb comprises four to six thick, fleshy scales, the metamorphic leaves of which are packed with reserve materials to support the plant's future growth. In addition, the exterior of the bulb is covered with other specialized scales (tunics), which originate from dead scales of previous years.

Tulip bulbs are protected by tunics to keep them safe from unsuitable environmental conditions. It is important to note the morphological features of tulip bulbs in order to distinguish between different species. The lowest part of the bulb is called the basal plate, which is disc-shaped and produces roots from its edge. The apical bud, located in the center of the basal plate of an adult bulb, develops into the flowering stem and leaves. Additional buds, or at least one bud, are found on the basal plate in the axils of fleshy scales, which grow into offsets. These offsets are additional bulbs of varying sizes for the next season, some of which may be of flowering size. In this way, tulip production is based on vegetative propagation, and all the offsets will produce new plants identical to the mother plant. Many tulip species are stoloniferous, and the buds on the basal plate that form the offsets grow outwards to form a hollow tube with a new bulb at the end.

The tulip has a unique stoloniferous habit that is particularly prominent in triploid and pentaploid species like *T. saxatilis* and *T. clusiana*, which rarely reproduce from seed. This not only facilitates the tulip's growth but also contributes to the formation of a growing colony [36 - 38].

The tulip plant's stem manifests in three main forms, namely the basal plate, the stem as an integral part of the stolon, and the stem of the flowering shoot along with the peduncle. In the first year, the stem only takes two forms: the basal plate as a modified, shortened, and broadened stem, and the stem section that fosters the growth and development of the stolon. The third form, the stem of the flowering shoot, does not appear until the tulip enters the adult phase and is composed of three parts, namely the stem between the lowest leaf and the basal plate of the bulb, a center part of the stem between the lowest leaf and the upper leaf that bears the assimilatory leaves, and an upper part, the peduncle, which is crowned by a flower [37].

Tulips have five different types of leaves. The first year, the plant produces only one "cotyledon" leaf. Then, in every spring until the flowering stage, one "petiole leaf" emerges above the ground. When the plant reaches the adult phase, it forms two to four "sessile stem leaves". However, some species may have fewer or more leaves, such as *T. regelii* with only one leaf and *T. schmidtii* with twelve leaves. The sessile stem leaves are typically fleshy, with a glaucous to green color, with membranous margins, and are often held alternate on the stem. They decrease in size up the stem, clasping it rather than having a distinct petiole. The other types of leaves, modified basal leaves, form the "tunics" and "the fleshy scales" of the bulb [36 - 38].

The flower is mostly upright, large, symmetrical, and supported by a sturdy stem. Its parts are arranged in alternating rings. The five-layered, three-part flower is made up of two rings of separate petals, two rings of stamens, and one ring of carpels. There are no nectar glands. The stamens and ovary are shorter than the petals and are located inside the flower [37, 38]. Flowers could be yellow, mandarin red, orange, pink-purple, and red, depending on the species. Tulip species bloom during the period from March to early June [35].

The ovary develops into a capsule with three compartments that can be globular, ellipsoidal, or trilocular. Within each compartment, two layers of seeds are attached horizontally to the curved edges of the carpels horizontally. These seeds are flat and have various shapes, ranging from triangular with two rounded edges to orbicular. The number of seeds is numerous [36 - 38].

Climate and Soil Requirement

The temperature required for tulip cultivation depends on the time of flowering. During the early cultivation phase, the soil temperature should not go beyond 16°C, and the air temperature between the plants should not exceed 18°C. For late plantings, the soil temperature should be around 9-10°C for the first 4-5 days. For December planting, the soil temperature should be 13°C, and the air temperature should be 15°C.

Tulip plants are not sensitive to changes in light. They do not show any visible reaction to such changes. However, it has been observed that the intensity of light affects the shape of the leaves. When exposed to high light intensities, the flower stem elongates and the bulb grows faster. Additional lighting may, therefore, be beneficial.

The optimum humidity range for tulip plants is 70-80%. Excess moisture can lead to botrytis, so ventilation should be provided when humidity increases.

Tulip plants thrive in well-ventilated areas with moderate humidity and temperatures. It is crucial to keep the soil constantly moist when growing tulips, but avoiding using chlorinated water is important as this can cause stunting. Drip irrigation is the best way to water tulip plants [39].

Cultivation

When cultivating tulip bulbs, it is recommended to use a well-cultivated, permeable, sandy-clayey, and lime-free soil that is free of stones. It is important to avoid planting in the same area repeatedly and to ensure that the soil pH is maintained at around 7. For optimum growth, it is suggested to grow tulips in areas with high altitudes and cold, snowy winters. A soil analysis should be conducted to determine the necessary fertilizer to be added to the soil.

When cultivating tulip bulbs, row planting should be considered a viable option between the months of October and November. It is advisable to adjust the planting depth based on the soil structure, with an average range of 8-10 cm depth being suitable in most cases [39].

Proper maintenance of tulip bulbs entails regular care and attention to detail. This includes the diligent removal of weeds and other plant species, ensuring that their roots are extracted from the surrounding environment and then destroyed. By implementing this practice, the tulip bulbs are able to thrive and flourish without the impediment of competing plants. It is imperative that this task is performed regularly and consistently to ensure optimum growth and health of the tulip bulbs [40].

To prevent the diversion of nutrients toward the flower and seed formation of bulbs, it is recommended that the buds are extracted and removed from the plant. Furthermore, during the final growth phase, the acrial segments of the onion plant can be subjected to pressure with roller-like tools, resulting in an increased growth size of the bulbs [40].

Onion harvesting commences once the leaves of the plant turn yellow and brown. The drying of the onion root tips and browning of the outer surface also signal that it's time to remove them. Tulip bulbs, on the other hand, can be extracted using machines. The onions that have been harvested are packed into crates and transported to warehouses [40].

Successful tulip cultivation requires specific soil conditions that are conducive to plant growth. In particular, it is recommended that the soil be stone-free, sandy-loam, and lime-free soils with an average pH of 7. Prior to planting, the soil should be thoroughly prepared and flattened to ensure it is free of clods. It is also important not to cultivate tulips in the same area every year. Rather, they should be rotated to a different location annually to optimize their growth [41].

It is imperative to replace or entirely renew the soil to avoid tulip fever disease. According to the literature, it is advisable to wait at least five years before replanting tulips in a previously used area. Replacing or renewing the soil is deemed necessary to prevent the spread and accumulation of disease-causing organisms and to restore the soil nutrients depleted by previous plant growth. It is industry practice to replace soil at regular intervals to maintain soil fertility and prevent the spread of disease [40].

For an optimal outcome, it is recommended that soil fertilizer is applied only after a thorough soil analysis to determine the amount of nutrients required by the plant. Fertilization should be carried out 2-3 weeks prior to planting using ammonium sulfate, accounting for 40 kg of compound fertilizer [40].

When cultivating tulip plants for use as cut flowers, the bulbs should be 12 cm. Planting density must be adjusted based on the species of plant and the stage of leaf development. It is recommended that small-leaved varieties be planted in close proximity to one another, while varieties with larger leaves should be spaced further apart. A planting density of approximately 200 bulbs per square meter is appropriate. Once planted, the bulbs should be covered with 1.5-2 cm of soil. In sandy soils, planting at a greater depth is feasible [39].

Diseases and Pests

Prior to planting, tulip bulbs require treatment to mitigate the risk of disease. Specifically, tulip bulbs must be soaked in a prepared solution to eliminate contaminants. This process is intended to ensure that the bulbs remain healthy and disease-free, facilitating optimal growth and development.

It is, therefore, advisable to treat tulip bulbs in this manner before planting them in the ground.

Pythium Root Rot and Soft Rot

Pythium, a fungal disease, is known to cause damage to crops within two weeks of planting. It is most severe in wet soils. The disease progresses rapidly when temperatures exceed 16 °C. As the disease originates from the soil, soil disinfection prior to planting is essential to minimize the incidence of the disease [42, 43].

Rhizoctonia Solani

Tulips are susceptible to a fungal disease known as *Rhizoctonia*, which can cause leaf damage characterized by the development of brown spots or lines, particularly during the sprouting phase. To prevent this disease, it is imperative to avoid deep planting of tulips. If symptoms of the disease are observed, disinfection measures must be carried out.

It is pertinent to note that *Rhizoctonia* is a fungal pathogen that can negatively impact plant health and lead to significant yield losses. Thus, it is essential to implement measures to mitigate the spread of this disease. In light of this, tulip growers and gardeners must be vigilant and proactive in applying preventive strategies, such as avoiding deep planting and implementing disinfection measures when necessary [44].

Gray Bulb Rot (Rhizoctonia tuliparum)

Rhizoctania tuliparum is a plant disease that adversely affects tulip bulbs and stems. This disease causes the formation of tubers ranging in size from 1 mm to 1 cm, exhibiting colors from off-white to reddish-brown. When the bulbs are cut crosswise, brown rings appear. In addition, the stems of the tulip plant will rot and eventually collapse as the disease progresses. In order to mitigate the impact of this disease, it is imperative to sterilize the soil before planting [45].

Botrytis Blight

The occurrence of "*Botrytis cinerea*", a fungal disease, poses a significant threat to plants such as tomatoes, peppers, and chrysanthemums that were previously grown in soil where tulips were cultivated. This disease causes the leaves to yellow and the bulbs to decay, diminishing the plant's health and yield.

Soil disinfection is recommended as the most effective preventive measure to avoid the disease's occurrence. Therefore, before planting, it is essential to disinfect the soil adequately to ensure the plant's protection against the disease [46].

Fire (Botrytis Blight)

It is caused by *Botrytis tulipae.* This particular affliction impedes the emergence of sprouts. Any sprouts that do arise will perish almost immediately. It is also referred to as gray mold and is characterized by spores that remain in the soil for an extended duration. To effectively combat this disease, the soil must be sterilized [40].

Basal Rot

F. oxysporum f. sp. *tulipae* is a soil-borne pathogen attacking tulip bulbs, and all other organs of the tulip shoot can also be infected with no specific preference. However, gummosis only occurs on infected bulbs and such symptoms have not been found around infected areas on other tulip organs. The tips of leaves turn yellow and the flower buds dry out. The pathogen can infect tulip bulbs at any stage of development [47]. Reducing the rate of wounds and bruises while digging, cleaning, and grading can be important in controlling the disease in bulbs because infections may occur if healthy and diseased bulbs come in contact with each other [48]. The soilless system is another way to manage *Fusarium* [49, 50]

Pythium Blight

It is caused by *Phytium* spp. The disease leads to the development of soft and watery areas on the roots, hindering plant growth [43].

Pests

Garlic Leaf Mite

Aceria tulipae Keifer, the garlic leaf mite, is one of the most important eriophyid-attacking bulbous crops. The first visible symptoms on infested tulip bulbs can be noticed about two months after harvest. Superficial, purple to red or yellow to cream spots grow on the normally white outer fleshy scale when mites enter the space between this fleshy scale and the dry brown husk. The bulbs infested heavily dry up, and inhibition of root and shoot development occurs. *A. tulipae* can be prevented by keeping storage temperatures low and planting early. Treatment of chemicals is the most effective when applied right after the bulb harvest [51].

Harvest

Tulips should be harvested when the flowers are closed but start to show their color. When harvesting tulips, break the stem right at the base of the flower bulb. The bulb is separated from the stem, and the stem is discarded.

Once the tulips have been harvested, they are carefully sorted into bundles of ten according to the length of their stems. This sorting is essential to ensure that the flowers are conveniently arranged and ready for easy handling. The bundles are then placed in a temperature-controlled environment to remove water and maintain freshness and quality. This process is critical in ensuring that the tulips retain their beauty, texture, and longevity, thus increasing their value in the marketplace [40].

CONCLUSION

The Liliaceae family, with 15 genera, is prevailing in the northern hemisphere and temperate Eurasia. The most commonly known genera are *Fritillaria* and *Tulipa*.

The highest number of taxa reported for *Fritillaria* is from Türkiye. *Fritillaria* is valued for its chemical components. However its germplasm is overexploited due to anthropogenic pressure. *Tulipa,* which is popular in landscaping, is distributed in Europe and Asia. Propagation methods, cultivation techniques, and disease and pest management are valuable for chemical properties and landscaping.

REFERENCES

[1] Tamura MN. Liliaceae. In: Huber H, Kubitzki K, Eds., Flowering Plants Monocotyledons: Lilianae (except Orchidaceae). Berlin, Heidelberg: Springer Berlin Heidelberg 1998; pp. 343-53.
[http://dx.doi.org/10.1007/978-3-662-03533-7_41]

[2] Bozyel ME, Merdamert-Bozyel E, Benek A, Turu D, Yakan MA, Canlı K. Ethnobotanical Uses of Liliaceae s.s. and Colchicaceae Taxa in Turkey. Int J Innov Approaches Sci Res 2021; 5(3): 163-74.
[http://dx.doi.org/10.29329/ijiasr.2021.379.4]

[3] WCVP. World Checklist of Vascular Plants, version 2.0. Facilitated by the Royal Botanic Gardens, Kew. 2024. Available from: http://wcvp.science.kew.org

[4] Ugurlu E, Secmen O. Medicinal plants popularly used in the villages of Yunt Mountain(Manisa-Turkey). Fitoterapia 2008; 79(2): 126-31.
[http://dx.doi.org/10.1016/j.fitote.2007.07.016] [PMID: 17878061]

[5] Ugulu I, Baslar S, Yorek N, Dogan Y. The investigation and quantitative ethnobotanical evaluation of medicinal plants used around Izmir province, Turkey. J Med Plants Res 2009; 3(5): 345-67.

[6] Ugulu I. Traditional ethnobotanical knowledge about medicinal plants used for external therapies in Alasehir, Turkey. Int J Med Aromat Plants 2011; 1(2): 101-6.

[7] Saraç DU, Özkan ZC, Akbulut S. Ethnobotanic features of Rize/Turkey province. Biological Diversity and Conservation 2013; 6(3): 57-66.

[8] Doğan A. Pertek (Tunceli) yöresinde etnobotanik araştırmalar. (Doctoral dissertation, Marmara Universitesi (Turkey). 2014.

[9] Kökçü B, Esen O, Uysal İ. Medicinal plants sold in Çanakkale/Turkey city center herbalists. Biological Diversity and Conservation 2015; 8(3): 80-91.

[10] Mükemre M, Behçet L, Çakılcıoğlu U. Ethnobotanical study on medicinal plants in villages of Çatak (Van-Turkey). J Ethnopharmacol 2015; 166: 361-74.
[http://dx.doi.org/10.1016/j.jep.2015.03.040] [PMID: 25819616]

[11] Bağcı Y. Sarıveliler (Karaman) ve çevresinde yetişen bitkilerin etnobotanik özellikleri. Selçuk Üniversitesi Fen Fakültesi Fen Dergisi 2016; 42(1): 84-107.

[12] Nadiroğlu M, Behçet L, Çakılcıoğlu U. An ethnobotanical survey of medicinal plants in Karlıova (Bingöl-Turkey). Indian J Tradit Knowl 2019; 18(1): 76-87.

[13] Rix EM, *Fritillaria* L. Flora of Turkey and the East Aegean Islands. In: Davis PH, Mill RR, Tan K, Eds. Edinburgh: Edinburgh University Press 1984; 8.

[14] Ori K, Mimaki Y, Sashida Y, Nikaido T, Ohmoto T. Steroidal alkaloids from the bulbs of *Fritillaria persica.*. Phytochemistry 1992; 31(12): 4337-41.
[http://dx.doi.org/10.1016/0031-9422(92)80470-Y]

[15] Kumar P, Partap M, Warghat AR. *Fritillaria roylei*. Himalayan Medicinal Plants Academic Press 2021; 57-66.
[http://dx.doi.org/10.1016/B978-0-12-823151-7.00010-6]

[16] Farooq A, Choudhary M, Gilani A, *et al.* A new anticholinergic steroidal alkaloid from *Fritillaria imperialis* of Turkish origin. Planta Med 1994; 60(4): 377-9.
[http://dx.doi.org/10.1055/s-2006-959507] [PMID: 7938275]

[17] Zhou JL, Xin GZ, Shi ZQ, *et al.* Characterization and identification of steroidal alkaloids in *Fritillaria* species using liquid chromatography coupled with electrospray ionization quadrupole time-of-flight tandem mass spectrometry. J Chromatogr A 2010; 1217(45): 7109-22.
[http://dx.doi.org/10.1016/j.chroma.2010.09.019] [PMID: 20926090]

[18] Kaneko K, Nakaoka U, Tanaka M, Yoshida N, Mitsuhashi H. Two steroidal alkaloids, hapepunine and anrakorinine, from the mature *Fritillaria camtschatcensis.*. Phytochemistry 1981; 20(1): 157-60.

[http://dx.doi.org/10.1016/0031-9422(81)85237-5]

[19]   Day PD, Berger M, Hill L, *et al.* Evolutionary relationships in the medicinally important genus *Fritillaria* L. (Liliaceae). Mol Phylogenet Evol 2014; 80: 11-9.
[http://dx.doi.org/10.1016/j.ympev.2014.07.024] [PMID: 25124097]

[20]   Türktaş M, Aslay M, Kaya E, Ertuğrul F. Molecular characterization of phylogenetic relationships in *Fritillaria* species inferred from chloroplast trnL-trnF sequences. Turk J Biol 2012; 36(5): 552-60.

[21]   Yıldız F, Aslay M, Kandemir A, Kaya O. Reproductive biology of *Fritillaria aurea* Schott (Liliaceae), a rare species endemic to Turkey. Diversity (Basel) 2022; 14(12): 1052.
[http://dx.doi.org/10.3390/d14121052]

[22]   Bizimbitkiler.. Available from: http://www.bizimbitkiler.org.tr accession: 30 12 2023.

[23]   Tekşen M. Doğadan herbaryuma: *Fritillaria* L. (Liliaceae). Herbarium Turcicum 2022; 0(2): 1-15.
[http://dx.doi.org/10.26650/HT.2022.1158469]

[24]   Has M. Morphological, anatomical and phytochemical studies on *Fritillaria imperialis* L. and *Fritiillaria persica* L. (*Fritillaria imperialis* ve *Fritillaria persica* L. türleri üzerinde farmasötik botanik ve fitokimyasal araştırmalar). Publication No 554427 Master's thesis Anadolu University, National thesis centre 2019. Available from: https://tez.yok.gov.tr/UlusalTezMerkezi/

[25]   Hartmann HT, Kester DE, Davies FT, Geneve RL. Propagation by specialized stems and roots Plant propagation: Principles and practices. 6th ed. New Jersey: Prentice Hall 1997; pp. 520-40.

[26]   Arslan N. Farklı soğan kesme yöntemlerinin *Fritillaria persica* L.'nın bazı özellikleri üzerine etkisi. J Agric Sci 2008; 14(03): 246-50.

[27]   Uluğ BV, Korkut AB, Sısman EE. Research on propagation methods of Persian lily bulbs [*Fritillaria persica* Linn.] with various vegetative techniques. Pak J Bot 2010; 42(4): 2785-92.

[28]   Kumar P, Partap M, Ashrita , Rana D, Kumar P, Warghat AR. Metabolite and expression profiling of steroidal alkaloids in wild tissues compared to bulb derived *in vitro* cultures of *Fritillaria roylei* – High value critically endangered Himalayan medicinal herb. Ind Crops Prod 2020; 145: 111945.
[http://dx.doi.org/10.1016/j.indcrop.2019.111945]

[29]   Petrić M, Subotić A, Trifunović M, Jevremović S. Morphogenesis *in vitro* of *Fritillaria* spp. Invited review. Floric Ornam Biotechnol 2012; 6: 78-89.

[30]   Yenikalayci A, Yalinkiliç NA, Bayram A. Effects of different growth media on bulb growth in Mus tulip (*Tulipa sintenisii* baker). Akademik Ziraat Dergisi 2023; 12(1): 15-20.
[http://dx.doi.org/10.29278/azd.1216688]

[31]   Ardakani AS. Intensive Damage of *Lilioceris chodjaii* on *Fritillaria imperialis* in Kohgiluyeh va Boyerahmad province, Iran. Adv Environ Biol 2014; 8(22): 791-5.

[32]   Alaserhat İ, Canbay A, Aslay M. Türkiye ters lale (*Fritillaria spp.*) koleksiyon bahçesinde zararlı olan böcek türleri (Harmful insect species in Turkey Inverted Tulip (*Fritillaria spp.*) Collection Garden). Bitki Koruma Bul 2016; 56(3): 259-66.

[33]   Speight MCD, Claussen C, Hurkmans W. Révision des syrphes de la faune de France : III - Liste alphabétique des espèces des genres Cheilosia, Eumerus et Merodon et Supplément (Diptera, Syrphidae). Bull Soc Entomol Fr 1998; 103(5): 401-14.
[http://dx.doi.org/10.3406/bsef.1998.17451]

[34]   Ünver S. The history of tulips in Turkey. Daffodil Tulip Year Book 1969; 34: 46-53.

[35]   Eker I, Babac MT, Koyuncu M. Revision of the genus *Tulipa* L. (Liliaceae) in Turkey. Phytotaxa 2014; 157(1): 001-112.

[36]   Hall AD. The Genus *Tulipa*. London: Royal Horticultural Society 1940.

[37]   Botschantzeva Z. Tulips: taxonomy, morphology, cytology, phytogeogr. Crc Press 1982.

[38] Wilford R. Tulips: species and hybrids for the gardener. OR: Timber Press 2006.

[39] Schneider JH. Rhizoctonia disease of tulip: characterization and dynamics of the pathogens. Wageningen University and Research 1998.

[40] Massodi NH, Hssain QA, Lone MA, Ganiae NA. Cultivation guide for Tulip & Hyacinth. Beyond Leer Publishing, an Imprint of Kohli Media LLP 2022.

[41] Fayaz K, Khan FU, Nazki IT, Nisa MU, Verty P, Singh VK. Effect of integrated nutrient application on yield and bulb production characters in Tulip (Tulipa gesneriana L.) cv."Red Beauty". Int J Curr Microbiol Appl Sci ISSN 2018; 2319-7692.

[42] Humphreys-Jones DR, de Rooy MJ. Control of *Pythium* root rot in five-degree tulips in the Netherlands and the United Kingdom. II Int Symp Flower Bulbs 1974; 47: 83-90.

[43] Gould CJ, Byther RS. Diseases of tulips 1979; 9: 3.

[44] Priyatmojo A, Yamauchi R, Naito S, Kageyama K, Hyakumachi M. Comparison of whole-cell fatty acid compositions of isolates of *Rhizoctonia solani* AG 2 from Tobacco and Tulip, AG 2–1 and AG-BI. J Phytopathol 2002; 150(4-5): 283-8.
[http://dx.doi.org/10.1046/j.1439-0434.2002.00756.x]

[45] Coats K, DeBauw A, Lakshman DK, Roberts DP, Ismaiel A, Chastagner G. Detection and molecular phylogenetic-morphometric characterization of *Rhizoctonia tuliparum*.. J Fungi (Basel) 2022; 8(2): 163.
[http://dx.doi.org/10.3390/jof8020163] [PMID: 35205917]

[46] Straathof TP, Mes JJ, Eikelboom W, van Tuyl JM. A greenhouse screening assay for *Botrytis tulipae* resistance in tulips. VIII Int Symp Flowerbulbs 2000; 570: 415-21.

[47] Saniewska A, Dyki B, Jarecka A. Morphological and histological changes in tulip bulbs during infection by *Fusarium oxysporum* f. *sp. tulipae*. Phytopathol Pol 2004; 34: 21-39.

[48] Price D. The occurrence of *Fusarium oxysporum* in soils, and on narcissus and tulip. II Int Symp Flower Bulbs 1975; 47: 113-8.

[49] Garibaldi A, Gullino ML. Chapter 21: *Fusarium* wilts of some ornamental compositae. In: Gullino ML, Katan J, Garibaldi A. Fusarium Wilts Greenh Veg Ornamental Crops. American Phytopathological Society. 2012; pp. 205-11.

[50] Gullino ML, Daughtrey ML, Garibaldi A, Elmer WH. *Fusarium* wilts of ornamental crops and their management. Crop Prot 2015; 73: 50-9.
[http://dx.doi.org/10.1016/j.cropro.2015.01.003]

[51] Conijn CG, Van Aartrijk J, Lesna I. 3.2. 12 Flower bulbs. World Crop Pests Elsevier 1996; 6: 651-9.

CHAPTER 7

Orchidaceae

Ezgi Oguz[1], Muhammet Cagri Oguz[1,*] and Mustafa Yildiz[1]

[1] Department of Field Crops, Faculty of Agriculture, Ankara University, Ankara, Türkiye

Abstract: The Orchidaceae family is the world's largest family of flowering plants. Species belonging to the Orchidaceae family have great economic importance as ornamental plants and food raw materials. Orchid species grow naturally in Türkiye. Orchid tubers attract great attention, especially in sahlep production. Collecting orchid tubers from nature for sahlep production causes the extinction of the species. For this reason, it is of great importance to increase knowledge and awareness about the cultivation of sahlep orchids. In this section, information is given about the characteristics of orchid species and the species distributed in Türkiye.

Keywords: Orchidaceae, Orchid, Sahlep, Tuber, Vanilla.

INTRODUCTION

The Orchidaceae family consists of approximately 1,000 genera and more than 35,000 plant species worldwide and is the world's largest family of flowering plants [1]. Although the Orchidaceae species is distributed in many regions of the world, it is especially dense in humid and tropical regions.

Species of the family have great economic importance as ornamental plants and food raw materials. Plant materials are collected from nature or cultivated for different uses. Orchid flowers are in high demand as ornamental plants and are widely cultured commercially. Especially *Cypripedium* (lady's slipper), *Epidendrum* (green fly orchid), *Habenaria* (fringe orchid), *Oncidium* (butterfly orchid), *Vanda*, *Vanilla*, and *Odontoglossum* (lady orchid) attract great attention due to the color and structure of their flowers. Besides, the tubers of the *Orchis* species are used to produce sahlep. Sahlep is used as a thickening and flavoring agent in ice creams and beverages. Sahlep orchids are in danger due to their intense and uncontrolled collection from nature. Vanilla (*Vanilla planifolia*) cultivation is of great importance in countries in the Western Hemisphere.

* **Corresponding author Muhammet Cagri Oguz:** Department of Field Crops, Faculty of Agriculture, Ankara University, Ankara, Türkiye; E-mail: m.cagrioguz@gmail.com

Vanilla is an important product used to add flavor to foods. *V. pompona* and *V. tahitensis* are widely grown for vanilla production. Additionally, leaves of *Calanthe veratrifolia* are used as dye raw materials. Besides, the tubers of *Habenaria susannae* and *Orchis latifolia* are used as food in many regions [2]. Although Orchidaceae species are perennial, they are non-woody plants. Some species are ivy-like. The species of the family include terrestrial, epiphyte, detritus, vine, rhizomes, or tuberous plants. They have annual rhizomes in terrestrial forms and perennial rhizomes in epiphytic species and roots that have turned into pseudo bulbs. While some species bear nutrient-storing tubers, some species have tape roots. The tape roots can benefit from oxygen and moisture in the air. In Orchidaceae species, strong branches form the primary shoot [3]. Branching occurs when one branch develops more strongly than the other. Weaker branches arise laterally and have a bifurcation pattern. This type of branching pattern is called sympodial (sympodialis). On the other hand, some species are plants with monopodial (monopodialis) growth habits. They grow upwards from a single point. Every year, they add leaves to the top, and the trunk grows accordingly. This type of growth is common in orchid genera. Monopodial growing species often develop green roots that hang down in long curtains and are used as additional photosynthetic organs. They have fleshy leaves that are effective in adapting to drought. The stem is generally leafy. They have simple, alternate, sometimes opposite or whorled, usually fleshy, linear to oval leaves covering the base, sometimes reduced to achlorophyllous scales. Leaves may have bract-like sheathed scales. The leaves are rarely hairy. Many species have layers of dead cells called velamen to protect them from water loss and hot conditions. The flowers of Orchidaceae species are usually single, rarely unilateral or bilateral [4]. Some flowers have a bracted structure, erect, symmetrical, with or without a stem. They generally have an epigynous ovary structure. The flowers are in single or double rows, in different numbers, joined together or in a column. The ovary is inferior and has one or rarely three segments. The seed capsule is numerous and small. The plant has three stigmas, and all or only two lateral ones are fertile. The fruit is in capsule form. The seeds are numerous, small, and distinctly winged. Especially in orchids, rostellum functions to encourage foreign pollination if the plant cannot self-fertilize. Rostellum is a tongue-shaped structure that exists between the anther and the pistil tube. If the plant is not pollinated, the rostellum dries out, and the flower can self-pollinate. This structure is one of the protection mechanisms developed by the plant for the continuation of the generation. Orchids are pollinated by bees, butterflies, moths, and insects such as weevils and grain borers [5]. Plants have different floral and scent characteristics to attract insects. Some orchid flowers resemble insects (*Phalaenopsis*, moth orchids), while others are perceived by insects as food or enemies. After the pollinator insect receives the orchid pollen, the pollen is released when it visits another orchid of the same species [6, 7]. Orchidaceae family species have been divided into five subfamilies based on recent studies [8]: Apostasioideae (two genera, *Neuwiedia* and *Apostasia*), Cypripedioideae (five genera: *Cypripedium*, *Mexipedium*, *Paphiopedilum*, *Phragmipedium,* and *Selenenedium*), Epidendroideae (has 15,000 species in 576 genera), Orchidoideae (7 tribes and 3,630 species; has 2 subclades with tribes *Orchideae* and *Diseaethen;* the other has tribes *Cranichideae, Chloraeeae,* and *Diurideae*), and Vanilloideae (15 genera and about 180 species: Pogonieae (77 species) also Vanilleae (with 172 species).

Apostasioideae

Apostasioideae has 15 species and two genera, *Neuwiedia* and *Apostasia* [8]. It is naturally grown in Sri Lanka, India, Nepal, Thailand, Vietnam, Cambodia, southern China, Japan, Malaysia, Indonesia, the Philippines, New Guinea, and northern Australia.

The genus *Neuwiedia* is a primitive terrestrial orchid distributed in the shade habitats of China, Asia, and some Pacific Islands. They are rhizomatous plants with long leaves. They have white and yellow flowers hanging on a branchless upright stem. Although the species of both genera have primitive features, they could be sibling genera to other orchid families [9]. *Apostasia* is commonly called lawn orchids [10]. They are grass-like evergreen plants. They have a star-like structure consisting of small yellow and white flowers on a branched flower stalk. They are naturally distributed in humid regions of China, India, Sri Lanka, and Southeast Asia.

Species of the Apostasioideae family are generally terrestrial plants. It is in the shape of a flake with leaves. The roots are partly stilt-like. It also has rhizomes and can bear capillary roots. The stem structure is upright, simple and with ascending branches. The leaf structure is spiral-shaped. They have leaves of different shapes, from oblong to oval, often curled. Although the leaves are hairless or slightly hairy, they can be herbaceous and slightly thick. The flowers of the Apostasioideae family species are generally bracted, leafy, glabrous, or slightly hairy. The flowers are in cluster form. The clusters with upright, simple, and branched stems bear colorful flowers. Each flower is located at the end of a short or long stem [11].

The flower stalk (pedicel) and the ovary are cylindrical or elliptical. The sepals are similar to each other. The flower parts are attached to the expanded flower receptacle of the stem. The flower basin narrows towards the base. It acts as a thick, fleshy, protruding spine on the outside. Apostasioid orchids have 3 stamens (except Cypripedioideae). However, other orchid subfamilies are single stamens

[12]. The stigma terminal may be slightly swollen, round, or pyramidal, with a flat top. It produces a large number of seeds. Its seeds are oval to elliptic in shape.

Cypripedioideae

Cypripedioideae is a subfamily of orchids known as lady slipper orchids or slipper orchids. Cypripedioideae includes the genera *Cypripedium, Mexipedium, Paphiopedilum, Phragmipedium,* and *Selendiedium* [13]. *Mexipedium,* a genus in the Cypripedioideae subfamily, is a monotypic genus consisting of a single species in a certain region of Mexico. *Phragmipedium* and *Selendiedium* are distributed in North, South, and Central America. *Cypripedium* is found in North America, parts of Europe, and Asia. *Paphiopedilum* is distributed in subtropical and tropical Southeast Asia and Southern China [14].

All members of Cypripedioideae are herbaceous but perennial plants. The leaves emerge from the stem in a spiral or two rows. There is no other tissue between the leaf and the shoot. The leaves are wide and have a striped structure. Shoots from the leaves close to the ground have grown thin and upright. The leaves are curled, and the leaf blade is plicate-shaped in the bud. The flowers are located in a spiral or in two rows at the end of a single stem. Flowers are single and clustered [15]. Plants of this species are characterized by their slipper-shaped sacs. These sacs perform an important method in flower pollination. The sac-shaped flowers force the insects past the stigma and stamens, allowing them to climb up the staminode. The insect climbs up and gets the pollen, which helps pollinate the flower inside. Despite their wide geographical distribution and different habitats and sizes, all members of the Cypripedioideae have the same basic floral morphology and pollination mechanism [15].

Epidendroideae

Epidendroideae contains more than 15,000 species in 576 genera. Besides, Epidendroideae are larger than all other orchid subfamilies combined. It is widespread in temperate and humid regions. Most Epidendroids live as hosts on other plants without forming roots in the soil. Such plants are typically tropical epiphytes. Plants grow as hosts rather than parasites. Furthermore, plants have evolved to make better use of light. They can stick to many parts of the host plant. In addition to humid tropical species, terrestrial epiphytes such as *Epipactis* are also included.

The subfamily Epidendroideae is divided into two classes or subgroups known as higher Epidendroids (vandoids) and lower Epidendroids. The lower Epidendroids contain polyphyletic tribes, particularly Arethuseae and Epidendreae [8]. Members of the Epidendroideae family are constantly updated in the light of morphological and genetic information [16]. Epidendroideae generally have spiral or toothed leaves on the stems. The flowers have a structure consisting of a single pair of anthers. The anther form can be erect or horizontal. The anther forms a right angle with the column axis or is directed backward in many genera. Pollen is waxy and hard. The apical part of the stigma lobe is strip-shaped. Their ovaries are usually monocular.

Vanilloideae

The subfamily Vanilloideae consists of 15 genera and approximately 180 species belonging to the tribes Pogonieae and Vanilleae. It is naturally grown in the tropical regions of Asia, Australia, and America. Pogonieae are commonly known as "pogonias". Pogonieae genera include *Cleistes*, *Cleistesiopsis*, *Duckeella*, *Isotria*, and *Pogonia*. They are terrestrial plants distributed in the temperate regions of Asia and North America. *Pogonia* species generally have a thin structure. There are leaves from the base of the plant to half of the stem. Plant height varies between 10 cm to 50 cm. The flowers are pink. The bears a single flower and the flower petals are elliptical or lanceolate. Different species are distributed in swamps or areas close to wetlands. On the other hand, *P. japonica* is native to the Asian continent and grows in moist open areas of Japan, Korea, and China.

Vanilleae genera include *Clematepistephium*, *Cyrtosia*, *Epistephium*, *Eriaxis*, *Erythrorchis*, *Galeola*, *Lecanorchis*, *Pseudovanilla*, and *Vanilla*. The Vanilleae tribe generally has long and fleshy thick leaves in the shape of ivy. The most economically important breed is *Vanilla*. *Vanilla* consists of 110 species. The most widely known member is *Vanilla planifolia* is native to Mexico. Vanilla products are commercially obtained from *Vanilla planifolia* [17]. The main components it contains are phenolic aldehyde and vanillin [18].

Vanilla is a vine-like plant. It can grow more than 35 meters. Their bodies are long and thin. Dark green, thick, and fleshy leaves are arranged along the trunk. In some species, the leaves have lost their function. There are long and strong roots capable of photosynthesis on the nodes of their trunks. The flowers are short-lived. Flowering occurs in the form of clusters in the leaf axils or on the stems. A single cluster produces 20-100 flowers. The flowers are close to white, white-yellow, and white-green tones. The flowers are large in size. Sepal and petal are similar to each other. The flowers are quite large and attractive and come in white, green, greenish-yellow, or cream colors. The sepals and petals of the flowers are similar. The lip is tubular. Most vanilla flowers have a beautiful scent. The biggest problem in economically grown vanilla is pollination. Therefore, the most economically reliable method is hand pollination [19]. In addition, due to the root structure of vanilla, trees that the plants can hold are needed in its cultivation. Vanilla fruit is long, fleshy, and shaped like 10-20 cm long capsules. Each capsule contains thousands of tiny seeds. Vanilla flavor can be obtained by using capsules and seeds together [19].

ORCHIDOIDEAE

Orchidoideae or Orchidoid orchids include approximately 3600 species [20]. Although previous studies reported that Orchidoideae consists of six different tribes, recent studies argue that Orchidoideae should consist of Orchideae, Cranichideae, Diurideae, and Codonorchideae tribes [8, 20]. Although the tribe *Codonorchideae* is a group of taxa consisting only of a common ancestor and all descendants, it has common derived features and characters with other tribes in phylogenetic branching (monophyletic). *Codonorchis* consists of a single genus found in South America. The Cranichideae tribe consists of eight subtribes. The Diurideae tribe consists of nine different taxa distributed in Australia [8]. Orchidinae consists of six subtribes. The most well-known and economically important subtribe is Orchideae. It is divided into two subtribes, Orchidinae and *Habenariinae*. The Orchidinae subtribe contains approximately 1,800 species [21].

Orchidoideae species are generally terrestrial. *Orchids* are perennial herbaceous plants and erect stems. The leaves grow in a spiral shape on the stem or at the base, toothless, smooth or curved. Flower shapes vary depending on the species. It can be found alone or in clusters at the end of the stem. Flowers carry both ovules and pollen. It is three-piece and bilaterally symmetrical. There are sepals and petals on the ovary. The petal is in the shape of a labellum. The fruit is in capsule form. Orchidaceae species can produce thousands of seeds. Seeds that do not carry enough nutrients for germination require a long time and the help of other microorganisms to grow and develop [22]. This period can extend up to ten years. For this reason, orchids collected from nature for commercial purposes are in danger of extinction in some regions.

Türkiye Orchids

The Orchidaceae family is naturally distributed in Türkiye with 24 genera and over 180 species [23]. In addition to the Orchidaceae subfamily, Epidendroideae species are naturally distributed in Türkiye. The most widespread Orchidaceae member in Türkiye is *Ophrys* L. with 54 species. The tubers of plants belonging to these species have high starch content and are used in sahlep production. *Orchids* in Türkiye and the nearby geography have terrestrial characteristics [24]. *Orchids* are spread in coastal areas in the northern, southern, and western parts of Türkiye [25]. Endemic orchid species are distributed in forest areas in eastern

Türkiye. The orchids *Ophrys, Orchis, Platanthera, Serapias, Aceras, Anacamptis, Barlia, Dactylorhiza, Cephalanthera, Coeologlossum, Gymnadenia, Epipactis, Limodorume, Spiranthes, Himantoglossum, Anacamptis, Steveniella*, and *Traunsteinera* are naturally distributed in Türkiye [6, 24]. Seventeen species of orchids are tuberous in Türkiye. *Aceras, Anacamptis, Barlia, Comperia, Serapias, Dactylorhiza, Himantoglossum, Neotinea, Ophrys, Orchis*, and *Platanthera* species have tubers and are used in sahlep production in Türkiye [12].

Aceras (Orchis anthropophora/Aceras anthropoforum) is native to Great Britain, central Europe, southwestern Europe, southeastern Europe, North Africa, and West Asia (Cyprus, Eastern Aegean Islands, Lebanon, Syria, and Türkiye) [26]. *Aceras* prefers moderately sunny meadows on well-drained, often calcareous soils. It also grows in mountainous regions that are not at high altitudes. *Aceras* is an herbaceous plant with long, thin, and abundant leaves. The flowers are divided into four lobes and are decorated with a human figure. The flowers are yellowish green with red edges and a long labellum. It is found around the Mediterranean and in central and western Europe, as far north as southern England.

Anacamptis is a genus of flowering plants in the orchid family. It spreads naturally in the Mediterranean basin and the region from Europe to Iran. Plants can grow up to 20-50 cm. Tubers are round. The leaves are linear and lance-shaped and clustered near the base. The flower bed is initially dense and pyramidal but becomes rectangular over time. The flowers are small, petals and sepals are equal. Labellum is flat, fan-shaped and three-lobed [27].

Barlia robertiana sahlep orchid has 8 species and 2 hybrid taxa worldwide. It consists of three groups: *Himantoglassum comperianum, zimantoglassum robertianum*, and *Himantoglassum hircinum*. It is a typical Mediterranean plant, spreading from Morocco to Anatolia, from the Atlantic coast to the north of Spain. Although it has been reported as a very rare species, *Barlia* has a wide distribution in countries such as Italy, Portugal, Morocco, Corsica, the Greek Islands, France, Cyprus, Yugoslavia, Malta, Algeria, and Albania. The species is registered in Türkiye and is mostly found in the provinces of Muğla and Antalya. *Barlia robertiana* (sahlep orchid) is a very rare species, although it spreads over a very wide area. The flowers are purple-colored, fragrant, and tuberous orchid species that can grow 20-60 cm tall [28]. *Barlia robertiana* seeds are quite small and cannot germinate naturally because they do not contain endosperm. Mycorrhizal association is essential for seeds to germinate naturally. *Comperia* was reclassified as a monotypic genus after being classified within the genus *Orchis (Orchis comperiana)*. The *Comperia comperiana* is in the same class as *Himantoglossum hircinum* (Lizard orchid) and *Himantoglossum robertianum* (giant orchid) in the *Himantoglossum* genus. The Komper orchid has distinctive hooded flowers. It has much in common with the Lizard orchid and Giant orchid but does not grow as large as the others. In good growing conditions, it can reach a maximum height of around 70 cm. The distribution of the Komper orchid includes Crimea (the southernmost part of Ukraine), Lesbos, Samos, Türkiye, Lebanon and Iran. Komper Orchid is one of the rare species of Türkiye.

Serapias vomeracea (locally named mule hoof, deaf ear, cow ear) is a common species in Türkiye. *Serapias* has one of the flower structures specific to orchid species. Dark red-purple flowers are in the form of long branches on top of each other. Curved flower petals have a tubular structure that attracts insects. Insects pass through the flower and provide pollination. Usually, *Serapias* can produce two or more tubers. Therefore, it is of great importance for sahlep cultivation. Seed tubers collected from their natural environment have a yield of 4-5 tubers under suitable growing conditions. Plant height varies from 10 to 40 cm. It is naturally found in scrub, heath, and meadows up to 1000 m above sea level.

Dactylorhiza is a genus of the Orchidoideae family. Tubers are flat, finger-shaped, and briefly lobed [29]. The stem is stiff or almost hollow and leafy. The leaves may or may not have purple spots. *Dactylorhiza osmanica* (Ottoman sahlep) is one of the endemic species in Türkiye. Plants grow naturally in moist, fresh meadows, forest edges, and stream banks at an altitude of 550 to 2400 meters [30].

Himantoglossum is a genus of flowering plants known as the 'Monk flower'. It spreads naturally in the region from Europe to Türkiye and Iran. The plant, which is seen in forests, maquis, and bushes, spreads naturally at altitudes of 300 to 1400 meters. The plant can grow up to 100 cm. The color of the leaves is purple, and the leaf shape is spear-shaped from the bottom to the wide tip. Flowers are spike-shaped and can grow up to 40 cm. Tubers are large and oval-shaped. The petals and sepals are close to each other and look like a hood. The genera *Comperia* and *Barlia* were merged into the genus *Himantoglossum* [26].

Neotinea tridentata is a tuberous orchid species. *Neotinea* is distributed in Crimea, Poland, Germany, Spain, and Türkiye [31]. Plant height is 15 to 45 cm. It has 3-4 lanceolate leaves near the base. The inflorescence is spherical to oval. The flowers are in a dense cluster and are rose-colored. The sepals have dark red veins. It is seen in meadows, maquis, and bush areas [27].

Ophrys is native to the Mediterranean basin, Europe, and Western Asia. They are small perennial plants with mostly two undivided round tubers. The leaves are usually at the base. The flower spike is relatively loose, and the flowers are showy. Sepals are bare, rose green, or whitish in color. The leaves are smaller.

They imitate the appearance, color, and smell of female bees to deceive male bees in order to ensure pollination [26, 27].

Platanthera includes approximately 150 species of orchids. *Platanthera* species are found in North America, Asia, Europe, North Africa, Borneo and Sarawak. Major centers of diversity are located in North America and East Asia [32]. *Platanthera* are perennial terrestrial plants. Some varieties may have tuberous roots. Leaves can be fleshy, oblong, oval, or lance-shaped. It can produce single flowers and cylindrical spikes. Flowers can be in shades of purple, yellow, and white. Due to its wide distribution in the world, it grows naturally in various habitats, from swamps to forests [33].

Sahlep is obtained from tuberous terrestrial orchid species that spread naturally in Türkiye. Sahlep is used as a thickening and flavoring agent in foods and beverages. Sahlep orchid tubers contain nearly 50% glucomannan, 25% starch, 10% protein, and a small amount of sugar. Glucomannan is also used as plant-based glue. The content and active substance in sahlep tubers vary in different climates and soil conditions. As a quality criterion, the glucomannan content of the tuber must be at least 40%. It has been reported that the glucomannan value is close to 60% in different climates and topographies [34]. Orchid tubers are mostly collected from nature for sahlep production. The fact that the collected tubers belong to protected orchid species causes some endemic and local plant species to be in danger of disappearing. It is known that sahlep obtained from orchids is obtained mostly in Türkiye and Iran and in small amounts in France and Greece. Some precautions have been taken to alleviate the damage caused by intensive and unconscious tuber collection. In recent years, awareness-raising activities have been carried out in Türkiye to collect orchids from nature under suitable conditions and to preserve their continuity. In addition, studies are carried out on the agricultural production of cultivated sahlep orchids. Cultivation of the economically important sahlep orchid is becoming widespread with appropriate planting and care procedures.

Sahlep Orchid Cultivation

Sahlep orchids can grow naturally in different climatic regions of Türkiye. However, adaptation problems may occur when producing orchid species and genera in regions with different climates. Therefore, knowing the climate requirements of the plant to be grown is effective in preventing yield losses. Sahlep plants have special growth and climate requirements. First of all, the soil should be light textured, sandy, sandy loam or clay loam. Drained soil that does not retain water in winter prevents the tubers from rotting. It is important that the soil is rich in phosphorus and has high potassium availability. At the beginning of soil preparation, 5 tons of organic animal manure should be mixed per decare before tilling the soil. Then, soil plowing should be carried out. In September, 15 kg N, 10 kg P_2O_5, and 15 kg K_2O should be applied per decare. In the same month, 30 cm high ridges are formed. The prepared seed bed is important for the good development of tubers and against flooding, as in the cultivation of other tuber plants. Tubers are planted on the prepared ridges, 10 cm apart in the row and 20 cm apart in the row. Planting tubers, care should be taken to plant them at a depth of 6-8 cm with the growth points facing upwards. Irrigation should be done according to climatic conditions. Along with irrigation, weeding operations can be carried out culturally. Orchids are thin and small plants and are sensitive to weeds. Weeding can be carried out 2-3 times during the production season. The biggest pests of sahlep orchids include mole crickets and earthworms. Early intervention measures should be taken in the spring months. Sahlep orchids are susceptible to *Alternaria* disease in areas with excessive rainfall and shade. Cultural importance includes items such as good soil cultivation, ridge formation, avoiding cultivation in shaded areas, and choosing suitable land against flooding. Harvest is carried out at full bloom time. Under ideal growing conditions, 2-3 tubers are formed. Harvesting is done manually. If 100-125 kg of tubers are planted per decare, an average tuber yield of 300-375 kg can be achieved.

CONCLUSION

The Orchidaceae family has important species both as ornamental plants and for the food industry. Besides, the populations of orchid species contain promising genotypes for the sustainability of orchid production. Wide range population will make a significant contribution to breeding studies as a genetic resource. However, most Orchidaceae members are endemic and bring with them the need for protection. Therefore, to protect and ensure the sustainability of species, uncontrolled harvest from nature must be prevented. Especially in Türkiye, the uncontrolled harvesting of orchid tubers from nature for sahlep production endangers many species. In this context, studies should be carried out on knowing the species characteristics and cultivating the appropriate orchid species/genus for the purpose. The sahlep production from the orchid tuber, seed production, breeding, and productivity studies must be increased under laboratory, greenhouse, and field trials for different climatic regions. These studies will make significant scientific and economic contributions.

REFERENCES

[1]   Attri LK, Bhanwra RK, Nayyar H. Pollination induced embryology studies in *Aerides multiflora* (ROXB.). Int J Botany Stud 2020; 5(4): 211-5.

[2]   Masters S. Turkish orchids: a diversity of species, and threats. The Orchid Review Orchids in Habitat 2013; 226-33.

[3] Pridgeon AM, Cribb P, Chase MW, Rasmussen FN. Genera Orchidacearum. Epidendroideae. OUP Oxford 2009; 5.
[http://dx.doi.org/10.1093/oso/9780198507130.001.0001]

[4] Prete CD, Miceli P. Histoanatomical and taxonomical observations on some central mediterranean entities of Orchis sect. Labellotrilobatae P.Vermeul. subsections Masculae Newski and Provinciales Newski (Orchidee). Caesiana. Quaderno 1999; 12: 21-44.

[5] Stern WL. Vegetative anatomy of subtribe Orchidinae (Orchidaceae). Bot J Linn Soc 1997; 124(2): 121-36.
[http://dx.doi.org/10.1111/j.1095-8339.1997.tb01786.x]

[6] Süngü Şeker Ş, Akbulut MK, Şenel G. Labellum micromorphology of some orchid genera (Orchidaceae) distributed in the Black Sea region in Turkey. Turk J Bot 2016; 40(6): 623-36.
[http://dx.doi.org/10.3906/bot-1512-7]

[7] Çalışkan Ö. Orta Karadeniz Bölgesi salep orkidesi türleri ve bazı yumru özellikleri. Anadolu Tarım Bilimleri Dergisi 2019; 34(1): 78-83.

[8] Chase MW, Cameron KM, Freudenstein JV, *et al.* An updated classification of Orchidaceae. Bot J Linn Soc 2015; 177(2): 151-74.
[http://dx.doi.org/10.1111/boj.12234]

[9] Zhang GQ, Liu KW, Li Z, *et al.* The Apostasia genome and the evolution of orchids. Nature 2017; 549(7672): 379-83.
[http://dx.doi.org/10.1038/nature23897] [PMID: 28902843]

[10] Jones DL. A complete guide to native orchids of Australia, including the island territories Reed New Holland. Sydney, NSW, Australia 2006.

[11] Kocyan A, Qiu YL, Endress PK, Conti E. A phylogenetic analysis of Apostasioideae (Orchidaceae) based on ITS, trnL-F and matK sequences. Plant Syst Evol 2004; 247(3-4): 203-13.
[http://dx.doi.org/10.1007/s00606-004-0133-3]

[12] Sezik EE. Orkidelerimiz: Türkiye'nin orkideleri. Sandoz kültür yayınları 1984.

[13] Jin X, Li J, Ye D, Wang Y, Li Z. Plants of subfamily Cypripedioideae. In: Ye D, Li J, Jin X, Eds. Atlas of Chinese Native Orchids. Singapore: Springer; 2023. p. 25–52.
[http://dx.doi.org/10.1007/978-981-99-4853-6_4]

[14] Nemer W, Rebbas K, Krouchi F. Découverte de *Cypripedium calceolus* (Orchidaceae) au Djurdjura (Algérie), nouvelle pour l'Afrique du Nord. Fl Medit 2019; 29: 207-14.

[15] Pemberton RW. Pollination of slipper orchids (cypripedioideae): a review. Lankesteriana 2013; 13(1-2): 65-74.
[http://dx.doi.org/10.15517/lank.v0i0.11539]

[16] Freudenstein JV, Chase MW. Phylogenetic relationships in Epidendroideae (Orchidaceae), one of the great flowering plant radiations: progressive specialization and diversification. Ann Bot (Lond) 2015; 115(4): 665-81.
[http://dx.doi.org/10.1093/aob/mcu253] [PMID: 25578379]

[17] Sinha AK, Sharma UK, Sharma N. A comprehensive review on vanilla flavor: Extraction, isolation and quantification of vanillin and others constituents. Int J Food Sci Nutr 2008; 59(4): 299-326.
[http://dx.doi.org/10.1080/09687630701539350] [PMID: 17886091]

[18] Takahashi M, Inai Y, Miyazawa N, Kurobayashi Y, Fujita A. Identification of the key odorants in Tahitian cured vanilla beans (*Vanilla tahitensis*) by GC-MS and an aroma extract dilution analysis. Biosci Biotechnol Biochem 2013; 77(3): 601-5.
[http://dx.doi.org/10.1271/bbb.120840] [PMID: 23470766]

[19] Mauseth JD. Botany: an introduction to plant biology. Jones & Bartlett Publishers 2014.

[20] Chen GZ, Huang J, Zhang GQ, Ma L, Chen SP. New subtribe Pachitinae (Orchideae) of Orchidaceae: Evidence from morphological and molecular analyses. Phytotaxa 2017; 329(2): 114-26.
[http://dx.doi.org/10.11646/phytotaxa.329.2.2]

[21] Jin WT, Schuiteman A, Chase MW, *et al.* Phylogenetics of subtribe Orchidinae s.l. (Orchidaceae; Orchidoideae) based on seven markers (plastid matK, psaB, rbcL, trnL-F, trnH-psba, and nuclear nrITS, Xdh): implications for generic delimitation. BMC Plant Biol 2017; 17(1): 222.
[http://dx.doi.org/10.1186/s12870-017-1160-x] [PMID: 28049439]

[22] Attri LK. Studies on Mycorrhizal Associations in an Orchid. Asian J Biol Life Sci 2023; 12(1): 179-86.
[http://dx.doi.org/10.5530/ajbls.2023.12.24]

[23] Güner A, Özhatay N, Ekim T, Başer HKC. Flora of Turkey and East Aegean Islands Edinburgh University press, Supplement 2000; 2(11): 656.

[24] Aybeke M. *Ophrys mammosa* subsp. mammosa Desf.'nın stolon anatomisi. Gümüşhane Üniversitesi Fen Bilimleri Dergisi 2022; 12(3): 818-25.

[25] İşler S, Sezik E. Muş Salebinin Menşei ve Muş Civarının Orkideleri. Yuzuncu Yil Univ J Agric Sci 2019; 29(3): 476-88.

[26] Çalışkan Ö. Orta Karadeniz Bölgesi salep orkidesi türleri ve bazı yumru özellikleri. Anadolu J Agric Sci. 2019; 34(1): 78–83.
[http://dx.doi.org/10.7161/omuanajas.474256]

[27] Kayıkçı S, Oğur E. Hatay İlinde Yayılış Gösteren Bazı Orkide Türleri Üzerine Bir İnceleme. Anadolu J Aegean Agric Res Inst. 2012; 22(2): 1–12.

[28] Altundag E, Sevgi E, Kara O, Sevgi O, Tecımen HB, Bolat I. *Himantoglossum robertianum* (Loisel.) P. Delforge (Orchidaceae) Türünün Morfolojisi. Anatomisi ve Yetişme Ortamı Özellikleri 2012; 153(1): 173-83.

[29] Foley M. Orchids of the British Isles. Cheltenham, UK: Griffin press Publishing Ltd 2005.

[30] Available from: http://194.27.225.161/yasin/tubives/index.php?sayfa=1&tax_id=9617

[31] Delforge P. Orchids of Europe, North Africa and the Middle East. Timber Press 2006.

[32] Bateman RM, James KE, Luo YB, *et al.* Molecular phylogenetics and morphological reappraisal of the Platanthera clade (Orchidaceae: Orchidinae) prompts expansion of the generic limits of *Galearis* and *Platanthera*. Ann Bot (Lond) 2009; 104(3): 431-45.
[http://dx.doi.org/10.1093/aob/mcp089] [PMID: 19383726]

[33] Peach DAH, Gries G. Mosquito phytophagy – sources exploited, ecological function, and evolutionary transition to haematophagy. Entomol Exp Appl 2020; 168(2): 120-36.
[http://dx.doi.org/10.1111/eea.12852]

[34] Farhoosh R, Riazi A. A compositional study on two current types of salep in Iran and their rheological properties as a function of concentration and temperature. Food Hydrocoll 2007; 21(4): 660-6.
[http://dx.doi.org/10.1016/j.foodhyd.2006.07.021]

CHAPTER 8

Zingiberaceae

Muhammet Cagri Oguz[1,*], **Ezgi Oguz**[1] and **Mustafa Yildiz**[1]

[1] Department of Field Crops, Faculty of Agriculture, Ankara University, Ankara, Türkiye

Abstract: The Zingiberaceae family has many economically important genera. This family contains agriculturally important spices and medicinal plants. Turmeric, ginger, galangal, and cardamom are among the medicinal and aromatic plants that attract great interest worldwide. Although the Zingiberaceae family has different genera, they have similar structures botanically. There are minor distinctive differences between the species. Differences in flowers, leaves, stems, fruits, and active ingredients are important in distinguishing the species from each other. The most important common feature in the Zingiberaceae family is the rhizome root structure. Especially rhizomes, which are both propagation material and harvest products of cultivated species, have high starch content. Rhizomes are offered to the market as fresh, dried, ground, and oil solutions. This chapter includes botanical and agricultural information about some Zingiberaceae genera that have attracted great attention in recent years.

Keywords: Cardamom, Ginger, Galangal, Turmeric, Zingiberaceae .

INTRODUCTION

Zingiberaceae is a large plant family consisting of approximately 1600 species and 50 genera [1]. Species of the Zingiberaceae family are naturally distributed in the tropical regions of the Southern and Northern Hemispheres [2]. The Zingiberaceae family is of great importance with its wide use as an ornamental plant and medicinal and aromatic properties. *Costaceae* is the closest relative of the Zingiberaceae family [3]. Important species belonging to the Zingiberaceae family include ginger (*Zingiber officinale*), turmeric (*Curcuma longa*), galangal (*Alpinia officinarum*), and cardamom (*Elettaria cardamomum*). Some species, such as *Alpinia* and *Hedychium,* are cultivated as ornamental plants. Ornamental plants include shell gingers, siam or summer tulip (*Curcuma alismatifolia*), ginger lily (*Hedychium spicatum*), *Kaempferia*, torch ginger (*Etlingera elatior*), *Renealmia*, and ginger (*Zingiber*). Especially the rhizomes of *Zingiber officinale* (ginger) and *Curcuma species* (turmeric) are the most consumed important spices in the world market.

* **Corresponding author Muhammet Cagri Oguz:** Department of Field Crops, Faculty of Agriculture, Ankara University, Ankara, Türkiye; E-mail: m.cagrioguz@gmail.com

Sibel Day (Ed.)

The seeds of the *Elettaria cardamomum* and *Aframomum* species plant are of great importance as spices and pharmaceutical compounds. Different plant parts of *Aframomum*, *Alpinia*, *Amomum,* and *Kaempferia* species are used as flavorings in meals. *Hedychium* and *Alpinia galanga* can be used in the perfume industry, and *Curcuma* is used as a coloring agent. *Globba* species, *Curcuma*, *Hedychium*, *Alpinia,* and *Etlingera* genera are cultivated as ornamental plants in tropical and subtropical regions. Besides important features, the Zingiberaceae family contains essential oils. Essential oils containing a wide variety of organic compounds, such as phenylpropanoids, are synthesized in *Zingiber* and *Curcuma* species. The most well-known compound, "curcumin", is found in *Alpinia*, *Curcuma,* and *Zingiber*. In addition, they contain aromatic acids, flavonoids, diterpenes, triterpenes, beta-carotene, lycopene, anthocyanins, and tannins.

General Characteristics of Zingiberaceae Plants

The Zingiberaceae family plants have pseudo-erect stems formed by leaf sheaths. In these species, the main stem stops growing after side branches grow. The main stem develops weaker than the side branches and creates a bifurcated branching pattern (sympodial). This development is generally seen in the Zingiberaceae family. Upright and large shoots are pseudo-stems consisting of arrowroots. The actual stem of the plant is short and thin. Flowers occur at the ends of branched leafy pseudo stems. *Etlingera* and *Alpinia* genera's pseudo stems can grow up to 8 meters in tropical regions.

Zingiberaceae has a few species that have flowers and leaves located on separate shoots. In tropical areas covered with dense vegetation, the plant height is tall and the flowers are close to the ground, while the flowers of plants in open areas are located at the ends of the stems. The leaves under the shoots on the stem are scattered and tufted. Although Zingiberaceae varies according to species, some species are ligule, elliptical, linear or broadly elliptical, hairy or hairless, open or curled leaf, with or without petioles. Petioles are of varying lengths. *Zingiber* is short, fleshy, and plump. Leaf sheaths are usually open, but closed leaf sheaths have also been found in *Roscoea* and *Cautleya* [4]. Blades vary in size; the largest usually develops in the middle of the shoot. They are elliptical in shape, rarely broadly elliptical or linear. Especially in *Alpinieae*, the blades are asymmetrical. During growth, one half of the blade rolls completely around the other [5].

Zingiberaceae flower structure is generally epigyne. The flower tray is sunken inward, and the female organ is located in the sunken part, while the other organs are located on the top. Male and female organs are located in the same plant. The flowers are variable axis (zygomorphic). The calyces are green covering leaves located outside the corolla (crown) and shaped tubular in the flower. The shape and size of the corolla varies depending on the breed. Corolla has three lobes and a tubular shape. The blooming is usually such that the main axis grows indistinctly. Although it resembles a raceme in appearance, the branches have a definite growth and form the actual raceme (thyrse) [6]. The flowers are arranged in two close rows, each corresponding to a leaf-like formation. Besides, flowers are usually modest and sometimes brightly colored. However, flowering may vary among genera and species. In some genera, the inflorescence is dense and the bracts are tightly overlapped. This type of flower has specialized leaves combined with reproductive structures. This structure, called bracts, is mostly different from green leaves. Bracts can be large, small, and in different colors, shapes, and textures.

In some genera of the Zingiberaceae family, bracts can be extremely large. In these cases, leafy appendages can develop. *Camptandra* and *Pyrgophyllum* are example genera with this condition. In *Curcuma* and *Zingiber* species, bracts form sac-shaped water-holding structures. For this reason, the resulting flower clusters develop continuously embedded in watery mucilage. In *Zingiber*, the development and formation of fruits take place in this viscous liquid substance [7].

The Zingiberaceae family generally has longitudinally opened and inward anthers. Although the lower ovary always appears to have three eyes in the early stages of development, a single ovary actually forms. The division of the pollen main cell is sequential, and the maturing pollen is always binucleated. In the Zingiberaceae family, embryo-sac development is of the polygonum type, and endosperm development is helobial. First, a cell wall forms between two nuclei in the formation of the helobial endosperm. Then, the endosperm develops, with one half extending through the cellular pattern and the other half encompassing the nuclear pattern [8].

The Zingiberaceae family fruit consists of a dry or sometimes fleshy capsule. It can be opened loculicidalally with three valves from top to bottom. The fruit consists of two or more carpels. Although the opening locations of the fruit are important in systematics, they are used to distinguish species [9]. Ripe fruits show a loculicidal opening from the back of each carpel from top to bottom. The number of seeds varies. Seeds are round or nearly round in shape. Seeds of various structures have flat and linear embryo structures that contain starch, are large, and contain abundant perisperm. The seeds are usually compounded in Hedychieae and Zingibereae. Alpinieae seeds, simple small grains with diameters less than 2.5 mm, are formed. While the seeds of Alpinieae do not contain starch, in other species, the perisperm contains large amounts of starch. As a general feature, hypogeal germination is dominant in Zingiberaceae. During germination, cotyledons or storage organs remain underground. The pulumula is pushed upwards and rises to the soil surface. Seeds of some genera, like Cardamom, have economic importance. The seeds in Zingiberaceae are simple, often flattened, and sometimes their outlines are irregular. Different types of spherical or ellipsoidal grains can be found.

Most of the Zingiberaceae genera that are economically important and produced in the field are propagated by rhizomes. Most *Globba* species produce bulbs in the axils of the lower bracts or below the stem instead of flowers, and propagation is possible with these bulbs. Sexual reproduction is gradually disappearing due to increasing ploidy levels in Zingiberaceae [10].

Zingiberaceae family roots generally have very short and wide cortexes. In species and genera with tuberous-rhizomes root structure, the active substance and nutritional tissue accumulate in this part. Rhizome size and branching vary according to species. In genera such as *Globba*, *Siphonochilus*, *Kaempferia*, *Roscoea*, the rhizome is small and underdeveloped. On the other hand, in the genus *Curcuma* the rhizome shows a lot of branching. The exodermis structure is formed by the corking of several rows of epidermis cell walls in the area above the absorbent hair area of the roots. The exodermis structure is present in some genera, such as *Elettaria* and *Hornstedtia*.

Zingiberaceae family plants distributed in tropical regions have stilt roots. Rarely are they high above the soil and close to turning into a woody structure. These roots rise straight in some species and obliquely in others. These types of stilt root plants carry branched rhizomes that serve as support to hold them more tightly to the soil. Rhizomes are permeable and help the roots of plants to breathe in swamp-like soils.

In the next section, general information is given about the characteristics and cultivation of *Zingiber officinale*, *Curcuma longa*, *Alpinia,* and *Elettaria*.

Ginger *(Zingiber officinale)*

Zingiber officinale (ginger) is a species of the Zingiberaceae. *Zingiber* has about 20 species [2]. Ginger, a species belonging to the *Zingiber* genus, is one of the most important spice plants in the world. The tubers and rhizomes are economically important parts of ginger. Rhizomes and tubers are perennial and serve as fleshy storage [11, 12]. Nowadays, there is an increasing demand for ginger. Southeast Asian countries are among the leading producers in meeting this demand. In addition to countries such as China, Nepal, Taiwan, the Philippines, and Thailand, ginger is extensively grown in Australia, Jamaica, and India. The world's largest producer and exporter of ginger is India [12].

Ginger plants rise directly from the roots. The plants have reed-like, green-leaved annual stems. There are 8-12 long, sheathed, lanceolate, pointed leaves on the stem. The flower structure is similar to the other varieties of the Zingiberaceae family. Flowers are covered with spirally arranged bracts [13]. The parts of the plant used in drug production are the rhizome and tubers. These parts have a high active ingredient and starch content. In addition to ginger rhizomes, stems and leaves have high antioxidant content, such as flavonoids and polyphenols [13].

Environmental conditions directly affect the flowering period of the ginger plant. The beginning of ginger flowering can occur over a wide period between April and July. This elongation is related to the humidity and temperature. The period between the beginning and end of flowering is approximately 80 days. Since flower formation and pollen viability are low in cross-pollinated ginger, few seeds are developed [14].

Ginger (*Zingiber officinale*) is naturally distributed in tropical and subtropical regions [15]. Ginger plants need a hot and humid climate for development. Although it can be easily grown in tropical regions, it is possible to grow it agriculturally in different climates and conditions. The vegetation period lasts approximately 240 days, and during this period, it can be grown by irrigation in regions with a total monthly rainfall distribution of 1300-1500 mm. Ginger planting can be accomplished using rhizomes and tubers [13]. Proper soil preparation before planting is one of the most important factors of successful agricultural production. Tillage is important to increase soil permeability, aerate the soil, and obtain ideal soil for sowing/planting. Soil preparation for ginger cultivation is carried out in autumn by plowing the soil to a depth of 30 cm. After the second superficial plowing process at a depth of 20 cm in the spring, the raking field is prepared for planting. Planting on prepared ridges that are 30 cm high and 1 meter wide can be beneficial [15]. This process provides suitable cultivation in heavy soils with drainage problems. On the other hand, increasing soil depth increases rhizome and tuber productivity [2]. It is difficult to meet the nutritional needs of ginger with organic fertilizers. For this reason, nitrogen, phosphorus, and potassium fertilizers should be applied. Nitrogenous fertilizer at 10-12 kg da^{-1}, 4-6 kg P$_2$O$_5$ and 2-3 kg da^{-1} K$_2$O can be applied at different stages of development. The application of nitrogenous fertilizer is divided into three parts: The first application is with planting, the second 45 days after planting, and the third 90 days after planting. Phosphorus and potassium should be applied with planting. Fresh rhizome yield in ginger cultivation varies between 500 and 2500 kg da^{-1} depending on the care, fertilization, and genetic potential of the varieties [12]. The soil should be free of stones and gravel, loose, and light for the comfortable development of rhizomes and tuber in ginger [11]. In addition, loamy, loamy-sandy, and soils with high organic matter content are important soil properties that increase ginger yield [16]. Seedling selection in ginger cultivation is one of the important factors affecting yield and cost. Large rhizomes for seedling will cause the cost to increase. The ideal ginger rhizomes for seedlings are 3-5 cm in length and weigh 20-25 g [15]. Additionally, seedlings must be free from diseases and pests. Potential problems can be prevented by treating the tubers with fungicide before planting [13]. Photoperiod conditions are the most important factors affecting the yield and quality of the ginger plant. Ginger generally requires bright sunlight, heavy rainfall, and high relative humidity [2]. The minimum and maximum growth temperature for ginger is 13-32°C; the optimum growth temperature is 19-28°C. Ginger is sensitive to cold, salt, and drought.

The water needed for the plant must be met by rainfall or irrigation. Since the soil suitable for ginger cultivation is permeable, frequent irrigation is required. The ginger is cultivated without irrigation in regular and frequent rainfall regions. Otherwise, ginger should irrigate 2-3 times during the vegetation period [11]. Drought is one of the important factors limiting rhizome yield in ginger. The fiber content of the rhizomes increases and the product quality reduces in case of water deficiency. Increasing the fiber ratio significantly reduces the quality. The first emergence from planted rhizomes occurs after 10-15 days. Under adverse conditions, this period may extend up to 50 days. While plant development continues for up to 130 days after emergence, dry matter accumulation in the above-ground parts continues for up to 200 days. However, since dry matter accumulation in the rhizomes can continue for up to 240 days, harvesting occurs approximately 250 days after the first emergence. The most suitable harvest time is considered to be the period after the leaves of the plant turn yellow and dry [15]. Rhizomes are washed and dried after harvest to prevent the fungus and mold. This stage makes rhizomes ready for processing.

The most important diseases and pests include weeds, soft rot, leaf spot disease, nematode pests, false stem borers, and rhizome insects. These biotic stress factors are effective among the Zingiberaceae family. Soft rot disease is the most important disease that causes the quality of rhizomes to decrease both in the field and in storage. On the other hand, *Pythium*, caused by *P. aphanidermatum* and *P. myriotylum* is widely found in ginger-cultivating countries. *Phyllosticta zingiberi* is the cause of leaf spot disease. *Meloidogyne* spp. causes gall disease; *Pratylenchus* spp. causes root lesions. Its effects include common symptoms such as stunting, chlorosis, and reduced tillering in plants. The colors darken and the decay of the area accelerates rhizomes infected with nematodes. *Conogethes punctiferalis* stem borer is the most serious insect pest of ginger [17]. *C. punctiferalis* causes the trunk and leaves to dry out and results in the death of the plant. *Aspidiella hartii* can cause great damage to mature and harvested rhizomes.

It feeds on the plant sap in the rhizomes and causes the rhizomes to dry out, as well as causing the seed rhizomes to lose their vitality. *A. hartii* symptom is the form of crusting on the rhizomes. *Holotrichia* spp. is a pest that feeds on soft rhizomes. It causes the roots and stems base to yellow and the plant to wilt [15].

Turmeric (*Curcuma longa*)

Turmeric (*Curcuma longa*) is a perennial herbaceous plant with yellow flowers and large leaves, also known as Indian saffron. Although naturally grown in South Asia, it is grown extensively in the tropical and subtropical regions of Pakistan, India, China, and Bangladesh. Turmeric is an important aromatic plant in traditional medicine and food industry. The "curcumin" contained in turmeric is of great economic importance [18].

Turmeric cultivation is similar in many characteristics to ginger. Turmeric can be cultivated under both rainfed and irrigation conditions in different climate regions. An average temperature of 20-35 °C and an altitude of 1500 m are suitable for turmeric cultivation. As with ginger, the most limiting factor for turmeric is water. When soil moisture falls below 50%, rhizome yield and active ingredient levels decrease. Soils with high organic matter content, humus, loam, and pH between 5.5 and 7.8 are suitable for turmeric cultivation. The soils with good drainage and no gravel or stones are ideal for the development of rhizomes.

Turmeric develops few fertile seeds due to its flower structure and seed development. This situation limits reproduction by seeds. For this reason, turmeric rhizomes are used as seedlings. The biggest difference between turmeric and ginger rhizomes is color. In addition, there are also differences in the active ingredient contents. Ideal soil preparation for turmeric cultivation is achieved by simple tillage/weeding before planting. Approximately 15 tons of organic fertilizer can be given per decare. Moreover, 5-7 kg da^{-1} N, 10-12 kg da^{-1} P, and 10-12 kg da^{-1} K_2O fertilizer can be applied with planting. Planting in beds created at a height of 20-30 cm in the field ensures good development of the rhizomes. The distance between the beds is at least 50 cm, and the bed width is 1 meter. The most suitable material to use for planting is mature rhizomes. Ideal seedling rhizomes should weigh an average of 50 grams and contain 1-2 buds. Sowing depth should not be more than 10 cm. Irrigation is important for successful development. The most important maintenance tasks include mulching. Mulching is an ideal cultural measure for weed control and soil moisture conservation. In addition, the throat-stuffing process provides a suitable environment for the development of rhizomes. Leaves that turn yellow at the completion of the vegetation period are an indicator of harvest time. Crop yield varies from 8 to 12 tons, depending on variety and growing conditions. Diseases and pests include leaf blotch, leaf spot, shoot borer, leaf roller, rhizome rot, and rhizome scale.

Galangal (*Alpinia*)

Alpinia galanga and *Alpinia officinarum* are called galangal or greater galangal. *Alpinia* generally have rhizome and tillering perennial plants. The plant is spear-shaped, pointed, and hairless. The galangal stem is in the form of an upright structure consisting of open-leaf sheaths. The flower structure consists of 2-6 flowers in cluster-shaped bracts, oval, 1-2 cm long, in green-white tones. The fruit has capsules that are close to round and 1-1.5 cm in diameter. The plant can grow up to 4 meters. The colors of rhizomes are the most important characteristic feature. The rhizomes have a red-brown outer shell and an orange-brown interior. *Alpinia* can be distinguished from turmeric and ginger with colors [19].

Although *Alpinia* species are generally called galanga, there are botanical differences between *A.galanga* and *A. officinarum. Alpinia galanga* has more tuberous and multi-branched aromatic rhizomes. The plant can grow up to 2 meters. Rhizomes are 3-5 cm in diameter, jointed, brown-red, and contain aromatic substances. The flowering period is between May and August. The fruiting period is between September and November. The fruit color is close to red, and the aroma resembles cardamom [20]. *A. officinarum* has long, cylindrical, hard, and branched rhizomes with an average length of 1 m. The rhizome is smaller in diameter, *i.e.*, 2 cm. Rhizome has hairy roots and a brown-red color. Flowering time varies depending on the region and growing conditions. Generally, flowering begins between April and September. The capsules are red and spherical. The fruiting period varies between May and November. Although *A.galanga* and *A.officinarum* have botanical similarities, there are significant differences in their pharmacological effects and the composition of their active ingredients [21]. Borneol, 1,8-cineole, eugenol, galangin, camphor, ß-bisabolene, and quercetin are the most important active ingredients in the essential oil content of the *Alpinia* species.

Galangal can be found in wild, semi-wild, and cultivated states. Shady places are suitable for agricultural production. Excessive sunlight exposure causes the plant to lose moisture and cause leaf burn. The soil structure should be permeable, sandy, loamy, and rich in organic matter. Galangal can grow naturally in tropical regions. Galangal flowers are generally sterile and have a very low rate of fertile seeds. The rhizomes of the plant are used as seedlings. Galangal can be planted on mounds prepared at a height of 30 cm for the rhizomes to develop. After planting, organic fertilizer, chemical fertilizer, and lime can be applied to the pits (to regulate acidity). The first emergence occurs approximately one month after planting. The development of the plant is completed in an average of 120 days. Water logging in the field makes rhizomes susceptible to diseases. Therefore, the field soil must be well drained. Soil moisture below 45% reduces rhizome quality. Late harvesting of rhizomes that have reached harvest maturity causes the fiber amount of the rhizomes to increase and their quality to decrease. A delay in harvesting increases the fibrous structure of the rhizomes. This situation prevents the use of galangal as a spice [20]. However, 15-month-old rhizomes are used as a medicinal drug. Galangal rhizomes with high fiber content allow their evaluation for their medicinal and active ingredients [22].

The most important disease in galangal is root rot. Root rot poses a threat to all rhizome-producing members of the Zingiberaceae. Poor soil structure and low water permeability are the main causes of root rot. On the other hand, fungi belonging to the *Pucciniales* order can cause galangal rust disease. The symptoms of the disease can be seen from the spots on the leaves. It begins as white fluffy spots on the leaves in shaded areas where irrigation and fertilization are irregular. Then turns yellow and resembles rust.

Cardamom (*Elettaria* & *Amomum*)

Cardamom is the general name of the *Elettaria* and *Amomum* genera. Cardamom is a large-leaved perennial plant genus that grows in India and Southeast Asian countries with warm climates. India, Sri Lanka, Iran, Tanzania, Kuwait, Indonesia, and Nepal produce the most cardamom in the world. These plants can grow up to 5 meters. Cardamom fruits are 1-2 cm long and yellow, green, white, brown and black colors. Mainly, cardamom is divided into two groups based on pod color and seed characteristics: green cardamom (*Elettaria cardamom)* and black cardamom (*Amomum costatum* and *Amomum subulatum)* [19]. The seeds have high antioxidant and active ingredient content. Unlike ginger, turmeric, and galangal, the economically important plant part is seeds. After harvesting, the fruits are dried, and the seeds are obtained. Cardamom seeds are rich in active ingredients such as 1,8-cineole, a-pinene, a-terpineol, a-terpinyl acetate, linalool, and linalyl acetate.

Cardamom is easy to grow in tropical regions. 10°C to 35°C is the ideal temperature range. Efficiency and product quality increase in semi-shaded and humid areas. It can be grown without irrigation in tropical regions where annual rainfall is 1500 to 4000 mm. However, it is difficult to grow outside of humid, hot, and tropical regions. Cardamom is sensitive to water stress. Soils rich in organic matter, humus, and loam and with a pH value of 4 - 7 are ideal for cardamom cultivation [23].

Cardamom can be propagated vegetatively as with other genera of the Zingiberaceae family. Instead of seed production, vegetative production is more efficient and practical. 1-1.5 years-old cardamom seedlings are transplanted into the field and cultivated. Cardamom seedlings are planted in holes dug approximately 50 cm deep and 30 cm in diameter in spring. According to regions and climates, cardamom variety planting can be done at distances of 2×1, 2×2, and 2×3 meters. Covering the soil surface with mulch after planting is of great importance to combat fungi and weeds. Another important factor affecting cardamom yield is fertilization. Fertilizer containing 8 kg of N, 8 kg of P, and 15 kg of K per decare is recommended. Fertilization can be applied in two different periods. The first fertilization, which falls in the middle of seedling development, affects capsule development. The second fertilization affects the formation of clusters [24].

Cardamom cultivation can be done without irrigation in regions with high annual rainfall. During hot periods when soil moisture drops below 50%, irrigation every 2 weeks reduces yield losses. On the other hand, regular drip irrigation increases flowering, fruit formation, and seed yield. The cardamom species fruit production begins in the 2nd or 3rd year of plant development. Economic efficiency is achieved starting from the 3rd year. Economic life can last up to 10 years with good care. The formation of fruits is completed in approximately 40 days. Cardamom yield varies depending on growing and climatic conditions. The average capsule yield is 45-50 kg da^{-1}. The most important pests for cardamom species include thrips, hairy caterpillars, mites, aphids, and nematodes. The most common diseases are capsule rot and katte disease. Like other members of the Zingiberaceae family, cardamom is sensitive to cold and drought.

CONCLUSION

Cardamom, turmeric, ginger, and galangal have attracted great attention worldwide in recent years. This section will contribute to agricultural production and scientific studies with information on planting, care, diseases, and pests of species. Although it can be grown easily in tropical and subtropical regions, evaluating the possibilities of growing it in humid regions and greenhouses will provide significant economic gains. Farmers need to be informed and supported on this issue.

REFERENCES

[1]   Christenhusz MJM, Byng JW. The number of known plants species in the world and its annual increase. Phytotaxa 2016; 261(3): 201-17.
       [http://dx.doi.org/10.11646/phytotaxa.261.3.1]

[2]   Jakribettu RP, Boloor R, Bhat HP, *et al.* Ginger (*Zingiber officinale* Rosc.) Oils. Essential oils in food preservation, flavor and safety. Academic Press 2016; pp. 447-54.

[http://dx.doi.org/10.1016/B978-0-12-416641-7.00050-X]

[3]   Sass C, Iles WJD, Barrett CF, Smith SY, Specht CD. Revisiting the Zingiberales: using multiplexed exon capture to resolve ancient and recent phylogenetic splits in a charismatic plant lineage. PeerJ 2016; 4(4): e1584.
        [http://dx.doi.org/10.7717/peerj.1584] [PMID: 26819846]

[4]   Spearing JK. Note on closed leaf sheaths in Zingiberaceae Zingiberoideae. Notes from the Royal Botanic Garden, Edinburgh 1977.

[5]   Kress WJ. The phylogeny and classification of the Zingiberales. Ann Mo Bot Gard 1990; 77(4): 698-721.
        [http://dx.doi.org/10.2307/2399669]

[6]   Hickey M, King C. Glossary of botanical terms, The Cambridge illustrated. 2001.

[7]   Holttum RE. The Zingiberaceae of the Malay peninsula. Gard Bull (Singapore) 1950; 13: 1-249.

[8]   Larsen K, Lock JM, Maas H, Maas PJM. In: Kubitzki K, Ed, Flowering plants Monocotyledons: Alismatanae and commelinanae (except gramineae). Springer Berlin Heidelberg 1998; pp. 474-95.

[9]   Toker CM. Plant morphology book. Ankara University Biology department 2004.

[10]   Marschner H. Mineral nutrition of higher plants. Academic press 1995.

[11]   Jaidka M, Kaur R, Sepat S. Scientific cultivation of ginger (*Zingiber officinalis*). Adv Veg Agron 2018; 191-7.

[12]   Udounang PI, Ekwere OJ, Akata OR. Effect of different tillage practices on the growth and yield of ginger (*zingiber officinale* rosc.) in obio akpa-akwa ibom state, south eastern nigeria. J Agric Food Sci 2022; 6(1): 36-45.

[13]   Melati M, Palupi ER, Bermawie N. Floral biology of ginger (*Zingiber officinale* rosc.). Int J Curr Res Biosci Plant Biol 2015; 2(4): 1-10.

[14]   Zhou YQ, Liu H, He MX., Wang R, Zeng QQ, Wang Y, Zhang QW. A review of the botany, phytochemical, and pharmacological properties of galangal. In: Grumezescu AM, Holban AM, Eds. Natural and artificial flavoring agents and food dyes 2018; 351-396.
        [http://dx.doi.org/10.1016/B978-0-12-811518-3.00011-9]

[15]   Monnaf MA, Rahim MA, Hossain MMA, Alam MS. Effect of planting method and rhizome size on the growth and yield of ginger. J Agrofor Environ Sci 2010; 4(2): 73-6.

[16]   Zahid NA, Jaafar HZE, Hakiman M. Micropropagation of ginger (*Zingiber officinale* Roscoe) Bentong'and evaluation of its secondary metabolites and antioxidant activities compared with the conventionally propagated plant. Plants 2021; 10(4): 630.
        [http://dx.doi.org/10.3390/plants10040630] [PMID: 33810290]

[17]   Ujang Z, Nordin NI, Subramaniam T. *Ginger* species and their traditional uses in modern applications. J Inf Technol 2015; 23(1): 59-70.

[18]   Choudhary AK, Rahi S. Organic cultivation of high yielding turmeric (*Curcuma longa* L.) cultivars: a viable alternative to enhance rhizome productivity, profitability, quality and resource-use efficiency in monkey–menace areas of north-western Himalayas. Ind Crops Prod 2018; 124: 495-504.
        [http://dx.doi.org/10.1016/j.indcrop.2018.07.069]

[19]   Wilson L. Spices and flavoring crops: tubers and roots. In: Caballero B, Finglas PM, Toldrá F, eds. Encyclopedia of food and health. 2016.
        [http://dx.doi.org/10.1016/B978-0-12-384947-2.00781-9]

[20]   Qi S, Ji F, Yao Q. Study on chemical constituents of *Alpinia galanga* rhizomes. Food and Drug 2010; 12(1): 39-41.

[21]   Zhou YQ, Liu H, He MX, *et al.* A review of the botany, phytochemical, and pharmacological properties of galangal. In: Alexandru Mihai Grumezescu AM, Holban AM, Eds., Natural and Artificial

Flavoring Agents and Food Dyes 2018; pp. 351-96.
[http://dx.doi.org/10.1016/B978-0-12-811518-3.00011-9]

[22] Peter KV. Handbook of herbs and spices. Woodhead publishing 2006; 3.
[http://dx.doi.org/10.1533/9781845691717]

[23] Ramadan MF. Introduction to Cardamom (*Elettaria cardamomum*): Production, Processing, and Properties. Cardamom (*Elettaria cardamomum*): Production, Processing and Properties Cham. Springer International Publishing 2023; 1-9.
[http://dx.doi.org/10.1007/978-3-031-35426-7_1]

[24] Buckingham JS, Petheram RJ. Cardamom cultivation and forest biodiversity in northwest Vietnam. Agricultural Research and Extension Network. Overseas Developmewnt Institute. Newsletter 2004; (50): 10.

SUBJECT INDEX

A

Allium genus 54
alpinarii Özhatay & Kollmann 55
anatolicum Özhatay & B.Mathew 55
antalyense Eren, Çinbilgel & Parolly 55
armenum Boiss. & Kotschy 55
armerioides Boiss. 55
arzusense Eker & Koyuncu 55
asperiflorum Miscz. 55
balansae Boiss. 55
baytopiorum Kollmann & Özhatay 55
brevicaule Boiss. & Balansa 55
Amaryllidaceae family 53, 54, 66, 72
Anthropogenic pressure 1, 12, 13, 14, 137
Araceae 19, 20, 21, 23, 25, 27, 28, 29, 32, 35, 42, 45
family 19, 20, 21, 27, 28, 29, 32, 35, 42, 45
Arolycoricidine 68
Apostasioideae 143
Adaptation 2, 3, 4, 5, 14, 102, 149
Agronomic 24, 27, 62
aspects 25

B

Basal plate 2, 3, 7, 8, 9, 59, 132,
Botrytis blight 114, 136
Breeding 4, 19, 25, 27, 62, 88, 108, 114, 115, 150
Bulbs 1, 2, 3, 6, 7, 8, 9, 10, 11, 12, 21, 24, 25, 27, 54, 58, 59, 60, 61, 62, 63, 68, 71, 72, 114, 123, 124, 125, 127, 132, 133, 134, 135, 136, 137, 142, 156
Bulbocapnine 68

C

Cardamom 153, 156, 160, 161, 162
Climate requirements 60, 149
Colchicaceae family 76, 85
Conservation efforts 1, 13
Corm rot 108, 114
Crocus genus 99
Cultivation 1, 11, 22, 25, 26, 27, 28, 61, 62, 65, 71, 72, 85, 88, 93, 104, 105, 106, 112, 114, 115, 121, 125, 133, 134, 137, 141, 146, 148, 149, 150, 156, 157, 158, 159, 161, 162

D

Diseases 7, 12, 25, 26, 28, 45, 58, 59, 61, 62, 72, 76, 86, 93, 99, 108, 114, 121, 127, 135, 158, 160, 161, 162
Dormancy 4, 20, 27, 60

E

Ecosystem 4, 12, 14, 24, 26, 54
Ellipsoidal 133, 156
Epidendroideae 143, 144, 145, 146
Environmental requirements 1, 10
Endemic taxa 54, 55, 62, 66, 122, 130

F

Flowering 5, 6, 7, 8, 9, 10, 11, 19, 21, 23, 28, 53, 66, 68, 69, 71, 72, 101, 102, 104, 107, 108, 109, 111, 113, 123, 125, 126, 132, 133, 141, 145, 147, 148, 155, 157, 160, 162
Filiform 23, 102, 111
Fritillaria genus 122

G

Galangal 153, 160, 161, 162
Galanthus genus 66
Gladiolus 3, 10, 11, 93, 94, 108, 109, 110, 111, 112, 113, 114, 115

www.ingramcontent.com/pod-product-compliance
Lightning Source LLC
Chambersburg PA
CBHW041420290326
41932CB00042B/28